Property and Liability Insurance Principles

Property and Liability Insurance Principles

Edited by

Mary Ann Cook, CPCU, MBA, AU, AAI

Ann E. Myhr, CPCU, MS, ARM, AU, AIM, ASLI

7th Edition • 3rd Printing

The Institutes
720 Providence Road, Suite 100
Malvern, Pennsylvania 19355-3433

7th Edition • 3rd Printing • December 2018

Library of Congress Control Number: 2018955330

ISBN 978-0-89462-277-9

Foreword

The Institutes are the trusted leader in delivering proven knowledge solutions that drive powerful business results for the risk management and property-casualty insurance industry. For more than 100 years, The Institutes have been meeting the industry's changing professional development needs with customer-driven products and services.

In conjunction with industry experts and members of the academic community, our Knowledge Resources Department develops our course and program content, including Institutes study materials. Practical and technical knowledge gained from Institutes courses enhances qualifications, improves performance, and contributes to professional growth—all of which drive results.

The Institutes' proven knowledge helps individuals and organizations achieve powerful results with a variety of flexible, customer-focused options:

Recognized Credentials—The Institutes offer an unmatched range of widely recognized and industry-respected specialty credentials. The Institutes' Chartered Property Casualty Underwriter (CPCU®) professional designation is designed to provide a broad understanding of the property-casualty insurance industry. Depending on professional needs, CPCU students may select either a commercial insurance focus or a personal risk management and insurance focus and may choose from a variety of electives.

In addition, The Institutes offer certificate or designation programs in a variety of disciplines, including these:

- Claims
- Commercial underwriting
- Fidelity and surety bonding
- General insurance
- Insurance accounting and finance
- Insurance information technology
- Insurance production and agency management
- Insurance regulation and compliance
- Management
- Marine insurance
- Personal insurance
- Premium auditing
- Quality insurance services
- Reinsurance
- Risk management
- Surplus lines

Ethics—Ethical behavior is crucial to preserving not only the trust on which insurance transactions are based, but also the public's trust in our industry as a whole. All Institutes designations now have an ethics requirement, which is delivered online and free of charge. The ethics requirement content is designed specifically for insurance practitioners and uses insurance-based case studies to outline an ethical framework. More information is available in the Programs section of our website, TheInstitutes.org.

Flexible Online Learning—The Institutes have an unmatched variety of technical insurance content covering topics from accounting to underwriting, which we now deliver through hundreds of online courses. These cost-effective self-study courses are a convenient way to fill gaps in technical knowledge in a matter of hours without ever leaving the office.

Continuing Education—A majority of The Institutes' courses are filed for CE credit in most states. We also deliver quality, affordable, online CE courses quickly and conveniently through CEU. Visit CEU.com to learn more. CEU is powered by The Institutes.

College Credits—Most Institutes courses carry college credit recommendations from the American Council on Education. A variety of courses also qualify for credits toward certain associate, bachelor's, and master's degrees at several prestigious colleges and universities. More information is available in the Student Services section of our website, TheInstitutes.org.

Custom Applications—The Institutes collaborate with corporate customers to use our trusted course content and flexible delivery options in developing customized solutions that help them achieve their unique organizational goals.

Insightful Analysis—Our Insurance Research Council (IRC) division conducts public policy research on important contemporary issues in property-casualty insurance and risk management. Visit www.Insurance-Research.org to learn more or purchase its most recent studies.

The Institutes look forward to serving the risk management and property-casualty insurance industry for another 100 years. We welcome comments from our students and course leaders; your feedback helps us continue to improve the quality of our study materials.

Peter L. Miller, CPCU
President and CEO
The Institutes

Preface

Property and Liability Insurance Principles is the textbook for the first course in The Institutes' Associate in General Insurance (AINS) designation program. Designed for learners at the beginning to intermediate level, this course provides the foundation for the rest of the AINS program.

The text is divided into three segments. Segment A explains what insurance is, who provides it, how it is regulated, and how to measure an insurer's financial performance. Segment B describes the functions of marketing, underwriting, ratemaking, and claims, all of which are essential to providing insurance. Segment C examines the risk management process and its purpose, the elements of loss exposures, and the characteristics and provisions of insurance policies.

The Institutes are grateful to Ken Bergeron, MBA, CPCU, ARM, and all the insurance professionals, course leaders, and course sponsors who provided guidance and review during the planning of this text. Their assistance helped ensure that the text is accurate and reflects current industry practice.

For more information about The Institutes' programs, please call our Customer Success Department at (800) 644-2101, email us at CustomerSuccess@TheInstitutes.org, or visit our website at TheInstitutes.org.

Mary Ann Cook, CPCU, MBA, AU, AAI

Ann E. Myhr, CPCU, ARM, AU, AIM, ASLI

Contributors

The Institutes acknowledge with deep appreciation the contributions made to the content of this text by the following persons:

Doug Froggatt, CPCU, AINS

Kevin Kibelstis, CPCU, AINS, AIS

Christian Schappel

Contents

Segment A

Understanding Insurance

Educational Objectives

After learning the content of this assignment, you should be able to:

▷ Describe the benefits and the costs of insurance to individuals, organizations, and society.

▷ Explain how insurance operates in different roles.

▷ Distinguish among the common types of personal and commercial insurance.

▷ Describe the various types of private insurers providing property and liability insurance.

▷ Describe United States federal and state government insurance programs.

▷ Distinguish among the following insurance functions:

- Marketing
- Underwriting
- Claims
- Risk control
- Premium audit

Understanding Insurance

BENEFITS AND COSTS OF INSURANCE

Insurance is a prominent risk management technique, and several risk financing measures involve the use of insurance to some degree. When potential techniques for meeting risk management goals are being assessed, the benefits and costs of insurance should also be carefully considered.

Insurance can help individuals and organizations achieve risk financing goals, such as paying for losses, managing cash flow uncertainty, and complying with legal requirements. But beyond that, insurance provides several benefits to individuals, organizations, and society in general by encouraging an insured's loss control activities, providing insurers with a source of investment funds, and reducing social burdens by helping insureds recover after a loss. There are costs to insurance, however, ranging from premiums paid by insureds and insurers' operating costs, to opportunity costs and the possibility of increased losses.

The Benefits of Insurance

The best-known benefit of insurance, helping insureds regain their footing after a loss, is often considered its main purpose. Provided that the loss is to a covered loss exposure and involves a covered cause of loss, an insurer will indemnify the insured, subject to any applicable deductibles and policy limits. While this benefit holds great importance, insurance provides numerous other benefits that insurance professionals should be aware of.

Managing Cash Flow Uncertainty

Insurance also enables an individual or organization to manage cash flow uncertainty. The insured can be confident that as long as a loss is covered, the financial effect on the insured's cash flow will be reduced to any deductible payments or any loss amounts that exceed the policy limits. The remainder of the loss will be paid by the insurer, reducing the variation in the insured's cash flows.

Meeting Legal Requirements

Insurance also helps an insured meet legal requirements that might apply, whether for personal or commercial insurance customers. For example, all states have laws that require employers to pay for the job-related injuries or illnesses of their employees, and employers generally purchase workers compensation insurance to meet this financial obligation. An example of a legal requirement for individuals is personal auto insurance, which is often required in states that have compulsory auto insurance laws for anyone who wishes to own or drive an automobile.

Insurance can often be used or required to satisfy both statutory and contractual requirements, such as providing proof of insurance, that arise from business relationships. For example, building contractors are usually required to provide evidence of liability insurance before a construction contract is granted.

Promoting Risk Control

Insurance often provides an insured with the incentive to undertake cost-effective risk control measures. This incentive usually takes the form of risk-sharing mechanisms, such as deductibles, premium credit incentives, and contractual requirements, but it has also begun to take the form of collected data that can be used to prevent or limit losses before they happen.

Internet of Things (IoT)
A network of objects that transmit data to and from each other without human interaction.

For instance, with a growing number of devices connected to the **Internet of Things**, it is possible to use information gathered to monitor an insured device's maintenance needs. If a manufacturer's most important piece of machinery is in danger of breaking down, proper use of collected data could notify the insured beforehand, enabling repairs or updates to be made before the situation progresses to an insured loss.

Another example is the use of telematics in personal autos. By providing discounts to verified safe drivers, insurers can reduce the number of accidents; the amount of losses they have to pay; and, as a result, the premiums required of insureds. Risk control measures can save not only financial resources but also lives. Therefore, society as a whole benefits.

Enabling Efficient Use of Resources

Without insurance, people and businesses that face an uncertain future would have to set aside sufficient funds to pay for future losses. However, insurance makes it unnecessary to set aside a large amount of money to pay for the financial consequences of loss exposures that can be insured. In exchange for a comparatively small premium, individuals and organizations can free up additional funds. As a result, the money that would otherwise be set aside to pay for possible losses can be used to improve an individual's quality of life or to contribute to the growth of an organization.

Providing Support for Insureds' Credit

Insurance can provide support for an insured's credit by facilitating loans to individuals and organizations. Insurance guarantees that the lender will be able to receive payment for the loan it has provided, even if the collateral for the loan (such as a house or a commercial building) is destroyed or damaged by an insured event.

Providing a Source of Investment Funds

Having a robust insurance plan can help an insured financially because the funds that would otherwise be needed to pay for large potential losses can instead be invested in bonds, the stock market, or development projects.

Similarly, insurers can invest the funds that they collect in premiums until they are needed to pay insureds' claims. These investments can provide money for projects such as new construction, research, and technology advancements. Investment funds promote economic growth and job creation that, in turn, benefit individuals, organizations, and society, as well as provide profit that allows insurers to keep insurance premiums at a reasonable level.

Reducing Social Burdens

Finally, insurance can help reduce social burdens. For example, the social costs of natural disasters, such as large hurricanes or coastal storms, are increased by uninsured losses suffered by individuals and organizations that can amount to billions of dollars. Insurance helps to reduce the burden on the state or federal government by indemnifying the affected parties.

Compulsory auto insurance is another example, because it provides compensation to auto accident victims who might otherwise be unable to afford proper medical care or who might be unable to work because of the accident.

The Costs of Insurance

Although insurance, on the whole, is a net benefit for insureds and society at large, it also comes with some costs, including these:

- Premiums paid by insureds
- Operating costs of insurers
- Opportunity costs
- Increased losses

The premiums paid by insureds are necessary to generate the funds insurers use for loss payments. Despite the fact that insurance premiums, by law, must not be excessive, insureds may believe that their premiums are too high, most likely because the benefits of insurance may be intangible unless the insured suffers a covered loss and the subsequent claim is paid. But, as noted previously, if insurers can wisely invest the premiums they are paid, the resulting financial gains can be used to mitigate some of this cost for insureds.

The operating costs incurred by insurers, unfortunately, cannot be reduced as easily. As with any other business, an insurer has operating costs that must be paid to continue the day-to-day operations of the company. Insurers' operating costs include salaries, producers' commissions, advertising, building expenses, equipment, taxes, licensing fees, and so forth.

The opportunity costs of insurance are that the capital and labor being used in the insurance industry could be used elsewhere and could create other productive contributions to society. For insureds, the funds they use to pay their insurance premiums could be used for more immediate needs, such as new furniture or traveling, rather than protecting themselves from potential losses.

Finally, the existence of insurance may encourage losses. Although insurers have an economic incentive to provide and encourage risk control measures, insureds may have an economic incentive to claim losses. Fraudulent claims increase costs for both insurers (in terms of payment for fraudulent claims and the costs of investigating and resisting fraud) and insureds (who pay increased premiums to help cover the costs of those who defraud insurers).

MAJOR ROLES OF INSURANCE

Almost every person, family, and organization needs insurance of some type to protect assets against unforeseen events that could cause financial hardship. Sometimes, insurance is required to satisfy a contractual obligation, such as when a homeowner buys insurance on a home to protect the mortgage company's investment in the event the home is damaged or destroyed.

Almost everyone needs insurance, but not everyone fully understands it. What exactly is insurance?

One way to define insurance is to examine how it operates in each of these four major roles:

- As a risk management technique
- As a risk transfer system
- As a business
- As a contract

Insurance as a Risk Management Technique

Individuals, families, and organizations face loss exposures every day, many of which can have serious financial consequences. For example, a person operating an automobile may cause an accident, leading to thousands of dollars of damage to the property of others, plus medical expenses for the people involved. Businesses can also face an additional variety of loss exposures, such as damage to premises, injury to workers, and harm to customers from defective products or workmanship, but they also often have more risk management options available than personal insurance customers.

Sometimes, it makes more financial sense for a person or an organization to retain some loss exposures. For instance, a flat tire is a nuisance and an expense, but its financial impact is relatively minor. And because it is a common occurrence, purchasing insurance to cover the exposure could cost as much as a new tire.

At the other end of the spectrum, however, are loss exposures with the potential to create financial ruin—such as fires. Prudent persons and organizations must find ways to deal with these exposures other than retention.

Several risk management techniques are available to help mitigate the financial consequences of loss exposures. A person or an organization may choose to avoid a particular type of loss exposure. For example, a city dweller may avoid the loss exposures arising from the ownership, maintenance, and use of an automobile by not owning one and, instead, using public transportation or transportation network services. Loss exposures can also be controlled by loss prevention measures (such as the use of safety goggles and helmets by construction workers to reduce the frequency of injuries) and loss reduction measures (such as the placement of fire extinguishers in the home or workplace to reduce the severity of fire losses).

Some loss exposures are not easy to retain, avoid, or control. For example, Ming lives sixteen miles from his workplace, and no public transportation is available. He also needs a car for shopping, running errands, and seeing friends—so owning and operating a motor vehicle makes sense for him. However, this creates loss exposures for Ming; the bodily injury or property damage that might result from his negligent operation of the automobile could reach hundreds of thousands of dollars. He cannot afford to retain such loss exposures, and it is not practical to avoid them.

Though he may keep his vehicle well maintained and drive safely to control these loss exposures, he cannot guarantee avoiding or minimizing the financial consequences of a serious accident. For Ming, the best risk management technique may be transfer, so that the financial consequences of loss will be borne by another party. Ming could use forms of noninsurance transfer, but insurance is probably the most economically viable choice for him. Personal insurance customers often have fewer risk management options than larger commercial insurance customers.

The decision-making process used to determine which risk management technique best suits an insured's needs has become more reliant on technology and **big data**. Insurance professionals can use an abundance of new data to analyze an insured's history and needs. They can then recommend coverages, as well as risk control and loss prevention techniques, that could make the recommended coverages more affordable. This not only saves the insured money on the policy premium, but helps the insurer keep claims costs down.

Big data
Sets of data that are too large to be gathered and analyzed by traditional methods.

Insurance as a Risk Transfer System

Insurance enables a person, a family, or an organization to transfer the costs of losses to an insurer. The insurer, in turn, pays claims for covered losses from the premiums it has collected and, in effect, distributes the costs of the losses among all its insureds. In that way, insurance is a system of both transferring and sharing the costs of losses.

By transferring the costs of their losses to insurers through an insurance policy, insureds exchange the possibility of a large loss for the certainty of a much smaller, periodic payment (the premium that the insured pays for insurance coverage). Insurers, in turn, pool the premiums paid by insureds and use those funds to pay insureds who incur covered losses. The total cost of losses is thereby spread (or shared) among all insureds.

Insurers determine the total amount of premiums they must collect from insureds to cover future losses and expenses by considering past loss experience and the **law of large numbers**. Because insurers have large numbers of independent exposure units (the cars and houses of all their insureds, for example), they can predict the number of losses that all similar exposure units combined are likely to experience.

Law of large numbers

A mathematical principle stating that as the number of similar but independent exposure units increases, the relative accuracy of predictions about future outcomes (losses) also increases.

Property-casualty insurance

One of the two main sectors of the insurance industry, encompassing numerous types of insurance, most of which cover the financial consequences of damage to one's own property or legal liability to others.

Insurance as a Business

The insurance business can be divided into two sectors: property-casualty and life-health. The **property-casualty insurance** sector consists of homeowners, automobile, and commercial general liability insurance. Life-health insurance, meanwhile, consists of numerous types of insurance that cover the financial consequences of death, injury, and sickness.

Private insurers vary enormously in size and structure, the products they sell, and the territories they serve; collectively they represent a substantial segment of business in the United States. Despite their size and number, however, private insurers do not fill every insurance need. In some instances, federal and state governments step in to meet the property and liability insurance needs of the public.

State governments closely regulate the business of insurance through their insurance departments, requiring private insurers to be licensed (for most types of insurance) in the states where they sell insurance. Because regulation of licensed insurers encompasses all insurer operations, state insurance regulators review insurance rates, policy forms, underwriting practices, claims practices, and financial performance. If an insurer does not fully comply with state regulations, regulators can revoke its license.

State insurance regulators, insurance producers, stockholders, and insureds also need to be assured of an insurer's financial health. An insurer's revenue must, in the long run, match or exceed the amount it pays for claims and administrative expenses if the insurer is to remain financially viable.

The primary sources of revenue for insurers are premiums and the income produced from investing premiums between the time they are collected and the time they are used to pay covered claims. Insurers' income streams need to overcome several expenses, ranging from claim payments and loss settlement expenses to general expenses such as salaries, employee benefits, utilities, telephones, and computer equipment. However, the ability to pay these expenses and still make a reasonable profit is just one measure of an insurer's success.

Insurance as a Contract

An insurance policy is a contract between the insurer and the insured where the insured transfers the possible costs of covered losses to the insurer. In return for the premiums paid by insureds, insurers promise to pay for the losses covered by the insurance policy, which reduces the uncertainty or insecurity an insured may have about paying for potential losses. Insurance policies enable individuals, families, and organizations to protect their assets and minimize the adverse financial effects of losses, and the contractual nature of insurance policies gives legal force and protection to the rights and responsibilities of all of the parties.

Insurance policies must meet the same requirements as any other valid contract. That is, they must entail an agreement between competent parties for a legal purpose that involves the exchange of consideration. Additionally, insurance policies have certain special characteristics, including these:

- A contract of **utmost good faith**—Both parties to an insurance contract, the insured and the insurer, are expected to be ethical in their dealings with each other.

- A **contract of adhesion**—Because the insurer wrote or chose the policy and the insured generally has no say, if the policy wording is ambiguous, a court will generally apply the interpretation that favors the insured.

- A **contract of indemnity**—Insurance does not necessarily pay the full amount necessary to restore an insured who has suffered a covered loss to the same financial position, but the amount the insurer pays is directly related to the amount of the insured's loss and will not enable the insured to profit from the loss.

When structuring an insurance policy, insurers use one of two approaches: self-contained or modular. Self-contained policies usually include both property and liability coverages in a single document, such as the Insurance Services Office, Inc. (ISO) Personal Auto Policy. Modular policies, meanwhile, combine coverage forms and other documents to tailor a policy to the insured's needs. Commercial package policies and businessowners policies, for example, are modular policies.

Utmost good faith

An obligation to act in complete honesty and to disclose all relevant facts.

Contract of adhesion

Any contract in which one party is put in a "take-it-or-leave-it" position and must either accept the contract as written by the other party or reject the contract entirely.

Contract of indemnity

A contract in which the insurer agrees, in the event of a covered loss, to pay an amount directly related to the amount of the loss.

COMMON TYPES OF PERSONAL AND COMMERCIAL INSURANCE

The coverage provided by personal and commercial insurance policies enables individuals, families, and businesses to protect their assets and minimize the adverse financial effects of loss.

Personal insurance policies cover individuals and families against their personal (nonbusiness) loss exposures, while commercial insurance policies cover for-profit businesses or not-for-profit organizations against their commercial loss exposures. See the exhibit "Types of Insurance Policies—An Example."

Types of Insurance Policies—An Example

Rob and his wife, Laurie, own a sandwich shop in a suburban shopping center. They also own a home and two cars. Rob and Laurie are concerned that damage to their business or home could result in substantial financial loss. They have contacted their insurance agent to discuss these concerns and to design an insurance program to meet their personal and commercial needs.

The insurance agent will determine Rob and Laurie's insurance policy needs by examining their loss exposures. Because Rob and Laurie have both personal and commercial loss exposures, they will need both personal and commercial insurance policies.

The personal insurance policies will cover losses arising out of Rob and Laurie's personal loss exposures related to the ownership of the home and cars. For loss exposures arising from the sandwich shop, Rob and Laurie will need commercial insurance policies.

[DA00422]

Personal Insurance

Personal insurance policies fall into these general categories:

- Property insurance protects an insured's assets by covering the cost of repairing or replacing property that is damaged, lost, or destroyed. If net income is lost or extra expenses are incurred because of a loss, those may be covered, too.
- Liability insurance provides for payment on behalf of the insured for injury to others or damage to others' property for which the insured is legally responsible. It also covers the cost to defend the insured, up to the policy limit, against claims or suits alleging that the insured is legally responsible for injury or damage that the policy covers.

- Life insurance replaces the income-earning potential lost through death. It also helps to pay expenses related to an insured's death.

- Health insurance protects individuals and families from financial losses caused by sickness and accidents. Disability insurance is a form of health insurance that replaces an insured's income if the insured is unable to work because of illness or injury.

Personal insurance may be further divided into specific types of policies. See the exhibit "Common Types of Personal Insurance."

Common Types of Personal Insurance

- Homeowners
- Personal auto
- Personal watercraft
- Personal umbrella
- Life insurance
- Health insurance
- Annuities

[DA07568]

Property and Liability Insurance

A **homeowners policy** provides property and liability coverage for individuals and families. The property coverage protects an insured's home and its contents for damage caused by fire, wind, and other causes of loss. Most homeowners policies also include coverage for the theft or destruction of the home's contents. In addition, homeowners policies include personal liability coverage for allegations of negligence.

A **personal auto policy (PAP)** covers liability losses occurring from bodily injury to another person or damage to the property of others that results from an auto accident for which the insured is liable. It also covers vehicle damage resulting from a collision, while Other Than Collision coverage covers the vehicle for fire, theft, wind, contact with an animal, and other causes of loss.

The personal liability coverage in the homeowners policy and the auto liability coverage in the PAP exclude or limit coverage for operation of most watercraft. Therefore, a person who owns a boat may need a separate personal watercraft policy that covers both legal liability and physical damage.

Juries often award large sums of money in liability cases, and many homeowners have significant assets to protect. Because this may require some insureds to have higher limits of insurance than those available under personal liability or personal auto coverage, personal umbrella liability policies

Homeowners policy

Policy that covers most of the property and liability loss exposures that arise out of residential property ownership and occupancy, as well as property and liability loss exposures that individuals and families may have while they are away from their residences.

Personal auto policy (PAP)

An insurance policy that covers an individual or a family against loss exposures arising out of the ownership, maintenance, or use of automobiles.

provide an additional layer of liability coverage. Typical limits for a personal umbrella policy range from $1 million to $2 million, but higher limits are available if necessary.

Life and Health Insurance

The main purpose of life insurance is to replace the income-earning potential of a family's primary wage earner who died, but it also helps pay expenses related to an insured's death. There are two main categories of life insurance: term life insurance, which lasts for a defined period of time and does not accrue cash value, and permanent life insurance, which offers lifetime protection and does accrue cash value over time.

With health coverage, various forms of health insurance can be purchased on an individual or a group basis. Medical insurance covers medical expenses that result from illness or injury. Disability income insurance provides periodic income payments to an insured who is unable to work because of sickness or injury. Long-term care insurance provides coverage for nursing-home care and home healthcare.

Commercial Insurance

Loss exposures that arise from business operations can be covered under commercial insurance policies. See the exhibit "Common Types of Commercial Insurance."

Common Types of Commercial Insurance

- Commercial package
- Business owners
- Commercial auto
- Commercial property
- Commercial inland marine
- Commercial crime
- Commercial general liability
- Ocean marine
- Professional liability
- Environmental liability
- Commercial umbrella liability
- Workers compensation

[DA07569]

Many business organizations purchase a commercial package policy (CPP) or a businessowners policy (BOP), both of which provide business owners with property, crime, and liability coverages. In the past, a business owner would have had to purchase several separate policies, rather than just one, to get all of the necessary coverages.

Commercial auto insurance covers an insured's legal liability resulting from the insured's ownership, maintenance, or use of an automobile. Legal costs to defend the insured are also included, up to the policy limits. Auto physical damage coverage provides protection for the loss of use of or damage to a vehicle listed on the policy because of a covered cause of loss, such as fire, theft, or collision with an animal.

Commercial property insurance covers damage to buildings and/or their contents resulting from fire, vandalism, and other causes of loss. Coverage is generally limited to property located on or near the insured's premises.

Ocean marine insurance covers ships and their cargo against losses like fire, lightning, and "perils of the sea." Most cargo that travels by water is insured as "ocean marine" or "wet marine." Cargo transported by land is typically called "inland marine" or "dry marine." Commercial inland marine insurance covers mobile equipment and property used away from the insured premises by commercial enterprises. This coverage protects goods in domestic transit and property used in transportation and communication, as well as property used on job sites, such as backhoes and other mobile equipment.

Commercial crime insurance protects the insured against theft of job-site contents, such as cash registers, computers, and inventory. It also insures money that might be stolen in a robbery during business hours or in a burglary that occurs while the business is closed, and it can cover theft of employer property by employees.

Commercial general liability (CGL) insurance offers broad protection against claims alleging that the insured is legally liable for bodily injury or damage to the property of others. For example, a retail store could be responsible if a customer falls on the store's wet floor and is injured. Also, if a customer is injured by a product the store sold, the CGL policy might cover defense costs as part of the store's legal liability. Even if a suit is groundless, the CGL policy offers protection and peace of mind to the business owner.

Professional liability insurance covers professionals such as accountants, attorneys, or consultants for harm resulting from errors or omissions arising out of their professional practices. It also covers doctors, professional trainers, and other healthcare professionals, such as physical therapists, for injury to their customers or patients that results from their errors or omissions.

Environmental liability insurance offers business owners protection against environmental damage that may occur as a result of business operations. It can help protect business owners from remediation and cleanup obligations triggered after an environmental incident, such as a leaking fuel tank. This

Commercial general liability (CGL) insurance

Insurance that covers many of the common liability loss exposures faced by an organization, including its premises, operations, and products.

type of coverage is desirable for businesses because the CGL policy will not cover most pollution-related claims.

Commercial umbrella liability coverage is similar to the personal umbrella coverage. It provides additional limits beyond those provided by the CGL, commercial auto, and other policies and protects the insured in the event of a large liability loss. It may also "drop down" to cover losses not insured under the underlying policies if the causes of loss are not specifically excluded in the umbrella policy.

Workers compensation insurance

Insurance that provides coverage for benefits an employer is obligated to pay under workers compensation laws.

Workers compensation insurance pays the cost of medical care, lost wages, and other state-mandated benefits when employees are injured on the job or acquire a job-related illness, such as asbestosis. Because employers are required by law to pay certain benefits to injured or ill employees, these benefits are payable regardless of who caused the injury or illness. In return for this no-fault coverage, the employee generally loses the right to sue his or her employer.

Apply Your Knowledge

A firm of computer-systems consultants would most likely purchase which one of the following types of coverage to protect them in the event that they provide incorrect advice that causes financial injury to a customer?

a.　Commercial general liability insurance

b.　Business auto insurance

c.　Environmental liability insurance

d.　Professional liability insurance

Feedback: *d.* Professional liability insurance covers professionals such as accountants, attorneys, or consultants for errors or omissions arising out of their professional practices.

TYPES OF PRIVATE INSURERS

Numerous kinds of private (nongovernment) insurers provide property and liability coverage for individuals, families, and organizations.

Private insurers may be classified based on a variety of factors, including their form of ownership. Proprietary insurers are formed to earn a profit for their owners, while cooperative insurers are formed to provide insurance at a minimum cost to their owners, who are the policyholders. Within these broad classifications are different types of private insurers, and we'll go over the differences and similarities among these:

- Stock insurers
- Mutual insurers
- Reciprocal insurance exchanges
- Lloyd's
- Surplus lines insurers
- Captive insurers
- Reinsurance companies

Stock Insurers

Many of the largest property-casualty insurers in the United States are **stock insurers**. One of the primary objectives of a stock insurer is returning a profit to its stockholders. These companies have been able to attract and retain stockholders by the expectation of investment returns. The stock form of ownership provides financial flexibility for the insurer. For example, a stock insurer can raise funds for expansion by selling additional shares of common stock.

Stockholders have the right to elect a board of directors, which has the authority to appoint a chief executive officer (CEO) and control the insurer's activities.

Stock insurer
An insurer that is owned by its stockholders and formed as a corporation for the purpose of earning a profit for the stockholders.

Mutual Insurers

Mutual insurers include some very large national insurers and many more regional ones. While classified as cooperative insurers, mutual insurers, like stock insurers, generally seek to earn a profit. To share profits, mutual insurers pay dividends to policyholders as a return of a portion of premiums paid. The policyholders of a mutual insurer have the right to elect a board of directors that performs the same functions as the board of directors of a stock insurer. Some mutual insurers have converted to stock insurers through a process called demutualization.

Some mutual insurers have the right to charge insureds an assessment, or additional premium, after the policy has gone into effect. Such an assessment might be made after the insurer has endured a series of losses from a catastrophic event, such as a hurricane. These insurers are known as assessment mutual insurance companies, and they are less common than in the past.

Mutual insurer
An insurer that is owned by its policyholders and formed as a corporation for the purpose of providing insurance to them.

Reciprocal Insurance Exchanges

Each member of a reciprocal insurance exchange, or interinsurance exchange, is both an insured and an insurer. Because a reciprocal's members, called subscribers, are not experts in running an insurance operation, they contract with an individual or organization to operate the reciprocal; this manager is called an attorney-in-fact. An agreement (known as a subscription agreement) authorizes the attorney-in-fact to act on behalf of the subscribers to market and underwrite insurance coverage, collect premiums, invest funds, and handle claims. The existence of an attorney-in-fact is one of the main features that distinguish a reciprocal from other types of insurers. Reciprocals make up a small percentage of the insurance companies in the U.S., but they include some major national and international insurers. Small regional reciprocals also operate on a state-by-state basis.

Lloyd's

Lloyd's (Lloyd's of London)
An association of investors, grouped in syndicates, who are represented by underwriters to write insurance and reinsurance.

Lloyd's (formerly Lloyd's of London) is an insurance and reinsurance marketplace whose operation resembles that of a stock exchange. Lloyd's is an unincorporated association. Members of Lloyd's are investors that hope to earn a profit from insurance operations that occur at Lloyd's. Each individual investor, called a "Name," belongs to one or more groups called syndicates.

Lloyd's has earned a reputation for accepting applications for unusual types of insurance, such as insuring the legs of a famous athlete against injury. However, the bulk of Lloyd's business does not involve such exotic coverages. Lloyd's functions as an alien insurer in the U.S. Underwriters at Lloyd's have licenses in the U.S., and it's usually one of the largest writers of premiums in the surplus lines market. Lloyd's is also a reinsurer in the U.S.[1]

Surplus Lines Insurers

Surplus lines insurer
A nonadmitted insurer that is eligible to insure risks that have been exported by a surplus lines licensee in accordance with a surplus lines law.

When new or unusual insurance needs arise, producers and consumers often turn to **surplus lines insurers**. Surplus lines insurance consists of insurance coverages unavailable in the standard market (usually because of pricing difficulties or an inability to meet underwriting requirements). For example, consider the case of a restaurant that has a history of grease fires in its kitchen. Its standard market insurer has decided not to renew its policy because of poor loss experience, and no other standard market insurer will accept an application for coverage. A surplus lines insurer may be willing to write insurance for this restaurant with a premium substantially higher than a standard market insurer would charge.

Also, as new insurance needs arise, the surplus lines market responds. Producers and consumers often turn to the surplus lines market when they have an immediate need for a new type of coverage. Surplus lines insurers can often respond quickly to these developing needs, while standard market insurers may take longer to analyze the need for new or revised coverage, and to file policy forms and rates for state approval.

Nonadmitted insurer
An insurer not authorized by the state insurance department to do business within that state.

Surplus lines insurers mirror stock insurers in how they are organized. Surplus lines insurance is written by **nonadmitted insurers**. Nonadmitted insurers are not required to file their rates and policy forms with state insurance departments, providing them with greater flexibility than that of standard (or admitted) insurers. Still, surplus lines insurers are subject to regulation. Some states maintain lists of nonadmitted insurers that are approved to accept business from the state; others keep lists of nonadmitted insurers that are not approved. See the exhibit "The Rise of Insurtech Companies."

The Rise of Insurtech Companies

Emerging technologies have led to the growth of insurtech (that is, the coupling of insurance and technology) companies. These companies can assist traditional insurers with offering innovative new products and services. Categories of insurtech companies include these:

- Microinsurance—Firms offering insurance to economically disadvantaged and other traditionally underserved segments of the population that are united in risk pools whose members are connected to the insurer through web-enabled platforms on cell phones and other devices

- Firms that facilitate the use of sensors, Internet of Things (IoT)-enabled devices, and other data-capture technology to help insurers and brokers more accurately assess and price individual risks

- Peer-to-peer insurance—Firms that use web-enabled platforms to facilitate the formation of self-selected risk pools whose members (usually friends, relatives, or like-minded individuals) pool premiums and collectively pay for members' insured losses

- On-demand insurance (also known as need-based insurance)—Firms that use web-enabled customer interfaces and sensor technology to offer coverage that allows near-total customization for customers

[DA12776]

Captive Insurers

Captive insurers have become an important alternative in the insurance-buying decisions of corporations. A captive helps eliminate problems some corporations face when necessary or desired insurance coverage is unavailable or costs more than the corporation is willing or able to pay. Captives might be able to provide insurance coverage at a lower cost than other private insurers because acquisition costs are eliminated. A premium paid to a captive remains within the corporate structure until it is used to pay claims, which contributes to an improved cash flow for the organization.

Captive insurer
An insurer formed primarily to cover the loss exposures of its parent or members.

Apply Your Knowledge

Eastfork Insurance is a private insurer that provides property and liability insurance to businesses. Its goal is to make a profit. In the past year, it achieved its goal by collecting more in premiums than it paid in losses and expenses. Now, Eastfork Insurance will provide dividend payments to its policyholders.

An insurance company that operates like this is classified as a:

a.   Stock insurer
b.   Mutual insurer
c.   Surplus lines insurer
d.   Captive insurer

Feedback: b. Eastfork Insurance is a mutual insurer because, while its goal is to make a profit, it will use that profit to pay dividends to its policyholders rather than stockholders.

Reinsurance Companies

Reinsurance

The transfer of insurance risk from one insurer to another through a contractual agreement under which one insurer (the reinsurer) agrees, in return for a reinsurance premium, to indemnify another insurer (the primary insurer) for some or all of the financial consequences of certain loss exposures covered by the primary's insurance policies.

Some private insurers provide **reinsurance**. One of the most important reasons a primary insurer might buy reinsurance is that reinsurance permits the primary insurer to transfer some loss exposures to the reinsurer. For example, an insurer that writes a large amount of property insurance in an area where tornadoes commonly occur can use reinsurance to reduce its exposure to windstorm losses.

Reinsurance also enables a small insurer to provide insurance for large accounts (such as large national or multinational corporations) whose insurance needs would otherwise exceed the insurer's capacity. For example, consider a primary insurer that writes a commercial liability policy for a large company that manufactures sports helmets. Because the potential for large liability losses resulting from injuries caused by defective helmets is great, the primary insurer might contract with a reinsurer to cover all of its liability losses for this insured over a certain amount, such as $1 million. Now, the primary insurer and the reinsurer share the liability loss exposures for this insured.

GOVERNMENT INSURANCE PROGRAMS

In some cases, property-casualty insurance for certain loss exposures can be obtained only through government insurance programs.

The United States federal government and individual state governments provide certain insurance programs for various reasons. Government can participate in these programs as an exclusive insurer, as a partner with private insurers, or as a competitor to private insurers. Some government property-casualty insurance programs are administered by state governments, while others are operated at the federal level.

Reasons for Government Insurance Programs

Government insurance programs exist for these main purposes:

- To fill unmet needs in the private insurance market
- To facilitate compulsory insurance purchases
- To provide efficiency in the market and convenience to insureds
- To achieve collateral social purposes

Fill Unmet Needs in the Private Insurance Market

When private insurers are unable or unwilling to satisfy certain insurance needs, government programs can provide insurance to meet legitimate public demands. By offering such programs, the government provides protection against loss that would otherwise not be provided.

Facilitate Compulsory Insurance Purchases

Another reason federal and state governments are involved in insurance is to facilitate compulsory insurance purchases. For example, workers compensation insurance has proven to efficiently manage workplace injuries. However, it is possible that some employers would not purchase workers compensation insurance if they were not required to do so.

Because states require employers to purchase this insurance (or provide proof of self-insurance), they must have a mechanism to ensure that workers compensation insurance is available at a reasonable cost. Another example is personal automobile liability insurance. As auto liability coverage is required in almost all states, each state has some type of mechanism in place to provide insurance for those drivers who cannot obtain coverage at a reasonable price in the private market. In the workers compensation and auto liability insurance markets, most consumers obtain coverage through private insurers.

Provide Efficiency in the Market and Convenience to Insureds

Two related rationales for government involvement in insurance are providing efficiency in the market and providing convenience to insureds. In economic terms, these two rationales are essentially the same. Providing convenience to insureds, by reducing either the time or the resources they need to expend to obtain the desired insurance coverage, adds to the efficiency of the market.

Legislators often find it is more efficient to establish government insurance plans for particular purposes than to invite and analyze bids from private insurers and then supervise and regulate the resulting plans. When insurance provided by the government is compulsory, spending money on marketing or paying sales commissions (two large expenses for insurers) is unnecessary. Governments sometimes try to avoid sales costs by setting up their own distribution channels. Alternatively, as is the case with the National Flood Insurance Program (NFIP), they market through established insurance producers who also market other insurance.

Achieve Collateral Social Purposes

The government may participate in insurance to accomplish social goals because insurance is often seen as a social good. By making use of the pooling mechanism, insurance can reduce risk to society. This is beneficial both to society and to the overall economy.

An issue arises when individuals do not have an incentive to purchase insurance, even though it would benefit society. If, for example, an organization conducted a cost-benefit analysis and determined that workers compensation insurance was too expensive, it would not want to purchase the insurance. However, workers compensation laws encourage injury prevention and injured workers' rehabilitation. Therefore, the government provides incentives for the purchase of insurance through a combination of regulation and provision of insurance at a reasonable price. Organizations respond to these measures by purchasing insurance, which, as well as benefiting the organization, benefits society.

Level of Government Involvement

There are three levels at which the government can participate in an insurance program:

- The government can be an exclusive insurer either because of law or because no private insurer offers a competing plan. For example, in a few states, all employers must obtain their workers compensation insurance from the state-owned insurer (called an exclusive, or monopolistic, fund).

- Government partnerships with private insurers can develop when private insurers are no longer able to adequately provide coverages they had typically offered previously. The NFIP is an example of a partnership under which the federal government underwrites the insurance policy but private insurers and insurance producers deliver the policies to consumers. The private insurers take a percentage of the premium as a sales commission and pass the remainder of the premium on to the NFIP.

- Government involvement may also take the form of operating an insurance plan in direct competition with private insurers. This type of involvement often evolves when the private insurance market has not failed, but is not operating as efficiently as regulators prefer. Examples include the competitive workers compensation funds offered in some states.

Common Examples of Federal and State Programs

The final distinction among government property-casualty insurance programs is whether a state government or the federal government is involved with the program. Common examples of federal government insurance plans include NFIP and federal crop insurance.

Examples of state government insurance programs include workers compensation plans, residual auto plans, and beach and windstorm plans. See the exhibit "Examples of Property-Casualty Insurance Offered by State Governments."

Examples of Property-Casualty Insurance Offered by State Governments

Plan	Characteristics of Government Plan	Relationship to Private Insurance
Fair Access to Insurance Requirements (FAIR) Plans	Make basic property insurance available to property owners who are otherwise unable to obtain insurance because of their property's location or any other reason.	• Organization varies by state. Typically it is an insurance pool through which private insurers collectively address an unmet need for property insurance on urban properties. • Does not replace normal channels of insurance; is only for consumers who could not obtain coverage in the private market.
Workers Compensation Insurance	Helps employers meet their obligations under state statutes to injured workers.	• Private insurers provide workers compensation insurance. • State government can operate as an exclusive insurer, as a competitor to private insurers, or as a residual market.
Beach and Windstorm Plans	Make property insurance against the windstorm cause of loss available to property owners who are otherwise unable to obtain insurance because of their property's location.	• Organization varies by state: some states are insurance pools of private insurers; other states are ultimately guaranteed with taxpayer funds. • Does not replace normal channels of insurance; is only for consumers who could not obtain coverage in the private market.
Residual Auto Plans	Make compulsory automobile liability coverage available to high-risk drivers who have difficulty purchasing coverage at a reasonable rate in the private market.	• Organization varies by state. Typically it is an insurance pool through which private insurers collectively address an unmet need for compulsory auto liability coverage. • Does not replace normal channels of insurance; is only for consumers who could not obtain coverage in the private market.

[DA07628]

OVERVIEW OF INSURANCE FUNCTIONS

While insurers are known for selling insurance policies and paying claims, they also do much more than that.

Insurers will always look to protect their customers, but they must balance this goal with that of earning a profit. To accomplish this balance, insurers perform multiple functions:

- Marketing
- Underwriting
- Claims
- Risk control
- Premium audit

While many insurers have established departments for each of these functions, some of the functions may be performed by individual producers, actuarial firms, third-party administrative firms, or other outside entities. Additionally, individual insurers may use different terms for these functions in the course of their daily routines.

Whatever name they go by and whoever may perform them, the efficient interaction of these functions is vital to the survival and continued success of an organization.

Marketing

Marketing determines the products or services customers want and need. The marketing function contributes significantly to an insurer's goals of meeting customers' needs and making a profit while doing so.

A successful marketing program usually has these components:

- Market research that helps determine the needs of potential customers
- Advertising that informs customers about the insurer's products and services
- Use of social media platforms to interact effectively with customers
- Selection of appropriate marketing systems
- Training to prepare the sales force to meet customer needs
- Setting sales goals and implementing strategies for achieving them
- Motivating, managing, and training the sales force to meet customer needs

Underwriting

The process of selecting insureds, pricing coverage, determining insurance policy terms and conditions, and then monitoring the underwriting decisions made.

Underwriting

The role of the **underwriting** function is to determine how much coverage the insurer should offer for a given loss exposure, as well as at what price and under what conditions the coverage should be offered. Underwriters typically follow the underwriting process, which involves gathering the necessary information to make an underwriting decision, making the decision, and then implementing it.

Underwriters must carry out a variety of activities to apply the underwriting process. These underwriting activities are central to the underwriting process:

- Selecting insureds
- Pricing coverage
- Determining policy terms and conditions

Underwriters carefully screen potential insureds to determine which ones to insure. They make their selections by applying the underwriting criteria set by the insurer to the loss exposures of customers who have applied for insurance policies. A successful underwriting function ensures that those applicants who are selected receive the level of coverage that adequately reflects their loss exposures at the appropriate price.

Increasingly, underwriters can rely on advances in technology to help them complete their tasks more quickly and more accurately. The use of artificial intelligence has grown, providing almost immediate review of information used by underwriters, such as risks present at a potential insured's worksite or coverages that might suit a client better than the policy currently being offered.

After a potential insured has been approved, underwriting determines the price for the insurance being offered. The goal is to charge a premium that is commensurate with the loss exposure. The premium should be adequate to enable the total premiums paid by a large group of similar insureds to pay the losses and expenses of that group while also allowing the insurer to earn a reasonable profit.

Selection of insureds and pricing of coverage are intertwined with a third underwriting activity: determining policy terms and conditions. This sets certain qualifiers in place, some that exclude coverage in certain circumstances and others that outline the responsibilities of insureds in the instance of loss of or damage to insured property (such as notifying authorities if a crime occurred).

Claims

Insurers expect to pay claims—without them, insurance would be unnecessary. When policyholders purchase insurance, they are buying protection for the potential financial consequences of covered losses. The insurer's claims function is responsible for keeping the promise to make payments to or on behalf of the insured for covered losses by providing prompt and professional loss adjustment services.

When evaluating a claim, the adjuster typically applies a claims handling process that includes these six activities:

1. Acknowledging a claim and assigning it to a claims representative
2. Identifying the policy
3. Contacting the insured or the insured's representative
4. Investigating and documenting the claim
5. Determining cause of loss and loss amount
6. Concluding the claim

Because more than half of what insurers spend goes to the claims function, its proper and efficient performance is important to an insurer's profitability. The growing use of data mining has helped insurers determine the average length of time each step in the claims process takes, providing an opportunity to improve efficiency where needed. Additionally, data mining can supply information that helps an insurer identify potential fraud or subrogation opportunities, enabling the insurer to assign such cases to experienced representatives.

Business process management (BPM)

A systematic, iterative plan to analyze and improve business processes through life-cycle phases to achieve long-term goals and client satisfaction.

Business process management (BPM) can be applied to the claims handling process to improve customer service, efficiency, and cost-effectiveness. To achieve its goal of optimizing the claims handling process, BPM begins with exploratory analysis of the current process and then develops models for improvement. Data analysis is used in gathering intelligence as well as developing models.

Risk Control

From an economic viewpoint, controlling risks is preferable to insuring them because it generally costs less to do so. For example, installing handrails along an elevated walkway would probably cost less than paying the medical expenses for anyone who falls off it. As a practical matter, insurance and **risk control** are likely to be used jointly for most large loss exposures, because preventing all losses is seldom possible.

Risk control

A conscious act or decision not to act that reduces the frequency and/or severity of losses or makes losses more predictable.

The risk control function supports underwriters in selecting which loss exposures to insure. Risk control representatives can use predictive analytics and other technology to obtain information beyond what the insurance application provides to underwriters; in turn, this can help improve decision making.

Additionally, risk control professionals can work directly with insureds, providing suggestions as to which loss control techniques would be most effective at lowering the amount of risk they face and, as a result, helping to lower the insured's premiums.

Premium Audit

When commercial insurance policies are written, it is not uncommon for the premium to be calculated using a loss exposure measurement that could change during the policy period (usually one year). Therefore, the **premium audit** function, which occurs at the end of a policy period, determines whether any adjustments to the premium are required, based on the insured's actual loss exposures during that period.

For example, the premium of a workers compensation policy, which covers expenses when an employee is injured on the job, is based on the total amount of the insured employer's payroll. However, because of new hires, raises, terminations, and retirements during the policy period, the employer won't know the actual size of its payroll until the end of the policy period. Only after the policy period is completed can the insurer and the insured determine how much the actual premium should be.

Premium audit

Methodical examination of a policyholder's operations, records, and books of account to determine the actual exposure units and premium for insurance coverages already provided.

Apply Your Knowledge

For each of these activities, identify the insurance function that is most closely associated with it:

Determining the premium for a new customer's personal auto policy

a.   Underwriting

b.   Risk control

c.   Marketing

d.   Premium audit

Feedback: a. This activity is an underwriting function.

Visiting a prospective insured's factory to inspect the fire suppression system

a.   Marketing

b.   Risk control

c.   Premium audit

d.   Claims

Feedback: b. This activity is a risk control function.

Advertising a new policy program for small businesses

a.   Risk control

b.   Premium audit

c.   Marketing

d.   Claims

Feedback: c. This activity is a marketing function.

Reviewing an insured's payroll records for the preceding year at the end of a policy period

a.   Risk control

b.   Marketing

c.   Claims

d.   Premium audit

Feedback: d. This activity is a premium audit function.

Determining the cause and amount of a policyholder's loss

a.   Marketing

b.   Underwriting

c.   Claims

d.   Risk control

Feedback: c. This activity is a claims function.

SUMMARY

Insurance can help individuals and organizations achieve risk financing goals, such as paying for losses, managing cash flow uncertainty, and complying with legal requirements. It also provides several benefits to individuals, organizations, and society in general by encouraging an insured's loss control activities, enabling efficient use of resources, providing support for insureds' credit, providing insurers with a source of investment funds, and reducing social burdens by helping insureds recover after a loss. There are costs to insurance, such as the premiums paid by insureds, operating costs of insurers, opportunity costs, and the possibility of increased losses.

Insurance may be viewed as a risk management technique, as a risk transfer system in which the insured transfers the risk of financial loss to the insurer, as a business, and as a contract between an insured and an insurer that states which losses the insured is transferring to the insurer and expresses the insurer's promise to indemnify the insured for those possible losses in exchange for a stated regular payment by the insured.

Many types of property-casualty insurance policies cover personal loss exposures, which are mainly related to an insured's residences, personal vehicles, or owned watercraft, while a variety of life and health policies protect the health, medical well-being, and lives of families and individuals. Commercial insurance policies often combine liability and property coverages into a single CPP or a BOP, providing protection for a wide array of loss exposures.

Different types of private insurers provide property and liability coverage to people and businesses. Private insurers can be classified as stock insurers, mutual insurers, reciprocal insurance exchanges, Lloyd's, surplus lines insurers, captive insurers, and reinsurance companies.

Government insurance programs exist to fill unmet needs in the private insurance market, to facilitate compulsory insurance purchases, to provide efficiency in the market and convenience to insureds, and to achieve collateral social purposes. There are three levels at which the government can participate in an insurance program—as an exclusive insurer, as a partner with a private insurer, or as an insurer that competes with private insurers. Government-run insurance programs may operate at the state or federal level.

Like many businesses, insurers pursue their goals by segmenting operations into functional areas, or departments. These departments cooperate to serve the primary functions of making insureds financially whole again after a loss and creating a profit for the insurer. An insurer's key functions are marketing, underwriting, claims, risk control, and premium audit. Each department must interact effectively with other departments for the insurer to achieve its goals.

ASSIGNMENT NOTE

1.   Lloyd's, "About Lloyd's in the U.S.," www.lloyds.com/lloyds-around-the-world/americas/us-homepage/about-us (accessed June 14, 2018).

Direct Your Learning ▶▶

2

Insurance Regulation

Educational Objectives

After learning the content of this assignment, you should be able to:

▷ Explain why insurance operations are regulated.

▷ Explain how individual states in the United States regulate the licensing of insurers.

▷ Summarize the regulation of insurance rates and policy forms by individual states in the United States.

▷ Explain how the individual states in the United States regulate insurance marketing activities and insurer solvency.

Insurance Regulation

2

WHY INSURANCE OPERATIONS ARE REGULATED

When purchasing insurance, consumers may have many questions and concerns about whether the coverage they are purchasing will really protect them. Insurance regulation is meant to address many of these concerns.

Insurance consumers' concerns include whether the policy forms give them the coverage they expect and need, whether the price is appropriate, and whether the insurer will have the resources needed to pay losses that may occur months or even years after a policy has been purchased. To protect individuals, organizations, and entire communities from these kinds of problems, all of the states in the United States regulate insurance. Regulation varies considerably from state to state. However, most states focus their regulatory efforts on the same key areas of insurer operations: licensing, insurance rates, insurance policies, market conduct, and insurer solvency.

Insurers are regulated primarily for three reasons:

- To protect consumers
- To maintain insurer solvency
- To prevent destructive competition

Protect Consumers

Insurance is regulated to protect consumers. Many insurance policies are complex legal documents that may be difficult for some consumers to analyze and understand. Regulators help protect consumers by reviewing insurance policy forms to determine whether they benefit consumers. Regulators can set coverage standards, specify policy language for certain insurance coverages, and disapprove unacceptable policies.

Insurance regulators also protect consumers against fraud and unethical market behavior by insurers and producers, such as selling unnecessary insurance, misrepresenting coverage to make a sale, or refusing to pay legitimate claims.

Regulators try to ensure that insurance is readily available, especially the insurance that is viewed as a necessity. For example, all states try to make personal auto insurance available by restricting the rights of insurers to cancel or refuse to renew personal auto insurance policies.

Maintain Insurer Solvency

Solvency

The ability of an insurer to meet its financial obligations as they become due, even those resulting from insured losses that may be claimed several years in the future.

Insurance is regulated to maintain insurer **solvency**. Insurance regulators try to maintain and enhance the financial condition of private insurers for several reasons:

- Premiums are paid in advance, and the period of protection extends into the future. If an insurer becomes insolvent, future claims might not be paid even though the premium has been paid. Consumers may find it difficult to evaluate insurers' financial ability to keep their promises.

- Regulation is needed to protect the public interest. Large numbers of individuals are adversely affected when insurers become insolvent. For example, an unusually large catastrophe that affects a large area can make an insurer's financial ability to pay claims uncertain, such as when Hurricane Andrew struck Florida in 1992 and caused seven insurer insolvencies.

- Insurers hold substantial funds for the ultimate benefit of policyholders. Government regulation is necessary to safeguard such funds.

Despite regulatory reviews, insurers have become insolvent. However, sound regulation minimizes the number of insolvencies.

Prevent Destructive Competition

Insurance is regulated to prevent destructive competition. Therefore, regulators are responsible for determining whether insurance rates are adequate.

At times, some insurers price their policies too low in an effort to attract customers away from higher-priced competitors. This practice drives down price levels in the whole insurance market. Therefore, when insurance rate levels become inadequate, some insurers may not collect enough money to pay all of their insureds' claims and may become insolvent. Other insurers might lose so much profit that they withdraw from the market or stop writing new business. An insurance shortage can then develop, and individuals and organizations might be unable to obtain the coverage they need.

For example, following periods of intense competition among insurers, pharmaceutical companies have found it difficult to obtain commercial liability insurance to cover the risk of product defects in the drugs they manufacture.

INSURER LICENSING

Most insurance companies must be licensed by the state insurance department before they are authorized to write insurance policies in that state.

In the United States, insurers are licensed as domestic insurers in the states where they are domiciled. When insurers wish to operate in additional states, they become licensed as foreign insurers. Insurers domiciled outside the U.S.

are licensed as alien insurers. Surplus lines insurers typically operate through a specially licensed producer.

In addition to requiring that insurance companies (most commonly stock, mutual, or reciprocal exchange insurers) be licensed, states also generally require that certain individual insurance professionals, such as producers and claims representatives, be licensed.

Insurer's Licensing Status

An insurer's licensing status in a given state may assume any one of several forms: that of a **domestic insurer**, a **foreign insurer**, or an **alien insurer**. Licensing standards vary among these several forms. For example, a domestic insurer's license generally has no expiration date, whereas licenses of a foreign insurer and an alien insurer generally must be renewed annually.

Becoming Licensed as a Domestic Insurer

Domestic insurers usually must meet the conditions imposed on corporations engaged in noninsurance activities as well as some additional conditions imposed on insurers. An applicant for a domestic insurer license must apply for a corporate charter and provide specific information, including (but not limited to) these items:

- The insurer's form of ownership
- The names and addresses of the individual incorporators
- The name of the proposed corporation and the territories and types of insurance it plans to market
- The insurer's total financing, including authorized capital stock (the total number of shares, if any, that a corporation can sell to raise money), and its policyholders' surplus

Forms of Ownership

Insurers can be classified by legal form of ownership. The three most common forms of insurer ownership in the U.S. are stock insurance companies, mutual insurance companies, and reciprocal insurance exchanges.

Insurers formed for the purpose of making a profit for their owners are typically organized as stock insurers. Stockholders supply the capital needed to form the insurance company or the additional capital the insurer needs to expand its operations. Stockholders expect to receive a return on their investment in the form of stock dividends, increased stock value, or both. Stockholders have the right to elect the board of directors. The board of directors creates and oversees corporate goals and objectives and appoints a chief executive officer (CEO) to carry out the insurer's operations.

Domestic insurer

An insurer doing business in the jurisdiction in which it is incorporated.

Foreign insurer

An insurer licensed to operate in a state but incorporated in another state.

Alien insurer

An insurer domiciled in a country other than the United States.

A mutual insurer is a corporation owned by its policyholders. Because a traditional mutual insurer issues no common stock, it has no stockholders. Its policyholders have voting rights similar to those of a stock company's stockholders, and, like stockholders, they elect the insurer's board of directors. Although initially formed to provide insurance for their owners, mutual insurers today generally seek to earn profits in their ongoing operations, just as stock companies do. A mutual insurer needs profits to ensure the future financial health of the organization. Mutual companies include some large national insurers and many regional insurers.

A reciprocal insurance exchange, also referred to as a reciprocal, is organized as an unincorporated association of members, called subscribers, that agree to insure one another and share profits and losses. The term "reciprocal" comes from the reciprocity of responsibility of all subscribers to each other. Each member of the reciprocal is both an insured and an insurer. Because the subscribers are not experts in running an insurance operation, they contract with an individual or organization to operate the reciprocal. This manager, called an attorney-in-fact, is typically a corporation with a board of directors that manages the reciprocal. See the exhibit "Forms of Insurer Ownership."

Forms of Insurer Ownership

Type of Insurer	Form of Ownership	Management
Stock insurer	Corporation owned by its stockholders	Board of directors, elected by stockholders
Mutual insurer	Corporation owned by its policyholders	Board of directors, elected by policyholders
Reciprocal insurance exchange	Unincorporated association of subscribers	Attorney-in-fact chosen by subscribers

[DA07488]

Capital and Surplus

Information about capital stock and surplus is important to licensing regulators because it indicates the insurer's financial soundness. A domestic insurer that is also a stock insurer must meet certain minimum capital and surplus requirements, which vary widely by state and by amounts and types of insurance written. A domestic insurer that is also a mutual insurer has no capital derived from the sale of stock. Therefore, the minimum financial requirement applies only to surplus. Most states require mutual insurers to have an initial surplus equal to the minimum capital and surplus requirement for stock insurers writing the same type of insurance.

Becoming Licensed as a Foreign or an Alien Insurer

In the U.S., an insurer is typically licensed as a domestic insurer in one state and as a foreign insurer in all other states where it wishes to operate. Less commonly, an insurer is domiciled outside the U.S. and is licensed as an alien insurer in the U.S. states where it wishes to operate.

To be licensed in an additional state (that is, as a foreign insurer), an insurer first must show the regulator in the additional state that it has satisfied the requirements imposed by its home state (its state of domicile, or the state where it is a domestic insurer). A foreign insurer also must generally satisfy the minimum capital, surplus, and other requirements imposed on domestic insurers within the state in which it is seeking to be licensed.

Alien insurers must satisfy the requirements imposed on domestic insurers by the state in which they want to be licensed. Additionally, they must usually establish a branch office in any state and have funds on deposit in the U.S. equal to the minimum capital and surplus required. The funds on deposit are available, if necessary, to pay claims asserted against the alien insurer through the U.S. legal system. See the exhibit "Licensing Status of a Hypothetical Insurer."

Admitted Insurers and Nonadmitted Insurers

Insurers that are licensed to do business in a state, whether as domestic, foreign, or alien insurers, are collectively referred to as **admitted insurers**. Under special circumstances, insurers that are not licensed in the particular state, referred to as nonadmitted insurers, may be permitted to sell insurance within that state. A nonadmitted insurer may be an admitted insurer in other states, or it may even be an alien insurer.

Nonadmitted insurers are frequently referred to as surplus lines insurers. Surplus lines insurers are usually permitted to sell only insurance that is not readily available from admitted insurers because of specialty, risk, or several other factors. Under **surplus lines laws**, a nonadmitted insurer is permitted to transact business only through a specially licensed surplus lines producer. The nonadmitted insurer must still meet some of the regulatory requirements of a licensed insurer, but these do not typically include restrictions on rates and policy forms.

Producers and Claims Representatives

In addition to licensing insurers, all states require licensing of certain insurer representatives or employees. Agents, brokers, and claims representatives are often required to pass an examination on insurance laws and practices to earn a license. These examinations, along with continuing education requirements, are an attempt to ensure that these insurance professionals have a minimum level of insurance knowledge and meet ethical standards.

Admitted insurer

An insurer to which a state insurance department has granted a license to do business within that state.

Surplus lines law

A state law that permits any producer with a surplus lines license issued by that state to procure insurance from an eligible surplus lines insurer if the applicant cannot obtain the desired type of insurance in the admitted market.

Licensing Status of a Hypothetical Insurer

Insurer A, a regional insurer domiciled in Ohio, is licensed as a domestic insurer in Ohio and as a foreign insurer in its other states of operation.

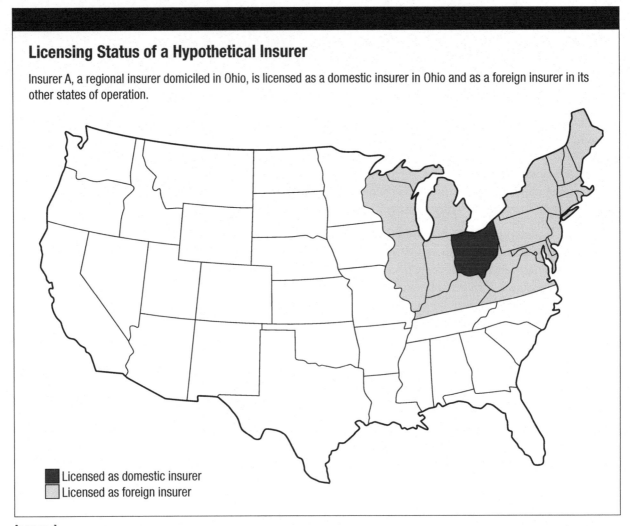

■ Licensed as domestic insurer
▢ Licensed as foreign insurer

[DA07504]

INSURANCE RATE AND FORM REGULATION

Individual states in the United States regulate insurance rates to strike a balance between reasonable profits for insurers and reasonable prices for consumers. Additionally, states regulate insurance policy forms to ensure that they are readable, understandable, and fair.

A solvent, profitable insurance market that provides insurance products at affordable rates is important to the citizens of every state. From coverage on their homes and autos to workers compensation, individuals need insurance. Organizations of all types and sizes cannot operate without insurance. Because insurance is important and often required for individuals and businesses, states enact laws to ensure that rates are sufficient for insurers and reasonable for consumers.

In addition to being able to afford to purchase insurance, consumers also need to be able to understand the insurance products they purchase. Therefore, states typically regulate insurance policy forms to enable consumers to read and understand them. Most states review policy provisions to ensure that they are fair and reasonable.

There are, however, certain types of insurance, such as coverage for complex commercial organizations or unique risks, exempted from regulation.

Insurance Rate Regulation

Setting insurance rates is the regulatory area that may receive the most public attention. It is important to insurers that rates allow them to collect sufficient premiums to pay for the insured losses that occur, to cover the insurer's costs of operating, and to allow a reasonable profit.

When deciding to approve or disapprove an insurer's request for a rate, a state insurance commissioner usually considers three major criteria:

- Adequate—Rates should be sufficient to pay all claims and the expenses related to those claims, helping to maintain insurer solvency.

- Not excessive—Insurers are entitled to a fair return but not to excessive or unreasonable profit.

- Not unfairly discriminatory—Insurers are permitted to adjust premium rates based on the risk profile of different groups of insureds, but these rates must be fair and consistent. Insureds with similar loss exposures should be charged similar rates.

Different states meet these criteria by different types of rating laws that vary in the type and extent of control the state asserts over insurers' rates:

- Mandatory rate law—Rate law that imposes the strictest control of an insurer's rates.

- Prior-approval law—Insurers cannot charge a rate until it is filed and approved by state regulators.

- File-and-use law—Insurers must file proposed rates but can immediately use the rates while state approval is pending.

- Use-and-file law—Variation of the file-and-use law that provides more flexibility for insurers in setting rates. Rates must be filed within a specified period after they are used.

- Flex rating law—Increases the amount of flexibility for insurers in their rate determinations. Prior approval is only required when new rates exceed a certain percentage above previous rates.

- Open competition—Market prices driven by the economic laws of supply and demand, rather than regulatory decisions, determine insurance rates. However, state insurance departments typically have the authority to monitor competition and disapprove rates if deemed necessary. The major criteria that rates must be adequate, not excessive, and not unfairly discriminatory continue to apply.

Insurance Policy Form Regulation

Another area of insurance regulation involves insurance policy forms. Because many insurance policies are difficult to interpret and are often sold on a take-it-or-leave-it basis, many states require insurers to file their policy forms with the state insurance department.

Regulations regarding insurance policy forms are intended to meet two major objectives. The first objective is that insurance policies be clear and readable to insurance consumers. The second major objective is to detect and address any policy provisions that are unfair or unreasonable.

Exemptions From Rate and Form Regulation

State insurance regulations do not apply to all insurers and insurance. Some insurers and some types of insurance policies are exempt from regulation regarding premium rates and policy forms.

Surplus lines insurers are generally exempt from insurance regulations pertaining to policy forms and rates. These insurers are willing to provide coverage for risks that admitted insurers are unable or unwilling to offer. Because these insurers increase the availability of insurance, they have the freedom to use policy provisions and rates that are appropriate for a particular risk.

There are various types of coverage related to unique or difficult-to-place risks that are also exempt from regulation in some states. Examples of these coverages include inland marine, ocean marine, and aviation. Inland marine originated and evolved in order to cover risks that were considered uninsurable under standard commercial policies, such as coverage for works of art and other valuable property.

Many states have deregulated some commercial insurance coverages for large, sophisticated purchasers. There is significant variation in the definition of the size of business to qualify for exemption from rate and form regulation. One state, for example, may require an aggregate annual premium of $500,000, while another state could require $25,000. Many states do not exempt certain types of commercial coverage, such as workers compensation or commercial property, from regulation.

MARKET CONDUCT AND SOLVENCY REGULATION

States regulate how insurers conduct themselves in the marketplace and monitor their financial strength for the protection of the public and insurance consumers.

States have imposed consumer-protection and licensing laws that apply directly to insurers and other entities conducting business within their borders. Solvency regulations that establish insurer financial requirements and monitoring systems seek to protect the public from loss of insurance coverage in the event of an insurer's financial failure.

Market Conduct

Market conduct regulation focuses on how insurers treat applicants for insurance, insureds, and others who present claims for coverage. Most states have statutes that address market conduct, often called **unfair trade practices laws.** These laws usually involve sales, underwriting, and claims handling.

Sales

Many states have adopted unfair trade practices laws that prohibit certain business practices. State regulators can suspend or revoke the licenses of sales agents or brokers who engage in unfair trade practices, such as embezzling premiums. Although they vary by state, these laws typically prohibit such unfair trade practices as these:

- Misrepresentation and false advertising—Insurance agents and other insurance personnel cannot generate, issue, or circulate information that misrepresents the benefits, advantages, conditions, or terms of any insurance policy; misrepresents the dividends to be received on any policy; conveys false or misleading statements about dividends previously paid on any policy; or uses a policy name or title that misrepresents the true nature of the policy. Insurance personnel are also prohibited from making untrue, deceptive, or misleading advertisements, announcements, or statements about insurance or any person in the insurance business.

- Tie-in sales—Producers cannot require the purchase of insurance to be dependent on some other purchase or financial arrangement, a practice known as a tie-in sale. It's also an unfair trade practice for a lender to require that a borrower purchase insurance from the lender or any insurer or producer recommended by the lender. Each transaction must stand on its own.

- Rebating—Producers are not allowed to pay a portion of the premium or give any commission to a policyholder. Producers are also prohibited from offering to do other business with a policyholder in exchange for the purchase of a policy.

Market conduct regulation
Regulation of the practices of insurers in regard to four areas of operation: sales practices, underwriting practices, claims practices, and bad-faith actions.

Unfair trade practices law
State law that specifies certain prohibited business practices.

Unfair trade practices laws prohibit other practices that are deceptive or unfair to applicants and insureds. For example, these laws prohibit an insurer and its producers from making false statements about the financial condition of another insurer. Entering false information on an insurance application to earn a commission from the insurance sale is also an unfair trade practice. Both insurers and policyholders count on insurance transactions being conducted in good faith.

Underwriting

In the interest of protecting the public, every U.S. state regulates insurers' underwriting activities and places some constraints on the terms and conditions insurers can offer. An insurer that is guilty of unfair underwriting practices could be fined or its operating license suspended or revoked. Two important examples of this type of regulation are the prohibition of unfair discrimination and restrictions on cancellations and nonrenewals.

The ability to discriminate fairly among applicants is one of the most important elements of underwriting because it allows insurers to charge insureds a premium commensurate with their loss exposures. However, state insurance regulations prohibit unfair discrimination in insurance, including underwriting activities. The challenge lies in distinguishing between fair and unfair discrimination. Examples of unfair discrimination include canceling, refusing to issue, or refusing to renew coverage for an applicant or insured solely on the basis of geographic location (sometimes known as redlining), gender, marital status, or race.

When it comes to restrictions on cancellation and nonrenewal, most states require that an insurer notify the insured within a specified period, such as thirty days, before a policy is to be canceled or nonrenewed. This notice is intended to give the insured an opportunity to replace the coverage. While these types of restrictions help insurance serve its purpose of protecting policyholders, they also limit how quickly an underwriter can stop providing coverage for an insured who has become undesirable.

Claims

Most states also have statutes that prohibit unfair claims practices, which include these:

- Knowingly misrepresenting facts about coverage to insureds or claimants
- Failing to promptly acknowledge communications from insureds and claimants
- Failing to promptly investigate and settle claims
- Failing to settle claims in good faith, promptly, fairly, and equitably when liability is reasonably clear
- Offering insureds or claimants substantially less money than a claim is worth, thereby forcing them to sue to recover the rightful amount

- Failing to affirm or deny coverage of claims within a reasonable time after completing an investigation

- Attempting to settle or settling claims based on an application that was materially altered without the insured's notice, knowledge, or consent

- Unreasonably delaying a claim payment or investigation by requiring both a formal proof of loss form and a subsequent verification that duplicates the proof of loss information

- Failing to provide forms necessary to present claims within fifteen calendar days of a request

- Failing to adopt and implement reasonable standards to ensure that repairs are performed in a workmanlike manner when the repairs are performed by a repairer owned by the insurer or that the insurer requires the claimant to use

Regulatory examinations of insurers identify some of these abuses, but others are exposed only when an insured or a claimant lodges a complaint. Every state insurance department has a consumer-complaints division to enforce its consumer-protection objectives and help insureds deal with problems they encounter with insurers and their representatives. State insurance departments investigate consumer complaints and may hold formal hearings as part of the investigation process. Claims representatives must be able to justify their actions and provide proper documentation when asked to do so by state insurance regulators. If the claims representative or insurer cannot justify the practices under scrutiny, it may face a reprimand, fine, license suspension, substantial legal judgment, or some other legal penalty.

Apply Your Knowledge

Richard, a salesman for a car dealership, also holds an insurance agent's license with Delmond Insurance. Julia purchases a car from Richard, who insists that Julia insure her car with Delmond. When she refuses, Richard tells Julia that the loan on her new car will be denied unless she purchases a policy from Delmond.

The unfair trade practice Richard is engaging in is:

a.   Rebating.
b.   A tie-in sale.
c.   False advertising.
d.   Misrepresentation.

Feedback: b. Richard is guilty of engaging in a tie-in sale—tying the sale of insurance to the financing of the car.

Licensing

One way states regulate insurance is by issuing licenses to insurers, producers, claims representatives, and other insurance personnel.

By issuing a license to an insurer, a state indicates that the insurer meets minimum standards of financial strength, competence, and integrity and that it has complied with the state's insurance laws and is authorized to write certain types of insurance. Once licensed, the insurer is subject to all applicable state laws, rules, and regulations.

To function legally as an insurance agent, a producer must be licensed by the state(s) in which he or she wants to sell insurance. Some states issue separate licenses for agents (representatives of the insurer), brokers (representatives of the customer), and solicitors (usually office staff). Generally, solicitors can seek prospects but not bind insurance coverage. Insurance producers operating without a license are subject to civil, and sometimes criminal, penalties.

To obtain a state insurance agent's license, a candidate generally must pass an examination on insurance principles, insurance coverages, and insurance laws and regulations. Some states require candidates to accumulate a minimum number of hours of classroom study before taking this examination. Producers' licenses generally have a specified term, such as one or two years, and can be renewed by paying a fee specified by the state. Most states also require producers to provide evidence that they have completed approved continuing education courses before the state will renew their licenses.

Insurance consultants, who give advice about insurance policies, may be required to be licensed, and requirements for a consultant's license vary by state. Passing separate examinations is usually required to be an insurance consultant in both life-health and property-casualty insurance.

Some states require claims representatives to be licensed so that those who make claims decisions for insurers are aware of prohibited claims practices, have at least a minimum level of technical knowledge and skill, and understand how to handle insureds' claims fairly. Licensing of claims representatives in most states includes an examination. The licensing process also typically involves a background check and ethics requirements to help protect consumers who file claims from unfair, unethical, and dishonest claims practices. Public adjusters, who represent insureds for a fee, are generally required to be licensed to ensure technical competence and to protect the public.

Insurer Solvency

Reserve

The amount the insurer estimates and sets aside to pay on an existing claim that has not been settled.

Another area of insurance regulation is insurer solvency. A noninsurance company is considered solvent if it has the resources to pay its bills and meet similar financial obligations. Because an insurer has promised to pay many unknown losses in the future, states require it to have financial **reserves** well in excess of its ordinary expenses in order to be considered solvent.

Solvency involves an insurer's ability to meet financial obligations as they become due—even those resulting from insured losses that might be claimed several years in the future. Primary causes of insolvencies include insufficient loss reserves, inadequate pricing, and rapid growth. Other, less common causes include investment problems, fraud, and catastrophic claims. To verify insurer solvency, insurance regulators conduct **solvency surveillance**.

Regulators use four methods to verify an insurer's solvency:

- Establish financial requirements by which to measure solvency
- Conduct on-site field examinations to ensure regulatory compliance
- Review annual financial statements
- Administer the Insurance Regulatory Information System (IRIS)

Establish Financial Requirements

Regulators establish financial requirements against which all similarly licensed insurers are measured. To obtain and keep a license as an admitted insurer, each insurer must meet certain minimum financial requirements, such as capital and surplus requirements. Specific financial requirements vary widely by state.

Conduct Field Examinations

State laws usually require that insurers undergo on-site field examinations at least once every three to five years. This examination usually occurs under the direction of the insurance department of the state where the insurer's home office is located.

A team of state examiners, working at the insurer's home office, reviews a wide range of activities, including claims, underwriting, marketing, and accounting procedures. Of particular interest to the examiners is the insurer's financial condition. The examining team carefully analyzes the insurer's financial records to ensure that the company is meeting all state financial reporting requirements.

Review Annual Statements

Insurers are required to submit annual financial statements to state insurance departments in a prescribed format. The **National Association of Insurance Commissioners (NAIC)** has prescribed a format called the **NAIC Annual Statement**, which requires detailed information on premiums, expenses, investments, losses, reserves, and other financial information. Regulators analyze these statements to assess insurers' financial strength.

Administer IRIS

Regulators administer the **Insurance Regulatory Information System (IRIS)**, which helps them identify insurers with potential financial problems.

Solvency surveillance

The process, conducted by state insurance regulators, of verifying the solvency of insurers and determining whether their financial condition enables them to meet their financial obligations and to remain in business.

National Association of Insurance Commissioners (NAIC)

An association of insurance commissioners from the fifty U.S. states, the District of Columbia, and the five U.S. territories and possessions, whose purpose is to coordinate insurance regulation activities among the various state insurance departments.

NAIC Annual Statement

The primary financial statement prepared by insurers and required by every state insurance department.

Insurance Regulatory Information System (IRIS)

An information and early-warning system established and operated by the NAIC to monitor the financial soundness of insurers.

Designed by the NAIC, IRIS uses data from an insurer's financial statements to develop financial ratios that assess the insurer's overall financial condition. If the insurer's ratios are outside predetermined norms, IRIS identifies the company for regulatory attention. IRIS is meant to be an early warning system that might enable regulators to rehabilitate an insurer or, if rehabilitation is not practical, to minimize the damage from liquidation.

If regulators determine that an insurer is insolvent, the state insurance department places it in receivership. If the insurer cannot be rehabilitated, it is liquidated according to the state's insurance code. At that point, the state's **guaranty fund** may be available to reduce the effects of the insurer's insolvency. A guaranty fund cannot prevent insurer insolvency, but it does provide funds for the unpaid claims of insolvent insurers licensed in a particular state.

Guaranty fund

A state-established fund that provides a system for the payment of some of the unpaid claims of insolvent insurers licensed in that state, generally funded by assessments collected from all insurers licensed in the state.

SUMMARY

Insurers are regulated primarily for these three reasons:

- To protect consumers
- To maintain insurer solvency
- To prevent destructive competition

Insurers must meet various requirements to be licensed as domestic insurers in the states where they are domiciled. Additionally, insurers must also be licensed as foreign insurers in other states where they wish to operate. Nonadmitted insurers may transact certain types of business through licensed surplus lines producers. In addition to requiring that insurers be licensed, states also require that certain insurance professionals, including producers and claim representatives, become licensed.

States regulate insurance rates to ensure that they are adequate, not excessive, and not unfairly discriminatory. States also regulate insurance policy forms to meet standards of clarity, fairness, and readability. However, there are certain types of insurance, such as large commercial policies or unique coverages, that are exempt from state regulation.

States regulate insurers' marketing activities and solvency to protect consumers. Market conduct regulation, which includes laws prohibiting unfair trade practices and unfair claims practices, applies to sales, underwriting, and claims. State licensing is required for insurers and for many of those involved in selling insurance or representing insurers, such as producers, claims representatives, and insurance consultants. Insurers are also subject to solvency laws that monitor the financial strength of insurers to ensure that obligations to customers and claimants can be met.

3

Insurer Financial Performance

Educational Objectives

After learning the content of this assignment, you should be able to:

▷ Explain how the management of a property-casualty insurer's income and expenses determines its profitability.

▷ Summarize the information found on the balance sheet and the income statement of a property-casualty insurer.

▷ Analyze a property-casualty insurer's profitability information using these financial ratio calculations:

- Loss ratio

- Expense ratio

- Combined ratio

- Investment income ratio

- Overall operating ratio

▷ Given a case regarding a property-casualty insurer's financial ratio calculation(s), determine the significance of those calculation(s) on the insurer's overall financial performance.

Insurer Financial Performance

INSURER PROFITABILITY AND INCOME AND EXPENSE MANAGEMENT

Sound management of an insurer includes careful attention to its financial performance. An important aspect of an insurer's financial performance is its profitability and whether it generates enough profit to survive and grow.

To survive long term, an insurer must generate more income than it spends; that is, an insurer's revenue must exceed its expenses. In a given month or year, an insurer's expenses might exceed its revenues, requiring the insurer to pay some of those expenses with accumulated funds. Such a pattern, however, will eventually deplete accumulated funds, and the insurer will fail. Like any other business, an insurer must manage its revenue and expenses to produce an overall income gain (revenue minus expenses) from its operations and to ensure profitability.

Managing Insurer Income

Insurers charge their insureds premiums for insurance coverage, part of which insurers invest to earn additional income. Consequently, insurers receive income from these two major sources: the sale of insurance and the investment of funds.

The sale of insurance generates underwriting income, which is the amount remaining (either a gain or a loss) after underwriting losses and expenses are subtracted from premiums. The investment of funds generates investment income, which is the amount remaining (either a gain or a loss) after investment expenses are subtracted from the gross amount earned on investments during a period. While some insurers receive other income from the sale of specialized services or other incidental activities, most of the income an insurer receives is either underwriting income or investment income.

During a particular calendar year, an insurer calculates its written premiums by totaling the premiums charged on all policies written with effective dates of January 1 through December 31 of that year. Written premiums are the total premiums on all policies put into effect, or "written," during a given period. For example, when a policy is written to become effective on July 1 for a premium of $600, that entire $600 is counted as written premiums on July 1, even though the insurer may not have collected it yet. If the policy is changed on September 12, resulting in a $75 refund, the insurer's written premiums are reduced by $75 on September 12. Although written premiums provide a source of cash for insurers, rules of accounting allow insurers to recognize only earned premiums on their income statement.

Earned premiums are the portion of the written premiums that apply to the part of the policy period that has already occurred. The remaining portion of written premiums applies to the policy period that has not yet occurred and is therefore called unearned premiums, representing insurance coverage yet to be provided.

Earned and unearned premiums can be compared to a non-insurance business transaction; for example, how a magazine subscription might operate. When a subscriber pays a $24 annual subscription fee for a monthly magazine, the publisher does not "earn" the entire $24 subscription amount until the magazine has been provided for twelve months. If the subscriber cancels the subscription after receiving only six monthly issues, the publisher might refund $12, or half of the subscription amount—the "unearned" portion. Likewise, when an insured pays a premium of $600 on July 1 for a one-year policy, the $600 premium is not fully "earned" until the end of the twelve-month coverage period. The entire $600, however, is considered written premiums for the current calendar year.

As the exhibit shows, only half of the $600 annual premium paid on July 1 is earned as of the end of the calendar year because only six months, or half of the protection period, has passed. Therefore, at the end of the calendar year, the insurer calculates $300 of earned premiums and $300 of unearned premiums for this policy. See the exhibit "Earned Premiums—One-Year Policy Issued on July 1 for $600."

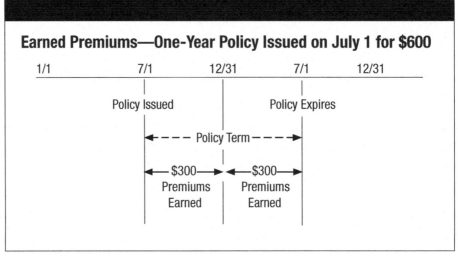

Earned Premiums—One-Year Policy Issued on July 1 for $600

[DA02103]

During the next calendar year, between January 1 and July 1, the unearned portion of the premium is earned as coverage is provided by the insurer. If this policy is not renewed on July 1 of the second year, the insurer records no written premiums for this policy in the second year (remember that the entire $600 was considered to be written during the first year). The insurer records only the earned premiums of $300 from the previous year's written premium. See the exhibit "Examples of Written, Earned, and Unearned Premiums."

Examples of Written, Earned, and Unearned Premiums

Annual policy with $600 premium is effective July 1.

At the end of Calendar Year 1:

    Written premiums   = $600.

    Earned premiums   = $300 (6 of the 12 months of coverage have elapsed).

    Unearned premiums   = $300 (6 of the 12 months of coverage have not elapsed).

At the end of Calendar Year 2 (assuming the policy is not renewed):

    Written premiums   = $0.

    Earned premiums   = $300 (the remaining 6 months of coverage have elapsed).

    Unearned premiums   = $0 (there is no more coverage; all the premium is earned).

If instead the annual policy were effective December 1 of that year, then the written premium would be the same, the full $600; but the earned premium would be $50 (1 of the 12 months has elapsed), and the unearned premium would be $550 (for the other 11 months). At the end of that calendar year, assuming the policy was not renewed, the earned premiums would be $550, and the written and unearned premiums would be $0.

[DA07662]

Underwriting Income

Underwriting income is an insurer's gain or loss as determined by subtracting the insurer's paid losses and **loss adjustment expenses (LAE)** from its earned premiums (the revenue from the insurer's underwriting operations). The losses paid by an insurer's policies plus the expenses associated with controlling and adjusting those losses are the primary underwriting expenses.

When calculating underwriting income for the year, or for any other period, an insurer must determine the portion of its written premiums that is earned premiums and the portion that is unearned premiums during the period, because if the policy were subsequently canceled by the insurer or the policy-holder, the unearned income would not be earned. Consequently, the use of written premiums could create a false impression of profitability.

Loss adjustment expense (LAE)

The expense that an insurer incurs to investigate, defend, and settle claims according to the terms specified in the insurance policy.

Investment Income

Because an insurer collects premiums from its policyholders and pays claims for its policyholders, an insurer handles large amounts of money. Insurers invest available funds to generate additional income. Investment income can be substantial, particularly during periods of high interest rates or high returns in the stock market. Insurers have investment departments that manage funds to earn the highest possible return from investments while ensuring that funds are secure and available to meet the insurer's obligations.

An insurer has investment funds available for two reasons. First, an insurer is legally required to maintain a certain amount of funds, called policyholders' surplus, to meet its obligations even after catastrophic losses. When the insurer is operating profitably, its policyholders' surplus is generally available for investment.

Second, the insurer usually receives premiums before it pays claims on the corresponding policies. Thus, an insurer can invest premiums and earn additional income until those funds are needed to pay claims. However, when an insurer settles claims, it must have funds readily available to meet its obligations. Similarly, if a policy is canceled before the end of the policy period, the insurer must have funds available to refund the unearned premiums.

Managing Insurer Expenses

An insurer's expenses fall into two broad categories: expenses associated with underwriting activities and expenses associated with investment activities. Expenses associated with underwriting activities include payment for losses, loss adjustment expenses, and other underwriting expenses. Some insurers also pay dividends to their policyholders. Expenses associated with investment activities include salaries and other general expenses related to running the investment department.

Underwriting Activity Expenses

The major expense category for most insurers is payment for losses arising from claims. Claims are demands for payment made by insureds based on the conditions specified in their insurance policies. For property-casualty insurers, loss payments often represent 70 percent to 80 percent of their total costs.

Claims are not necessarily settled immediately after a loss occurs. Sometimes the loss is not reported right away. When the loss is reported, the insurer's claim representative investigates the loss and verifies whether it is covered before the insurer pays the claim. Liability claims may involve lengthy legal proceedings. Some losses occur in one year but are settled in a later year. In any given year, an insurer knows only the amount of losses it has paid so far, but not a definite amount it will ultimately pay on claims.

To compare revenue and expenses, an insurer must calculate not only its **paid losses** but also its **incurred losses**. A paid loss is a definite amount. Paid losses do not include those losses in the process of settlement or **incurred but not reported (IBNR) losses**. Therefore, another method of measuring losses is to calculate incurred losses for a particular period using a basic illustration:

Incurred losses = Paid losses + Loss reserves

Insurers also incur loss adjustment expenses. For property insurance claims, a claim representative must identify the cause of the loss and decide whether the loss is covered by the policy. If the loss is covered, a claim representative must determine the covered amount. For liability claims, a claim representative must determine whether the insured is legally responsible for the bodily injury or property damage that is the basis of the claim and, if so, for how much. Determining the legal responsibility of the insured for a loss might require a complex and costly investigation. In addition to paying covered losses, liability insurers often pay the costs to defend the insured in the event of a lawsuit, regardless of whether the insured is ultimately held responsible for the damages. Thus, loss adjustment expenses associated with a liability claim can be substantial.

In addition to losses and loss adjustment expenses, the costs of providing insurance include significant "other underwriting expenses," which can apply to multiple departments and can be categorized as these: acquisition expenses; general expenses; and premium taxes, licenses, and fees.

Acquisition expenses—the category of other underwriting expenses associated with acquiring new business—are significant. All property-casualty insurers have a marketing system to market and distribute their products. This system includes individuals involved directly with sales (usually called agents, brokers, producers, or sales representatives) and the administrative staff who manage and support the sales effort.

Many people who directly generate insurance sales for insurers receive a commission. Others receive a salary, or a combination of salary and commission, and sometimes also a bonus based on sales, profit, or some other measure of productivity. While some insurers operate completely or in part without salespeople (usually through direct response systems such as mail, telephone, and the Internet), these insurers must still employ and pay staff to manage and administer their marketing operations. Additionally, various personnel and technical resources are needed to review insurance applications, issue insurance policies, and manage billings. Advertising expenses may also be a significant component of insurer acquisition expenses.

General expenses are the category of other underwriting expenses that insurers incur when underwriting and issuing insurance policies. Although these expenses do not relate directly to activities such as claims, marketing, and underwriting, they are crucial to the insurers' operations. These general expenses are associated with staffing and maintaining functional departments such as accounting, legal, statistical and data management, actuarial,

Paid losses

Losses that have been paid to, or on behalf of, insureds during a given period.

Incurred losses

The losses that have occurred during a specific period, no matter when claims resulting from the losses are paid.

Incurred but not reported (IBNR) losses

Losses that have occurred but have not yet been reported to the insurer.

customer service, information technology, and building maintenance. In addition, insurers must provide the necessary services to support these functions.

Premium taxes, licenses, and fees are another category of other underwriting expenses. In the United States, states levy premium taxes, which are usually a percentage of all premiums generated by the insurer in a particular state. Insurers must hold and pay for licenses in most states in which they operate.

Dividends

The portion of an organization's profits that is paid to shareholders.

Some insurers choose to return a portion of premiums to policyholders as **dividends**, which may be paid out on a regular basis or may be associated with a special circumstance. Mutual insurers may pay a dividend to policyholders when operating results have been good. Dividends may also be paid by any insurer as a marketing technique. Insurers who want to provide the lowest cost to their policyholders may prefer to accomplish that by paying dividends only after their operating results warrant such payments. In this way, the insurer's solvency is better protected than it would be by charging low rates up front with little margin for error.

Investment Activity Expenses

An insurer's investment department includes a staff of professional investment managers who oversee the company's investment program and provide accounting of all invested funds. The investment department devises investment strategy and implements it by purchasing and selling stocks, bonds, and other investments. Investment expenses include staff salaries and all other expenses related to the investment department's activities. Insurers deduct these expenses from investment income on their financial statements to calculate the net investment income. Gains or losses realized from the sale of invested assets are added to net investment income, resulting in net investment gain or loss, which represents an insurer's total results from investment activities.

Net investment income = Investment income − Investment expenses

Insurer Profitability

Profitability is the ultimate goal of all insurers. Adding net underwriting gain or loss for a specific period to net investment gain or loss for the corresponding period shows an insurer's overall gain or loss from operations—its profitability. Examining the result of this calculation gives a more complete picture of an insurer's profitability than net underwriting gain or loss because net investment gains generally help to offset underwriting losses.

Overall gain or loss from operations = Net investment gain or loss + Net underwriting gain or loss

An insurer's net income before taxes is the sum of its total earned premiums and investment income minus its total losses and other expenses in the corresponding period. Some adjustments for other income items might be necessary. For example, the insurer might have to write off some uncollected premiums, or it might have to add premiums that were written off during the previous period but were ultimately collected during the current period. Adjustments might also be necessary for a gain or loss on the sale of equipment or other items. Mutual insurers would also deduct dividends to policyholders from their income.

Like other businesses, insurers pay income taxes on their taxable income. Taxable income might differ from net income before taxes because of the special requirements of the tax code. For example, a portion of interest earnings from qualified municipal bonds is not taxed, and deductions for certain expenses are limited. Insurers often adjust their investment strategy in response to changing tax laws.

After an insurer has paid losses and reserved money to pay additional losses, expenses, and income taxes, the remainder is net income, which belongs to the owners of the company. The owners may receive a portion of this remainder as dividends. For a publicly held company, such dividends are payable to the shareholders.

The amount that remains after dividends are paid becomes an addition to the insurer's surplus. Surplus enables the insurer to grow and expand its operations in the future. An insurer that generates adequate return (or profit) will attract and maintain the investment funds it needs to survive and grow.

UNDERSTANDING INSURER FINANCIAL STATEMENTS

To meet their objectives of profitability and continuity for the long term, insurers must carefully monitor their financial performance. Insurers must record and report financial information in a consistent manner, using various financial statements.

To monitor financial performance, insurers and others, including regulators and financial rating organizations (such as A.M. Best Company and Standard & Poor's Corporation), examine insurers' financial statements. Insurers must prepare accurate financial statements that describe the company's financial position in an objective, standardized format. To protect the public's interests, regulators impose requirements on insurers' financial statements to ensure that they do not overstate their true financial condition. Two important financial statements are the balance sheet and the income statement.

Balance Sheet

The balance sheet shows an insurer's financial position at a particular point in time and includes the insurer's assets, liabilities, and policyholders' surplus. See the exhibit "Calladell Insurance Balance Sheet as of December 31, 20XX."

Calladell Insurance Balance Sheet as of December 31, 20XX

(All figures are in $ millions.)

Admitted Assets:

Cash and short-term investments	20.1
Bonds	67.2
Common stock	42.8
Total Admitted Assets	130.1

Liabilities:

Loss reserve and loss expense reserve	16.5
Unearned premium reserve	5.0
Other liabilities	60.1
Total Liabilities	81.6
Policyholders' Surplus	48.5
Total Liabilities and Policyholders' Surplus	130.1

[DA07654]

Assets

Insurers accumulate funds when they receive premium and investment income. Insurers do not immediately need all of their premium income to pay claims and operating expenses. In the meantime, insurers invest them in income-producing **assets**.

Assets typically accumulated by an insurer include cash, stocks, and bonds; property, such as buildings, office furniture, and equipment; and accounts receivable from policyholders, agents, brokers, and reinsurers. Financial reports filed with state insurance regulators require an insurer's assets to be classified as either admitted assets or nonadmitted assets.

Admitted assets are types of property that regulators allow insurers to show as assets on their financial statements. Because these types of assets could easily be liquidated, or converted to cash at or near the property's market value, regulators allow admitted assets to be shown on insurers' financial statements. In addition to cash, admitted assets include stocks, bonds, mortgages, real estate, certain computer equipment, and premium balances due in less than ninety days.

Nonadmitted assets cannot be readily converted to cash at or near their market value if the insurer were to liquidate its holdings. For this reason, regulators do not allow insurers to show them as assets on their financial statements. Nonadmitted assets include premiums that are more than ninety days overdue.

Assets

Types of property, both tangible and intangible, owned by an entity.

Admitted assets

Assets meeting minimum standards of liquidity that an insurer is allowed to report on its balance sheet in accordance with statutory accounting principles.

Nonadmitted assets

Types of property, such as office furniture and equipment, that regulators do not allow insurers to show as assets on financial statements because these assets cannot readily be converted to cash at or near their market value.

Liabilities

An insurer has a financial obligation to its policyholders: It must satisfy legitimate claims submitted by insureds and other parties. The major **liabilities** of an insurer arise from this financial obligation to pay claims. Three types of liabilities are found on an insurer's financial statements:

- Loss reserve and loss expense reserve
- Unearned premium reserve
- Other liabilities (typically small, miscellaneous obligations)

The **loss reserve** is considered a liability because it represents a financial obligation owed by the insurer. It is the insurer's best estimate of the final settlement amount on claims that have not yet been settled. Although establishing loss reserves for claims whose value is not yet definite might seem impossible, insurers use their experience, the law of large numbers, and their actuarial and statistical expertise to make reliable estimates of future claim settlement values. Insurers also set up the loss expense reserve to estimate the cost of settling the claims included in the loss reserve.

The **unearned premium reserve** is the total of an insurer's unearned premiums on all policies at a particular time. The unearned premium reserve is a liability because it represents insurance premiums prepaid by insureds for services that the insurer has not yet rendered. If the insurer ceased operations and canceled all of its policies, the unearned premium reserve would represent the total of premium refunds that the insurer would owe its current policyholders.

The "other liabilities" category is much smaller than the loss reserve, the loss expense reserve, and the unearned premium reserve. However, some insurers have a significant obligation reflected in the liability for reinsurance transactions.

Policyholders' Surplus

Policyholders' surplus measures the difference between what the company owns (its admitted assets) and what it owes (its liabilities). It provides a cushion that is available should the insurer have an adverse financial experience. While premiums may include a margin for error, that margin might not be sufficient to offset unexpected losses, particularly catastrophic losses. If losses exceed expectations, the insurer must draw on its surplus to make required claim payments. Policyholders' surplus also provides the necessary resources if the insurer decides to expand into a new territory or develop new insurance products. Thus, the amount of policyholders' surplus an insurer holds is an important measure of its financial condition.

Although a balance sheet shows an insurer's assets and liabilities only as of a particular date, the figures change constantly. Insurers establish unearned premium reserves for premiums they receive. The unearned premium reserve for each policy declines with the passage of time. Also, losses occur and

Liabilities
Financial obligations, or debts, owed by a company to another entity, usually the policyholder in the case of an insurer.

Loss reserve
An estimate of the amount of money the insurer expects to pay in the future for losses that have already occurred and been reported, but are not yet settled.

Unearned premium reserve
An insurer liability representing the amount of premiums received from policyholders that are not yet earned.

Policyholders' surplus
Under statutory accounting principles (SAP), an insurer's total admitted assets minus its total liabilities.

insurers establish loss reserves. New policies are written, and old policies expire or are renewed. Meanwhile, the insurer buys and sells stocks, bonds, and other investments as needed to meet its obligations while earning investment income. Therefore, an analysis of an insurer's assets and liabilities is only current at the date of the balance sheet, which presents a snapshot of the financial position of the insurer at that point in time.

Income Statement

An insurer's income statement shows the insurer's revenues, expenses, and net income for a particular period, usually one year. It compares the revenues generated with the expenses incurred to produce those revenues. The income statement lists these items:

- Revenues—earned premiums
- Expenses—incurred losses, loss adjustment expenses, and other underwriting expenses (acquisition expenses; general expenses; and premium taxes, licenses, and fees)
- Net underwriting gain or loss—earned premiums less total expenses
- Net investment income—investment income less investment expenses
- Net income before income taxes—net underwriting gain (loss) plus net investment income

In the income statement depicted for Calladell Insurance, its revenues from earned premiums during the year totaled $14.5 million. In the same year, the insurer's expenses totaled $20.3 million. These expenses included incurred losses; loss adjustment expenses; acquisition expenses; general expenses; and premium taxes, licenses, and fees. Because its losses and underwriting expenses exceeded its earned premiums, Calladell experienced a net underwriting loss of $5.8 million. However, Calladell also earned net investment income of $13 million during the year. Therefore, Calladell Insurance realized a net income gain of $7.2 million before income taxes. See the exhibit "Calladell Insurance Income Statement for the Year Ending December 31, 20XX."

Calladell Insurance Income Statement for the Year Ending December 31, 20XX

(All figures are in $ millions.)

Revenues:	
Earned Premiums	14.5
Expenses:	
Incurred losses	13.4
Loss adjustment expenses	3.1
Other underwriting expenses:	
Acquisition expenses	2.0
General expenses	1.4
Premium taxes, licenses, and fees	0.4
Total expenses	20.3
Net Underwriting Gain (Loss)	(5.8)
Net Investment Income	13.0
Net Income Before Income Taxes	7.2

[DA07655]

ANALYZING INSURER FINANCIAL RATIO CALCULATIONS

Comparing two items produces a ratio that highlights a particular aspect of financial performance. Several such ratios are widely used in the insurance industry by many people and organizations.

Property-casualty insurers examine their financial performance ratios to identify strengths and weaknesses in their operations. Investors analyze the ratios to identify the insurers that are most attractive as investments. Regulators examine the ratios to determine whether insurers have the financial strength to remain viable in the long term and to meet their financial obligations to policyholders and other parties. Insurance producers gauge an insurer's financial condition as one factor when selecting insurers with which they place business. Individual insurance company ratios are developed and calculated by insurers' actuaries using a variety of financial reporting programs and statistical gathering tools. The accuracy of the gathered and reported financial information, analyzed via ratios, is particularly important from both regulatory and investment perspectives.

These ratios are used to measure an insurer's profitability:

- Loss ratio
- Expense ratio
- Combined ratio
- Investment income ratio
- Overall operating ratio

Loss Ratio

Loss ratio

A ratio that measures losses and loss adjustment expenses against earned premiums and that reflects the percentage of premiums being consumed by losses.

The **loss ratio** compares an insurer's incurred losses and loss adjustment expenses to its earned premiums for a specific time period.

Maintaining a reasonable loss ratio helps ensure an insurer's profitability. Insurers may set a target for their loss ratio and then analyze the ratio periodically by examining the components of the loss ratio and determining any necessary changes to help meet the target ratio. For example, at the beginning of a year, management decided to target a 70 percent loss ratio for the year. As each month progressed, the loss ratio was recalculated, based on the company's experience to date, to determine whether the insurer was meeting the targeted 70 percent.

The result of the loss ratio is converted into a percentage and the ratio indicates the proportion of earned premiums that is used to fund corresponding losses and their settlement. If an insurer is not meeting its loss ratio target, it should review each component of the loss ratio to determine changes it might implement to better meet its target and improve its financial health.

An insurer could examine the total losses it incurred and consider how it might reduce that amount. An insurer could review the types of insurance that it writes and evaluate the loss potential for those types or the territories where it writes that insurance. For example, auto insurance in California is highly susceptible to losses, so an insurer might consider the effect of reducing the volume of personal and commercial auto insurance it writes in California and increasing the volume of auto insurance it writes in areas less susceptible to losses. Likewise, the insurer might consider its exposure to catastrophic storms. If it writes a high volume of property insurance along the Florida coasts that are susceptible to hurricane-driven winds, the insurer might consider increasing the volume it writes in areas less susceptible to hurricane winds.

In consideration of the loss adjusting expense component of its loss ratio, an insurer should examine any circumstances that could increase its loss adjustment expenses. An insurer might have higher than average loss adjustment expenses in general—perhaps because of its overhead costs or legal fees incurred, and need to reassess its claim processes in these areas. Alternatively, handling losses in areas hit hard by catastrophes requires additional spending because of damage to the infrastructure in the catastrophe area. Computer transmission equipment, cell phone towers, and telephone lines may not be available; therefore manual estimating of losses, handwritten loss drafts, and manual delivery services may result in the need for more processing staff, added costs, and additional loss adjusting expenses. These issues suggest that insurers should limit their volume of business in catastrophe areas. Any excessive loss adjusting expenses reduce an insurer's overall profit.

An insurer should also examine its earned premium and determine whether its pricing is appropriate based on the losses and loss expenses it incurs. An insurer might be able to improve its profitability by increasing its premiums, if it can do so and still remain competitive. If increased pricing is not an option, an insurer might improve its earned premium by expanding to write other types of insurance that might have less competition and have the potential to increase the insurer's earned income. Offering new, innovative types of insurance might offer a solution.

As it reviews each component of the loss ratio, an insurer should consider how any changes it implements could affect the loss ratio and, ultimately, its financial health.

Financial analysts use various tools to calculate loss ratios following a prescribed formula, as illustrated:

$$\text{Loss ratio} = \frac{\text{Incurred losses (including loss adjustment expenses)}}{\text{Earned premiums}}$$

Expense Ratio

The **expense ratio** compares an insurer's incurred underwriting expenses to its written premiums in a specific time period.

When converted into a percentage, the expense ratio indicates the proportion of an insurer's written premiums that is used to pay acquisition costs; general expenses; and premium taxes, licensing, and fees. This ratio indicates an insurer's general cost of doing business as a proportion of the premiums it has written. (Investment income and investment expenses are not part of either the loss ratio or the expense ratio.)

The expense ratio gives a general picture of how efficiently an insurer is operating. Insurers examine their expense ratios routinely to manage their cash flow and control expenses. An insurer might set a target amount for its expense ratio, such as 25 percent. It would then monitor its earned premiums and its underwriting expenses and make any changes to better meet its target ratio.

The written premium component of the expense ratio might suggest that an insurer should increase its written premiums while managing its growth by staying the course with a plan developed previously to support its growth mode.

Expense ratio
An insurer's incurred underwriting expenses for a given period divided by its written premiums for the same period.

By examining the expense ratio, an insurer might determine that it needs to reduce its acquisition costs. For example, an insurer might discontinue an agency incentive program that generates higher acquisition costs in commissions for new business, but from which the business that results is not profitable or is less profitable because it is not retained for subsequent policy terms.

Alternately, the general expense component of the expense ratio might suggest that the insurer should reduce costs in that area. For example, an insurer might offer an employee incentive program to encourage employees to work more efficiently and make fewer errors. Or, an insurer might install modern cost-saving devices, such as thermal, sealed reflective windows and automatic, timed light switches, in its buildings to reduce its utility costs. This reduction of expenses helps to increase the insurer's overall profit.

Written premiums are used in the expense ratio instead of earned premiums (as in the loss ratio) because many of the underwriting expenses insurers incur involve acquisition expenses, which occur at the beginning of the policy period. Written premiums recognize the entire premium as soon as it is written; therefore it is appropriate for comparing expenses to revenues. Financial analysts use various tools to calculate expense ratios following a prescribed formula, as illustrated:

$$\text{Expense ratio} = \frac{\text{Incurred underwriting expenses}}{\text{Written premiums}}$$

Combined Ratio

Combined ratio

A profitability ratio that indicates whether an insurer has made an underwriting loss or gain.

The basic **combined ratio** is determined by adding the loss ratio to the expense ratio. The combined ratio is one of the most commonly used measures of insurer profitability, as it reflects the efficiency with which an insurer is being run by comparing its premiums earned (cash inflows) to its total cash outflows (incurred losses and loss adjustment expenses) generated by its insurance underwriting operations.

When combined ratios are calculated by organizations, the results are decimal expressions such as 0.70 or 1.15. In insurance-industry vernacular, these ratios are typically expressed without the decimals, such as "70" or "115," much as one might express that a baseball player is "batting 333" when the mathematical calculation of getting one hit in each three at-bats results in a batting average of 0.333. An insurer's combined ratio of 70 percent indicates that for every $1.00 in premium it earned, it paid $0.70 for losses and expenses.

For profitability, insurers set target combined ratios that are ideally less than 100. Insurers, regulators, investors, and others use insurers' combined ratios to determine how closely an insurer's actual loss experience compares to its expected loss experience.

The combined ratio is considered the accepted measure of an insurer's under-writing performance, even though it does not take into account the insurer's investment income. The lower the combined ratio, the better it is for an insurer. Most insurers consider a combined ratio under 100 to be accept-able, because it indicates a profit from underwriting, even before investment income is considered. In fact, many insurers regularly experience a combined ratio over 100 and attempt to offset underwriting losses with investment income. Overall financial performance includes the results from both an insurer's underwriting activities and its investment activities.

Within the insurance industry, the combined ratio is used to compare profit-ability among insurers of varying sizes (an insurer's size does not affect the ratio). Consequently, the combined ratio is meaningful to investors and regu-lators, and it provides a measure to be used in benchmarking and in trending. For example, if the industry as a whole experiences difficulty because of losses or a poor economic environment in terms of expenses for a particular year, most insurers' combined ratios for that year would reflect this. An insurer that maintains a lower combined ratio for that year would stand out as an excep-tional insurer.

Financial analysts use various tools to calculate combined ratios following a prescribed formula, as illustrated:

Combined ratio = Loss ratio + Expense ratio

Investment Income Ratio

The **investment income ratio** compares the amount of net investment income (investment income minus investment expenses) with earned premiums over a specific period.

Investment income ratio

Net investment income divided by earned premiums for a given period.

The investment income ratio indicates the degree of success achieved in an insurer's investment activities. The more successful an insurer's investment activities are, the higher the ratio. The investment income ratio is affected by an insurer's ability to manage its investments and select a balanced blend of investments (stocks, bonds, real estate, and so forth) so that investment income (dividends, interest, and other earnings) is regulated over time. The investment income ratio is also affected by the phases in the underwriting cycle and by other financial market considerations. When the property-casualty insurance industry goes through a trough in the underwriting cycle, insurers' competitive price cutting results in reduced underwriting profit, making investment income crucial to insurers' profitability. Conversely, when stock prices plummet and other investments in the market are depressed (as in a recession), underwriting gains are essential to insurers' profitability and financial well being.

Financial analysts use various tools to calculate investment income ratios fol-lowing a prescribed formula, as illustrated:

$$\text{Investment income ratio} = \frac{\text{Net investment income}}{\text{Earned premiums}}$$

Overall Operating Ratio

The overall operating ratio is the combined ratio (loss ratio plus expense ratio) minus the investment income ratio (net investment income divided by earned premiums) and can be used to provide an overall measure of the financial performance of an insurer for a specific period.

Actuaries subtract the investment income ratio from the combined ratio because, realistically, investment income offsets an insurer's losses and underwriting expenses. For example, if the combined ratio was 115 (a loss), and the investment ratio was 25 (a profit), then the overall operating ratio would be 90 (115 – 25). Of all the commonly used ratios, the overall operating ratio is the most complete measure of insurer financial performance.

To obtain a true picture of an insurer's financial health, overall operating ratios for a number of years should be analyzed. An insurer might have a single bad year that is offset by a pattern of profitability over a longer period.

Financial analysts use various tools to calculate overall operating ratios following a prescribed formula, as illustrated:

$$\text{Overall operating ratio} = \text{Combined ratio} - \text{Investment income ratio}$$

Apply Your Knowledge

Janet is a regional underwriting manager for Calladell Insurance and wants to determine how successful her team of underwriters has been in selecting profitable new business over the past nine months.

Which one of these ratios can Janet examine to best determine Calladell's underwriting profitability?

a.   Loss ratio

b.   Combined ratio

c.   Investment ratio

d.   Expense ratio

Feedback: b. The combined ratio is considered the accepted measure of an insurer's underwriting performance or profitability because it provides a snapshot of the insurer's income from its underwriting operations (earned premium) with the costs it incurs in generating the income (expenses) and the costs of providing the service promised in the insurance contract (loss payments and the expenses associated with those losses)—essentially, the insurer's costs of doing business. An insurer's revenue and underwriting expenses are unique compared with the revenue and expenses of other types of business. The loss ratio and expense ratio are important components of the combined ratio, but neither gives the full picture of the insurer's underwriting results or profitability.

If Calladell's combined ratio was 95, what would that mean to Janet?

a. This would indicate that Calladell's underwriting operation was profitable over the nine-month period.

b. This would indicate that Calladell's underwriting operation was not profitable over the nine-month period.

c. This would indicate that Calladell's underwriting expenses exceeded its underwriting profit for the nine-month period.

d. This would indicate that Calladell's underwriting profit exceeded its underwriting expenses for the nine-month period.

Feedback: a. A combined ratio of less than 100 (such as 95) indicates that Calladell achieved an underwriting profit over the nine-month period. To determine the relationship between underwriting expenses and underwriting profit, Janet would need to know the loss ratio and the expense ratio. A combined ratio of 95 percent would indicate to Janet that for every $1.00 in premium that Calladell earned, it paid $0.95 for losses and expenses.

KNOWLEDGE TO ACTION: FINANCIAL RATIOS AND INSURER FINANCIAL PERFORMANCE CASE

An analysis of an insurer's financial ratios provides a view of the insurer's profitability. Knowing how to apply financial ratios is an important skill. This activity will help you apply financial ratios in a business case. As you progress through this case study, you can check your understanding of the concepts by answering the Knowledge to Action questions.

Leightoff Insurance Company writes commercial property, commercial liability, and workers compensation insurance. Leightoff has suffered underwriting losses for each of the previous two years in its overall book of business and has hired a financial analyst, Maggie, to analyze the company's underwriting results using its financial ratios for the end of the current year. Maggie must be prepared to explain to Leightoff's management her analysis and any changes she recommends for future years.

Overview of the Procedure

To determine whether Leightoff achieved an underwriting gain for the year and, if so, the causes of this outcome, Maggie must perform these steps:

- Examine the company's loss ratio
- Examine the company's expense ratio
- Analyze the company's combined ratio

To complete the process, Maggie uses Leightoff's partial financial statement for the end of the year. For simplicity, assume that all of Leightoff's policies are renewed annually and that it issues its policies with a January 1 effective date. See the exhibit "Leightoff Insurance Income Statement for the Year Ending December 31, 20XX."

Leightoff Insurance Income Statement for the Year Ending December 31, 20XX

(All figures are in millions of U.S. dollars.)

Revenues:	
Earned premiums	28.7
Expenses:	
Incurred losses	18.5
Loss adjustment expenses	3.0
Other underwriting expenses:	
Acquisition expenses	5.2
General expenses	2.5
Premium taxes, licenses, and fees	0.3
Total expenses	29.5

[DA07661]

Examine the Loss Ratio

To determine Leightoff's combined ratio, Maggie must first calculate Leightoff's loss ratio. To perform the loss ratio calculation, Maggie reviews the income statement to obtain Leightoff's earned premium ($28.7 million), its incurred losses ($18.5 million), and its loss adjustment expenses ($3 million). She determines that Leightoff's loss ratio is 0.749, which is expressed as 75 percent. While this ratio is acceptable, Maggie determines that Leightoff could take some actions to reduce its loss ratio.

Knowledge to Action

Leightoff proposes to take the following actions in the next year. Determine which of these actions could improve Leightoff's loss ratio, and explain how the ratio would be affected.

a. Leightoff will implement a risk control services program that rewards commercial policyholders for implementing practices that reduce their commercial property, commercial liability, and workers compensation losses.

b. Leightoff will invest a greater volume of its policyholders' surplus in stocks to generate higher earnings.

c. Leightoff will add workers compensation services for its policyholders that exceed the benefits offered by its competition and enable it to charge higher premiums.

d. Leightoff will implement a "green" initiative for all of its buildings that includes installing solar panels and similar improvements to reduce heating and cooling costs.

Feedback: a. and c. To improve its loss ratio, Leightoff should find means to increase its earned premium and/or to decrease its losses and loss adjusting expenses. Implementing a risk control services program for policyholders could reduce the amount of losses that Leightoff must pay, and offering additional workers compensation services to its policyholders could enable Leightoff to charge higher premiums, leading to an increase in its earned premiums. Stock investments would not have an effect on the loss ratio, and a "green" initiative to control Leightoff's general expenses would not affect its loss ratio.

Examine the Expense Ratio

To determine Leightoff's combined ratio, Maggie must next calculate Leightoff's expense ratio. Because all of Leightoff's policies are annual and are issued effective January 1, they all expire on January 1 of the following year. Therefore, Leightoff's written premium is nearly equal to its earned premium at the end of the year (assume it is equal for the expense ratio calculation).

To perform the expense ratio calculation, Maggie reviews the income statement to obtain Leightoff's written (earned) premium ($28.7 million) and its incurred underwriting expenses. Leightoff's underwriting expenses include acquisition expenses of $5.2 million; general expenses of $2.5 million; and premium taxes, licenses, and fees of $0.3 million. Maggie determines that Leightoff's expense ratio is 0.279, which is expressed as 28 percent. While this ratio is acceptable, Maggie determines that Leightoff could take some actions to further reduce its expense ratio.

Knowledge to Action

Leightoff proposes to take the following actions in the next year. Determine which of these actions could improve Leightoff's expense ratio, and explain how the ratio would be affected.

a. Leightoff will hire an experienced investment manager to balance its investment portfolio and regulate its investment earnings.

b. Leightoff will implement a quality control program for its employees that rewards error-free work products and reduces the need for and cost of rework.

c. Leightoff will discontinue a costly agency visitation program requiring underwriters to travel extensively and will instead encourage the use of electronic communications.

d. Leightoff will implement a policy requirement that policyholders use arbitration instead of litigation to settle disputes on property values in loss settlements.

Feedback: b. and c. Leightoff should find ways to increase its earned premium and/or to decrease its "other underwriting expenses" (acquisition and general expenses, premium taxes, licenses, and fees). Implementing a quality control program for employees that rewards error-free work and reduces the cost of rework would help decrease Leightoff's general expenses. Discontinuing a costly agency visitation program would reduce its acquisition costs. Both of these actions would reduce Leightoff's expense ratio. An investment manager could help increase investment earnings or their stability, and an arbitration requirement for property value disputes could reduce loss adjusting expenses, but neither of these activities would affect Leightoff's expense ratio.

Analyze the Combined Ratio

To determine Leightoff's combined ratio, Maggie must use the amounts she has calculated for Leightoff's loss ratio (75 percent) and expense ratio (28 percent). Maggie calculates the ratio as 103 percent.

Knowledge to Action

Explain how each of these actions that Leightoff expects to implement could improve its combined ratio.

- Leightoff will review the profitability of each type of insurance it writes and increase the volume written of the most profitable types while reducing the volume written of the least profitable types by nonrenewing policies of those types that exceed a specified loss threshold.

• Leightoff will reward its most productive employees with pay increases and control its operating costs by requiring each department to reduce its expenses for the next year by 5 percent.

Feedback: Leightoff's combined ratio of 103 percent indicates that Leightoff has suffered an underwriting loss of 3 percent for the year. This means that for every $1.00 in premium it earned, Leightoff has paid $1.03 for losses and expenses. If Leightoff increased the volume of the most profitable types of insurance it writes and reduced the volume of the nonprofitable types it writes by nonrenewing policies with excessive losses, its earned premiums will increase and its losses and loss adjustment expenses will decline. The result will be an improved combined ratio. Rewarding productive employees will help with retention of valuable staff and reduce hiring costs, while a required reduction in departmental budgets can help lower other operating costs. These actions could improve Leightoff's combined ratio, which is a crucial measure of an insurer's profitability for investors and regulators.

SUMMARY

For an insurer to survive long term and grow, its revenue must exceed its expenses. An insurer must manage its revenue and expenses to produce an overall income gain (revenue minus expenses) from its operations and to ensure profitability.

The balance sheet, which measures an insurer's financial position, shows the insurer's assets, liabilities, and policyholders' surplus on a given date, such as the last day of the year. The income statement is a financial statement that shows an insurer's revenues, expenses, and net income for a particular period, usually one year.

Analyzing the relationship of different ratios, the components of the ratios, and how insurers' activities throughout the year can promote overall financial health can help both regulators and investors determine how well insurers are performing. An insurer's actuaries first develop and compile the ratios used in this analysis, including the insurer's loss ratio, expense ratio, combined ratio, investment income ratio, and overall operating ratio.

Understanding the significance of financial ratios and their components can help an insurer monitor its financial health and make necessary changes to improve its financial performance.

Segment B

4

Marketing

Educational Objectives

After learning the content of this assignment, you should be able to:

▷ Describe the factors that influence an agency relationship.

▷ Summarize the various types of insurance distribution systems and alternative marketing channels.

▷ Describe the functions performed by insurance producers.

▷ Describe the key factors an insurer should evaluate during the distribution-system and distribution-channel selection process.

Marketing

UNDERSTANDING FACTORS THAT INFLUENCE AN AGENCY RELATIONSHIP

Insurers depend on marketing personnel such as producers, agents, brokers, and sales representatives to keep them informed about the changing needs and desires of customers. Most insurance marketing systems involve a salesperson who represents either insurers or insureds, or both.

In an insurance context, "**producer**" and "agent" are synonymous terms that refer to any person who sells insurance (produces business) for one or more insurers. The terms "broker" and "sales representative" are also used for special categories of producers. An **agent** engages in an **agency** relationship with a **principal**. In insurance, the principal is often an insurer. Three factors influence an agency relationship:

- Legal roles
- Legal responsibilities
- Scope of authority

Legal Roles

The agency relationship requires absolute trust between the principal and the agent because it imposes serious legal obligations on both parties. While the agent has authority to act for the principal, the principal has control over the agent's actions on the principal's behalf. This authority and control are the two essential elements of an agency relationship.

The principal gives the agent authority to act as its representative within certain guidelines. The principal may authorize the agent to do anything the principal can do. For example, an insurer (the principal) can authorize its agent to collect premiums from insureds for new insurance policies and then require the agent to remit those premiums (sometimes after deducting a commission) to the insurer within a certain amount of time.

The agency contract, also known as an agency agreement, is a written agreement between an insurer and an agent that specifies the scope of the agent's authority to conduct business for the insurer. It gives the agent the right to represent the insurer and to sell insurance on the insurer's behalf. The contract specifies the compensation arrangement between the insurer and the agent. It also describes how the agency relationship can be terminated.

Producer

Any of several kinds of insurance personnel who place insurance and surety business with insurers and who represent either insurers or insureds, or both.

Agent

In the agency relationship, the party that is authorized by the principal to act on the principal's behalf.

Agency

A legal, consensual relationship that exists when one party, the agent, acts on behalf of another party, the principal.

Principal

The party in an agency relationship that authorizes the agent to act on that party's behalf.

Insurance agency contracts usually have no fixed expiration date and remain in force until one party cancels the contract after giving proper notice to the other party, as required by the contract.

Legal Responsibilities

In an agency relationship, the agent's fundamental responsibility is to act for the benefit of the principal. Just as the agent owes duties to the principal, the principal legally owes certain duties to the agent. An agency relationship also creates responsibilities to third parties.

Legal Responsibilities of the Agent to the Principal

The laws of agency impose five duties on all agents, including insurance agents:

*   Be loyal to the principal.
*   Obey the principal's lawful instructions.
*   Exercise a reasonable degree of care in actions on behalf of the principal.
*   Account promptly for any of the principal's money that the agent holds.
*   Keep the principal informed of all facts relating to the agency relationship. This is the duty of relaying information.

In insurance, an agency contract specifically addresses certain rights and duties of the agent. For example, the contract explicitly describes the insurance agent's right to make insurance coverage effective and any limitations on that right. The contract also specifies how the agent is to handle funds, including stipulations on how and when the agent must remit premiums to the insurer. Insurance agency contracts usually give the agent the right to employ subagents, who may act on behalf of the insurer according to the terms of the agency contract.

Legal Responsibilities of the Principal to the Agent

In the case of an insurance agent, the principal's duty to pay the agent for services performed requires the insurer to pay commissions and other specified compensation to the agent for the insurance the agent sells or renews. The principal also has a duty to indemnify, or reimburse, the agent for any losses or damages suffered without the agent's fault, but arising out of the agent's actions on behalf of the principal. If a third party sues the agent in connection with activities performed on behalf of the principal, the principal must reimburse the agent for any liability incurred, if the agent was not at fault.

However, no reimbursement is due if the agent acted illegally or without the principal's authorization, even though the principal may be liable to others for those acts. An important factor involved in this duty is the exposure of insurance agents to errors and omissions (E&O) claims, which may arise from an agent's negligent actions. For example, when an insurance agent gives a customer misleading or incorrect advice regarding the customer's insurance, the customer could bring an E&O claim against the agent if the customer suffers damage due to the agent's advice.

Responsibilities to Third Parties

The agent's authorized actions on behalf of the principal legally obligate the principal to third parties in the same way as if the principal acted alone. Therefore, from an insured's point of view, little distinction exists between the insurance agent and the insurer. Because the agent represents the insurer, the law presumes that knowledge acquired by the agent is knowledge acquired by the insurer.

If, for example, the agent visits the insured's premises and recognizes an exposure (such as vacancy of the building) that could suspend or void the insured's policy, the insurer cannot deny a claim to the insured merely because the agent failed to communicate that information to the insurer. According to agency law, the fact that the agent knew about the exposure means that the insurer is also presumed to know about it.

Scope of Authority

From a third party's perspective, an agent's authority can be either actual or apparent.

Actual Authority

Actual authority can be **express authority** or **implied authority**. Express authority applies not just to carrying out the principal's specific instructions, but also to performing acts incidental to carrying out those instructions. To determine the scope of express authority, courts examine the goals of the agency in light of all surrounding circumstances. For example, the power to sell generally includes authority to collect payment and to make customary warranties. However, to illustrate consideration of scope, a sales agent who has no possession or indication of ownership of merchandise has no authority to collect the purchase price. In most commercial situations, the agent has authority only to solicit orders or to produce a buyer with whom the principal can deal.

Binding authority, generally granted to the agent in the agency contract, is a form of express authority. Binding coverage is usually accomplished by issuing binders, which are agreements to provide temporary insurance coverage until a formal written policy is issued. Binders can be either written or oral. When an insurance agent binds coverage for a new client, the agent commits the insurer to covering an exposure for, and possibly paying a claim to, a customer who is unknown to the insurer. Binding authority involves important responsibilities for the agent, and agents are expected to use their binding authority carefully. See the exhibit "Binding Authority: An Example."

Actual authority
Authority (express or implied) conferred by the principal on an agent under an agency contract.

Express authority
The authority that the principal specifically grants to the agent.

Implied authority
The authority implicitly conferred on an agent by custom, usage, or a principal's conduct indicating intention to confer such authority.

Binding authority
An insurance agent's authority to effect coverage on behalf of the insurer.

> ### Binding Authority: An Example
>
> Assume Christopher owns an old car for which he has an automobile policy with no collision coverage. Christopher purchases a new car and calls his insurance agent, Lisa, to make sure the car is covered before he drives it off the dealer's lot. Reminding Christopher that he has no collision coverage, Lisa gives him a quote for collision coverage on the new car. Lisa and Christopher agree that Lisa will immediately add the new car to Christopher's policy, including collision coverage with a $250 deductible. Christopher agrees to pay the premium when he receives an invoice, and Lisa assures Christopher that "coverage is bound." Lisa then begins to process the paperwork necessary to issue a policy change (called an endorsement) that includes collision and other coverages on Christopher's new car. If Christopher should have an accident before receiving the policy endorsement, he would have collision coverage on his new car because Lisa issued an oral binder. The binder is temporary because it will be replaced by a policy endorsement.

[DA07549]

Custom is the most common source of implied authority. Agents can reasonably infer that they have authority to act according to prevailing custom unless the principal gives different instructions. Without different instructions, an agent's authority extends to, and is limited to, what a person in this agent's position usually does.

Apparent Authority

Apparent authority

A third party's reasonable belief that an agent has authority to act on the principal's behalf.

Unlike actual authority, a principal neither confers apparent authority on an agent nor creates it. **Apparent authority** is based on appearances and includes all the authority that a reasonable person acquainted with the customs and nature of the business could reasonably assume the agent has. It generally arises in one of two overlapping circumstances:

- A principal grants less authority than agents in the same position in that business usually have.
- The method of operation of the principal's business differs from that of other businesses of the same kind in the principal's area.

For example, principal Paul instructs agent Ann not to sell goods on credit if the total credit to a customer exceeds $200, an unusual restriction in Paul's business. Ann sells goods on credit to Lee for $250 with no actual authority to do so. Lee, however, neither knows nor had reason to know of the restriction. A third party could have reasonably believed that Ann had the usual authority in that situation. The authority was apparent, and Paul cannot deny it.

SUMMARIZING TYPES OF INSURANCE DISTRIBUTION SYSTEMS

Insurers use many types of distribution systems based on their organizational structure, business and marketing plans, growth goals, technological capabilities, staffing, and other resources.

Insurance distribution systems differ in their relationship to the insurer and customers, ownership of expirations, compensation methods, and functions performed. Insurers use several common distribution channels to promote products and services as well as to communicate with existing and prospective insureds.

These are the main insurance distribution systems:

- Independent agency and brokerage marketing system
- Exclusive agency marketing system
- Direct writer marketing system

Independent Agency and Brokerage Marketing System

The independent agency and brokerage marketing system uses agents and brokers who are independent contractors rather than employees of insurers. These independent agents and brokers are usually free to represent as many or as few insurers as they want.

Independent Agents and Brokers

An **independent agency** or brokerage can be organized as a sole proprietorship, a partnership, or a corporation. **Brokers** shop among insurers to find the best coverage and value for their clients. Because they are not legal representatives of the insurer, brokers are not likely to have authority to commit an insurer to write a policy by binding coverage, unlike agents, who generally have binding authority.

One vital distinction between independent agents and brokers and other distribution systems is the ownership of the **agency expiration list**. If the insurer ceases to do business with an agency, the agency has the right to continue doing business with its existing customers by selling them insurance with another insurer. The ownership of expiration lists is an agency's most valuable asset. The agency—not the insurer—owns the business (though insureds have the right to place their business with any insurer they wish, whether with that agent or elsewhere). An independent agency has the right to sell its expiration lists to another independent agent.

Independent agency

A business, operated for the benefit of its owner (or owners) that sells insurance, usually as a representative of several unrelated insurers.

Broker

An independent producer who represents insurance customers.

Agency expiration list

The record of an insurance agency's present policyholders and the dates their policies expire.

Compensation for independent agents and brokers is typically in two forms:

- A flat percent commission on all new and renewal business submitted
- A contingent or profit-sharing commission based on volume or loss ratio goals

The independent agency and brokerage distribution system can meet the needs of many different insurance customers and is spread geographically across the United States. Agents and brokers may also assist their customers in establishing and managing self-insurance programs, implementing risk control measures, and determining alternatives or supplements to insurance.

National and Regional Brokers

National and regional brokers generally represent commercial insurance accounts that often require sophisticated knowledge and service. In addition to insurance sales, large brokerage firms may provide extensive risk control, appraisal, actuarial, risk management, claim administration, and other insurance-related services. Large insurance brokerage firms operate regionally, nationally, and internationally. They can tailor insurance programs for customers or groups of customers who require a particular type of coverage for multiple locations. The brokers receive negotiated fees for the services they provide, or they receive fees in addition to commissions, subject to state regulation.

Independent Agency Networks

Independent agency network

A group of agencies that contractually link to share services, resources, and insurers to gain advantages normally available only to large regional and national brokers.

Independent agency networks—also known as agent groups, agent clusters, or agent alliances—operate nationally, regionally, or locally and, in the majority of cases, allow their agent-members to retain individual agency ownership and independence.

Managing General Agents

Managing general agent (MGA)

An authorized agent of the primary insurer that manages all or part of the primary insurer's insurance activities, usually in a specific geographic area.

The exact duties and responsibilities of a **managing general agent (MGA)** depend on its contracts with the insurers it represents. MGAs can represent a single insurer, although they more commonly represent several insurers. Some MGAs can be strictly sales operations, appointing and supervising subagents or dealing with brokers within their contractual jurisdiction. That jurisdiction can be specified in terms of geographic boundaries, types of insurance, or both. A few MGAs cover large multistate territories, although frequently only for specialty insurance.

An insurer operating through an MGA has several advantages:

- A low fixed cost
- Specialty expertise
- Assumption of insurer activities

Surplus Lines Brokers

Most agents and brokers are limited to placing business with licensed (or admitted) insurers. The circumstances under which business can be placed with an unlicensed (or nonadmitted) insurer through a surplus lines broker vary by state. Normally, a reasonable effort to place the coverage with a licensed insurer is required. The agents and brokers, who must be licensed to place surplus lines business in that state, might be required to certify that a specified number (often two or three) of licensed insurers have refused to provide the coverage. In some states, agents and brokers must provide letters from the insurers rejecting the coverage. Some state insurance departments maintain lists of coverages that are eligible for surplus lines treatment without first being rejected by licensed insurers. Some states also maintain lists of eligible surplus lines insurers, requiring producers to place business only with financially sound insurers. See the exhibit "Distribution Systems for Insurance Marketing."

Distribution Systems for Insurance Marketing

Distribution systems consist of the necessary people and physical facilities to support the sale of the insurance product and services.

Independent agency and brokerage marketing system

- Independent agents and brokers
- National and regional brokers
- Independent agent networks
- Managing general agents (MGAs)
- Surplus lines brokers

Exclusive agency marketing system

Direct writer marketing system

[DA12773]

Exclusive Agency Marketing System

The **exclusive agency marketing system** uses independent contractors called exclusive agents (or captive agents), who are not employees of insurers. Exclusive agents are usually restricted by contract to representing a single insurer. Consequently, insurer management can exercise more control over exclusive agents than over independent agents. However, some exclusive agency companies allow their agents to place business with other insurers if the exclusive agency insurer does not offer the product or service needed.

Exclusive agents are usually compensated by commissions. For exclusive agents, the focus is on new-business production, and a reduced renewal com-

Exclusive agency marketing system

An insurance marketing system under which agents contract to sell insurance exclusively for one insurer (or for an associated group of insurers).

mission rate encourages sales and supports growth. Though exclusive agents typically do not own expirations as independent producers do, some insurers that market through the exclusive agency system do grant agents limited ownership of expirations.

The exclusive agency insurer handles many administrative functions for the exclusive agent, including policy issuance, premium collection, and claim processing. Exclusive agents might offer loss adjustment services similar to those offered by independent agents and brokers; however, these agents might be restricted in their ability to offer some risk management services to their customers.

Direct Writer Marketing System

Direct writer marketing system

An insurance marketing system that uses sales agents (or sales representatives) who are direct employees of the insurer.

Sales agents in the **direct writer marketing system** may be compensated by salary, by commission, or by both salary and a portion of the commission generated. Because sales agents are employees of the insurers they represent, they usually do not have any ownership of expirations and, like exclusive agents, are usually restricted to representing a single insurer or a group of insurers under common ownership and management. Compared to independent agents and exclusive agents, insurer management exercises greater control over its employee sales agents. Sometimes a customer needs a type of policy not available from the direct writer insurer that the sales agent represents. When this happens, the sales agent may act as a broker by contacting an agent who represents another insurer and apply for insurance through that agent, who usually shares the commission with the direct writer sales agent. Insurance sold in this manner is referred to as brokered business.

Sales agents are largely relieved of administrative functions by their employers. These insurer-assumed functions include policy issuance, premium collections, and claim functions. Direct writer insurers should encourage their sales agents to develop new business. This can be accomplished by relieving producers of nonselling activities and compensating at a lower renewal rate.

Distribution Channels

The distribution channels used by insurers and their representatives are conduits for contacting and establishing communication with their customers and prospective customers.

Internet

As a distribution channel, the Internet and online access to insurance transactions by the insurer, its representatives, and the customer are experiencing rapid growth. Interactions range from exchanges of email to multiple-policy quoting, billing, and policy issuance. Customers also interact with insurers via web-based insurance distributors, also called insurance portals or aggregators. These portals deliver leads to the insurers whose products they offer through their websites. Portals benefit customers by offering the products and services of many insurance providers on one website. Although the leads that portals generate must subsequently be screened and fully underwritten by the insurers accepting the coverage, they can increase an insurer's market share and brand awareness.

Call Centers

The best-equipped call centers can replicate many of the activities of producers. In addition to making product sales, call center staff can respond to general inquiries, handle claim reporting, answer billing inquiries, and process policy endorsements. In some cases, a customer can begin an inquiry or a transaction on the Internet, then have a customer service representative at the insurer's call center access the Internet activity and answer the inquiry or conclude the transaction.

Direct Response

The direct response distribution channel markets directly to customers. No agent is involved; rather, the direct response relies primarily on phone or Internet sales. Direct response relies heavily on advertising and targeting specific groups of affiliated customers. With direct response, commission costs, if any, are greatly reduced. However, a disadvantage is that advertising costs are typically higher. The customer can sometimes "opt out" and speak with a call-center customer service representative or be assigned to a local servicing office. See the exhibit "Distribution Channels for Insurance Marketing."

Distribution Channels for Insurance Marketing

Distribution channels are communication conduits for promoting and servicing products as well as communicating with existing and prospective insureds.

- Internet
- Call centers
- Direct response
- Group marketing
- Financial institutions

[DA12774]

Group Marketing

Group marketing sells insurance products and services to individuals or businesses that are all members of the same organization. Distributing insurance to specifically targeted groups is known by a number of terms, including these:

- Affinity marketing—Insurers target various customer groups based on profession, interests, hobbies, or attitudes.

- Mass marketing or mass merchandising—Insurers design an offer for their policies to large numbers of targeted individuals or groups.

- Worksite marketing or payroll deduction—Employers can contract directly with an insurer or through a producer to offer voluntary insurance coverage as a benefit to their employees.

- Sponsorship marketing—A trade group sponsors an insurer in approaching a customer group. The sponsor participates in the profitability of the program.

Trade Associations

Trade associations serve their members through activities such as education, political lobbying, research, and advertising. The advertising programs are intended to create a favorable image of association members as a group and to make the public familiar with the logos and other association symbols. See the exhibit "Producers' Trade Associations."

Producers' Trade Associations

- Most independent agents are members of the Independent Insurance Agents & Brokers of America (IIABA), the National Association of Professional Insurance Agents (PIA), or both. The IIABA is often called the "Big I" because of the prominent letter "I" in its advertising logo. (In some states, IIABA and PIA have consolidated to form one state insurance agents' association.)

- The Council of Insurance Agents and Brokers (CIAB) includes independent agents and brokers associated with large agencies or brokerage firms that primarily handle commercial insurance.

- Many managing general agents are members of the American Association of Managing General Agents (AAMGA), which, like agents' and brokers' associations, also provides various services to its members.

[DA07561]

Financial Institutions

Insurers and producers can elect to market their products and services through a bank or another financial services institution, either exclusively or through additional distribution channels. Marketing arrangements can range from simple to complex. The prospect of diversifying into new markets appeals to many financial institutions.

Insurers view financial institutions as beneficial strategic partners because of these qualities:

- Strong customer base
- Predisposition to product cross-selling
- Strength at processing transactions
- Efficient use of technology for database mining geared to specific products and services

Omnichannel Marketing System

An omnichannel marketing system requires consideration of several issues:

- Maintaining consistent customer communications
- Providing a consistent customer experience
- Matching the type of insurance with an appropriate distribution system and channel
- Targeting customers with relevant data

Omnichannel marketing allows insurers to market to customers in multiple channels and meet the needs of customers seeking alternative methods to purchase insurance. By using an omnichannel approach, insurers can target various market segments using methods such as online, mobile applications, call centers, or other approaches based on the customers' preferred method of interaction. This approach is supported by developments in data analytics, which assists insurers in using customer data to make better and more consistent marketing decisions.

FUNCTIONS OF INSURANCE PRODUCERS

The functions insurance producers perform vary widely from one marketing system to another and from one producer to another within a given marketing system. Although technology has changed the process, producers are often the initial contact with insurance customers and provide expertise and ongoing services. This is particularly true for commercial insurance customers.

Insurance producers represent one or more insurance companies. As a source of insurance knowledge for their customers, producers provide risk management advice, solicit or sell insurance, and provide follow-up services as customers' loss exposures or concerns change.

Insurance producers typically perform these functions:

- Prospecting
- Risk management review

- Sales
- Policy issuance
- Premium collection
- Customer service
- Claim handling
- Consulting

Prospecting

Virtually all producers prospect. Prospecting involves locating persons, businesses, and other entities that may be interested in purchasing the insurance products and services offered by the producer's principals. Prospects can be located using several methods:

- Referrals from present clients
- Referrals from strategic partners, such as financial institutions and real estate brokers
- Advertising in multimedia and direct mail
- Interactive websites, social media, and mobile marketing
- Telephone solicitations
- **Cold canvass**

Cold canvass

Contacting a prospect without an appointment.

Large agencies and brokerages may have employees who specialize in locating prospective clients. However, a producer is typically responsible for his or her own prospecting. Insurers might also participate in prospecting, especially in the exclusive agent and direct writer marketing systems.

Risk Management Review

Risk management review is the principal method of determining a prospect's insurance needs. The extent of the review varies based on customers and their characteristics.

Individual or Family

For an individual or a family, the risk management review process might be relatively simple, requiring an interview or completion of an online questionnaire that assists in identifying the prospect's loss exposures, which are often associated with property ownership and activities. Using the results of the questionnaire, the producer suggests methods of risk control, retention of loss exposures, and insurance.

Businesses

The risk management review process for businesses is likely to be more complex because they have property ownership, products, services, employees, and liabilities that are unique to the size and type of organization. Substantial time is required to develop and analyze loss exposure information for a large firm with diversified operations.

A review of previous losses, or a "loss run," can guide the producer in helping the business owner develop risk management plans, track the results of current risk management efforts, identify problem areas, and project costs. Loss runs include, at a minimum, lists of losses and their total cost. For large commercial customers, the producer may work with the customer's Risk Management Department in identifying loss exposures and risk analysis. Based on this analysis, risk treatment decisions, including insurance coverage, can be made. The producer can then coordinate further coverage discussions between the customer and the insurer.

Sales

Selling insurance products and services is one of the most important activities of an insurance producer because it is essential to sustaining the livelihood of the agency or brokerage. Commission on business sold is the principal source of income for producers, and the ownership of policy expirations applicable to the business sold is the principal asset of an insurance agency.

Policy Issuance

At the producer's request, insurers issue policies and their associated forms, sending them either directly to policyholders or to the producer for delivery. In paperless environments, the policies and forms may be produced digitally, along with endorsements, bills, and loss history information.

Premium Collection

Producers who issue policies may also prepare policy invoices and collect premiums. After deducting their commissions, they send the net premiums to the insurers, a procedure known as the agency bill process.

To give the producer some protection against policyholders' late payments, premiums are usually not due to the insurer until thirty or forty-five days after the policy's effective date. This delay also permits the producer to invest the premiums collected until they are due to the insurer. The resulting investment income can be a significant part of the producer's remuneration.

Agency billing may be used for personal insurance policies, but it is more commonly used with large commercial accounts. For small commercial accounts and the vast majority of personal insurance, the customer is usually directed to send premium payments to the insurer, bypassing the producer in a procedure known as the direct bill process.

Customer Service

Most producers are involved to some degree in customer service. For independent agents and brokers, value-added services and the personalization of insurance packages are what differentiate them in the marketplace. For the producer of a direct writer, service might consist of providing advice, handling an endorsement request, providing coverage quotes, or referring a policyholder who has had a loss to the Claims Department.

Producers are expected to facilitate contacts between policyholders and the insurer, including these:

- Responding to billing inquiries
- Performing customer account reviews
- Answering questions regarding existing coverage and additional coverage requirements
- Corresponding with premium auditors and risk control representatives

Claim Handling

All producers are likely to be involved to some extent in handling claims filed by their policyholders. Because the producer is the policyholder's principal contact with the insurer, the policyholder usually contacts the producer first when a claim occurs.

In some cases, the producer might provide information on contacting the insurer. Alternatively, the producer might obtain some basic information about the claim from the policyholder, relay it to the insurer, and arrange for a claim representative to contact the policyholder. Frequently, insurers issue their policies with a "claim kit" that informs their policyholders about the proper procedures and contacts in the event of a loss.

Some producers are authorized by their insurers to adjust some types of claims. Most often, the authorization is limited to small first-party property claims. However, a few large agencies or brokerages that employ skilled claim personnel might be authorized to settle large, more complex claims. The limitations on the producer's claim-handling authority should be specified in the agency contract.

Claim handling by qualified producers offers two major advantages: quicker service to policyholders and lower loss adjustment expenses to the insurer. Conversely, if the producer is not properly trained in how to handle claims, overpayment of claims can offset the savings.

Consulting

Many producers offer consulting services, for which they are paid on a fee basis. Such services are usually performed for insureds, but they may also be performed for noninsureds or for prospects. Services might be provided for a fee only, or the producer might set a maximum fee to be reduced by any commissions received on insurance written because of the consulting contract.

Laws in some states prohibit agents from receiving both commission and a fee from the same client. Fees are billed separately from any insurance premiums due, whereas commissions are included in the premium totals billed.

SELECTING INSURANCE MARKETING DISTRIBUTION SYSTEMS AND CHANNELS

Any firm that sells a product has a distribution system to carry out some of its marketing functions. Distribution systems for intangible products, such as insurance, are more flexible and adaptable than those for tangible products because they are not constrained by large investments in physical facilities. This intangibility gives insurers options to meet a wide array of customers' needs as well as their own operational needs. Distribution channels provide even more options for communicating with existing and potential customers.

Insurance distribution systems and channels provide the necessary people, physical facilities, and conduits for communication between insurers and customers.

An insurer usually selects a distribution system before it begins writing business. Changing distribution systems for existing business can be difficult and expensive because of existing agency contracts and possible ownership of expirations. However, an insurer might decide to use a different distribution system when entering a new territory or launching a new insurance product. In contrast, distribution channels selected by insurers and their representatives are more readily changeable.

The key factors in selecting distribution systems and channels are based on customers' needs and characteristics as well as the insurer's profile. See the exhibit "Distribution Systems and Conduits for Insurance Marketing."

Distribution Systems and Conduits for Insurance Marketing

Distribution systems consist of the necessary people and physical facilities to support the sale of the insurance product and services.	Independent agency and brokerage marketing system • Independent agents and brokers • National and regional brokers • Independent agent networks • Managing general agents (MGAs) • Surplus lines brokers Exclusive agency marketing system Direct writer marketing system
Distribution channels are communication conduits for promoting and servicing products as well as communicating with existing and prospective insureds.	• Internet • Call centers • Direct response • Group marketing • Financial institutions

[DA06250]

Customers' Needs and Characteristics

The needs and characteristics of customers—both existing and those in target markets—are key factors in an insurer's selection of distribution systems and channels because their satisfaction drives their purchase decisions. These are examples of customer needs and characteristics:

- Products and services—What are customers' expectations regarding coverage, accessibility, price, and service? Customers with low service expectations, such as those who purchase minimum-coverage personal auto insurance, may be satisfied with the ease of shopping online for direct writers' policies. Conversely, a large commercial account's risk manager will seek the expertise of an agent or broker to provide advice, assist in coverage placement, and respond to changing needs as the organization's internal and external environments change.

- Price—To what degree is the price of products and services a factor for customers? Some consumers' paramount concern is the price of insurance. Others are concerned with price to a degree but are unlikely to make changes if they are satisfied with a product. Still others seek risk management alternatives that will minimize the adverse effects of losses for the organization over the long term.

- Response time—How quickly can inquiries and transactions be processed? Customers can quickly conduct many financial services transactions, and they often expect the same response from their insurance providers.

Insurer's Profile

An insurer's profile—including its strategies and goals, strengths, existing and target markets, geographic location, and the degree of control over producers it needs or desires—frames the business and marketing environments within which it operates. The insurer must evaluate these key factors when selecting distribution systems and channels.

Insurer Strategies and Goals

An insurer's strategies, defined by high-level organizational goals, provide purposeful direction for the organization. These strategies and goals often address issues regarding market share, sales, service, and the markets in which the insurer competes. They may also relate to acquisitions, strategic alliances, or mergers.

Changes in market strategies or aggressive goals can be a catalyst for an insurer to reexamine its distribution systems and channels if current approaches are inadequate to achieve required results. For example, a regional personal lines insurer that contracts independent agents as a distribution system may adopt a strategy to expand to the national market. Rather than contracting additional independent agents in the expanded geographic territory, the insurer assumes the role of a direct writer and uses an online distribution channel to reach customers through web-based insurance distributors. This approach can reduce long-term costs and accelerate the insurer's market-share growth.

Insurer Strengths

Organizations evaluate their internal and external environments to assess their strengths and weaknesses compared with external opportunities and threats. Once an insurer determines where its strengths lie, it selects those distribution systems and channels that maximize its opportunities to capture market share and minimize its weaknesses. In doing so, the insurer may analyze these factors:

- Financial resources—The initial fixed cost of entering a market through the exclusive agency system or direct writer system is greater than doing so through the independent agency system. The insurer must hire, train, and financially support the direct writer and exclusive agency producers at substantial cost before they become productive. Similarly, online distribution channels have high start-up costs for supporting information systems. In comparison, the cost of conducting a direct response campaign can be much lower. Consequently, insurers with the financial resources to initiate distribution systems and channels with high start-up costs have the option of competing in markets that are best served by those marketing methods.

Insurers without those financial resources may be limited in the target markets they can enter.

- Core capabilities—Core capabilities include the abilities of an organization's staff, processes, and technology. An insurer whose strength is successfully servicing large, complex commercial accounts can capitalize on the firm's core capabilities. Complex commercial accounts require personalized service and are well served by agents and brokers, who can provide advice and ongoing service to expand the types of businesses to which the insurer markets or its geographic market.

- Expertise and reputation of producers—Because agents and brokers are the point of contact with customers, their expertise and reputation can be a crucial strength or weakness for the insurer. The level of expertise required of a producer depends on the lines of insurance written. Specialty target markets, such as international manufacturing, high-net-worth individuals, and large public entities, require knowledgeable and prominent producers to advise them. Having producers with those attributes in a direct writer distribution system allows the insurer to expand into similar or secondary markets. An insurer attempting to enter specialty markets without the skill base on staff must compete for agents and brokers who can provide the needed expertise and reputation.

Existing and Target Markets

The characteristics of an insurer's existing book of business should be considered before any change in distribution system or channel. If agents or brokers own the expirations for current accounts, the insurer must either give up that business and start over or purchase the expirations from producers. Either option might be expensive, depending on the quality of the existing business.

Disruptions in communication channels can also result in policyholder dissatisfaction and lost accounts. As a result, insurers change market systems and channels for existing customers with great caution. However, some catalysts are sufficiently threatening to cause an insurer to change marketing approaches. For example, an insurer that is losing market share to an aggressive new competitor has ample incentive to change its approach to better address customers' needs and characteristics.

Customers' needs and characteristics are driving factors for an insurer that is considering changing its marketing approach or adopting an omnichannel approach for a new target market. If an insurer's existing distribution systems and channels do not adequately address the customers' profiles as determined through marketing research, the insurer is less likely to gain market share. To make an optimum choice, the insurer carefully balances the cost of changing its distribution systems and channels with expected benefits resulting from the new accounts it will write.

Insurers can apply data analytics approaches to more clearly define customer needs based on existing information regarding purchasing preferences, demographics, coverage needs, and other factors. This analysis can assist in determining appropriate distribution systems or channels for existing business and to target new markets.

Geographic Location

The geographic location of existing policyholders or target markets is a key concern in selecting a distribution system and channels because the insurer's fixed costs of establishing an exclusive or direct writer agent in a territory are substantial. Exclusive agent or direct writer marketing systems can be successful only when a sufficient number of prospects exist within a relatively small geographic area.

Because the cost of appointing an independent agent is generally lower than that of appointing an exclusive or direct writer agent, those systems can be used in sparsely populated areas or when customers in the target market are widely dispersed. Emerging digital technologies are also providing opportunities for insurers to reach these customers. This is especially true for personal lines or small commercial lines customers who may be better served through omnichannel marketing approaches, such as online or through call centers.

Degree of Control Required

The extent of control the insurer wants to exercise over its marketing operations may influence its choice of a distribution system:

- An insurer can exercise the greatest control over producers in the direct writer system. Under that system, the producer is an employee of the company, and the company can exercise control over both the results achieved and the methods used to achieve them. For example, an insurer can specify the number and type of new applications the producer must submit each month (results) as well as the marketing approaches the producer can use (methods).

- Under both the agency and brokerage system and the exclusive agency system, the producers are independent contractors; therefore, the insurer can control only the results they produce, not the methods they use to produce them. For example, an insurer can specify the number and type of new applications the producer must submit each month (results). To achieve those results, however, the agent or broker can engage in any advertising or marketing campaign that does not violate insurance regulations or contractual agreements with the insurer.

- Producers are not involved in the direct response system. Consequently, the insurer has complete control of its distribution system.

Degree of control becomes important in meeting the needs of some customers. For example, pharmaceutical manufacturers require specialized risk management advice that includes a risk control recovery plan in case a tainted drug or defective medical device is released to the public. The insurer may wish to control the nature of the risk management alternatives recommended to those insureds, preferring those that foster transparency and immediate response following products liability losses.

Other insurers value discretion in the producers who represent them. For example, an insurer that specializes in church insurance or distributes insurance through religious affinity groups will expect to have some control over the producers' use of social media. A producer's indiscretions posted in public forums can cause an insurer to lose accounts. Therefore, the insurer might choose a direct writer distribution system under which producers are employees and subject to the insurer's guidelines for media use.

SUMMARY

The legal relationship of agency empowers the insurance producer—the agent—to act on behalf of the insurer—the principal. An agent's authority can be either actual or apparent. An agent's actual authority can be express or implied. Binding authority, generally granted to the agent in the agency contract, is a form of express authority. Apparent authority generally occurs when a principal grants less authority than agents usually have, or when the principal's business operates differently from similar businesses in the area.

Insurance distribution systems consist of the necessary people and physical facilities to support the sale of insurance products and services. The main insurance distribution systems are these:

- Independent agency and brokerage marketing system
- Exclusive agency marketing system
- Direct writer marketing system

Insurers use distribution channels to promote products and services as well as to communicate with existing and prospective insureds.

Insurance producers represent one or more insurance companies and perform these typical functions:

- Prospecting
- Risk management review
- Sales
- Policy issuance
- Premium collection
- Customer service
- Claim handling
- Consulting

Insurers should evaluate various factors when selecting distribution systems and channels. These factors include customers' needs and characteristics, such as the products and services they require, the price they are willing to pay, and the response time they require.

Insurers' profiles serve as guidelines that affect their choice of distribution systems and channels. Insurers' profiles include their strategies and goals, strengths, existing and target markets, geographic location, and the degree of control required.

Direct Your Learning ▶▶

Underwriting and Ratemaking

Educational Objectives

After learning the content of this assignment, you should be able to:

▸ Distinguish among the underwriting activities typically performed by line and staff underwriters.

▸ Describe the steps in the underwriting process.

▸ Summarize the responsibilities of underwriting management.

▸ Explain how insurance rates are developed.

▸ Given the insurance rate and exposure units for a particular insurance policy, calculate the policy premium.

Underwriting and Ratemaking | 5

UNDERWRITING ACTIVITIES

Insurers assume billions of dollars in financial risk through coverage decisions based on underwriters' analysis of data drawn from both traditional sources and the increasingly significant universe of technology-driven big data. An insurer's underwriting activities—the coordinated efforts of **line underwriters** and **staff underwriters**—can therefore influence its profitability more than any other single factor.

Line underwriters evaluate new submissions and perform renewal underwriting, usually by working directly with insurance producers and applicants. Staff underwriters, meanwhile, manage risk selection by working with line underwriters and coordinating decisions about products, pricing, and guidelines. Collectively, these activities enable the insurer to avoid **adverse selection**, maintain adequate policyholders' surplus, and enforce underwriting guidelines, all of which contribute to the primary underwriting goal of sustaining profitable growth.

Let's examine the line underwriting and staff underwriting roles more closely.

Line Underwriting Activities

Line underwriters evaluate accounts for acceptability and make their decisions according to the **underwriting guidelines** outlined by staff underwriters. The individual activities these tasks entail include these:

- Selecting insureds—Line underwriters select new and renewal accounts (and evaluate existing ones) by identifying suitable applicants and charging appropriate premiums that accurately reflect the loss exposures covered. Techniques driven by customer-generated data, such as predictive analysis, generalized linear models, and credit-scoring models, often help line underwriters make these decisions. Line underwriters also look for unusual patterns of policy growth or loss and monitor real-time data, such as information from vehicle-based telematic devices, wearable sensors, and devices connected to the Internet of Things. Optimized insured selection helps line underwriters fulfill one of underwriting's chief purposes—to avoid adverse selection, which can significantly undermine profitability.

- Classifying and pricing accounts—Account classification entails grouping similar accounts so that they can be priced competitively while still allowing the insurer to make a profit and maintain an adequate **policyholders'**

Line underwriter
Underwriter who is primarily responsible for implementing the steps in the underwriting process.

Staff underwriter
Underwriter who assists underwriting management with making and implementing underwriting policy.

Adverse selection
In general, the tendency for people with the greatest probability of loss to be the ones most likely to purchase insurance.

Underwriting guidelines (underwriting guide)
A written manual that communicates an insurer's underwriting policy and that specifies the attributes of an account that an insurer is willing to insure.

Policyholders' surplus
An insurer's assets minus its liabilities, which represents its net worth.

surplus. Like account selection, this activity is often reinforced with data-driven decision making.

- Recommending or providing coverage—Line underwriters may make sure that existing accounts are adequately protected through non-insurance risk management techniques, such as retention or risk control, so that any coverage gaps are addressed. They might also collaborate with producers to ensure that applicants obtain the coverage they request. Finally, producers and applicants often want to know how coverage will respond to a specific type of loss; line underwriters respond (usually through the producer) by explaining the types of losses covered and the endorsements that can be added to provide coverage not included in standard policies.

- Managing a book of business—Some insurers' line underwriters are responsible for the profitability of a book of business accepted from a producer or written in a territory or line of business. In such cases, the line underwriter works to ensure that each book of business achieves established goals, such as product mix, loss ratio, and written premium.

- Supporting producers and customers—Because customer service activities and underwriting are often interwoven, line underwriters have a vested interest in ensuring that producers' and insureds' needs are met. Line underwriters usually work directly with producers to prepare policy quotations.

- Coordinating with marketing efforts—An insurer's marketing efforts and underwriting policy should be compatible.

Staff Underwriting Activities

Staff underwriters work closely with underwriting management to perform activities essential to profitable risk selection, such as these:

- Performing market research—Market research may entail evaluating the effect of adding or deleting entire lines of business, of expanding into additional states, or of retiring from states an insurer operates in; determining optimal product mix for a book of business; and examining premium-volume goals. Market research can also be refined using data-fueled predictive analysis methods.

Underwriting policy (underwriting philosophy)

A guide to individual and aggregate policy selection that supports an insurer's mission statement.

- Formulating underwriting policy— **Underwriting policy (underwriting philosophy)** translates an insurer's mission and goals into specific strategies that, in turn, determine the composition of the insurer's book of business. Insurers often develop their underwriting policy within the context of the market(s) they serve—the standard market, the nonstandard market, or the specialty market. Beyond these broad market selections, the goals for an insurer's book of business and resulting underwriting policy may be established according to types of insurance and classes of business to be written; territories to be developed; or forms, insurance rates (such as filed rates and surplus lines pricing), and rating plans to be used.

- Revising underwriting guidelines to reflect changes in underwriting policy—Some insurers' underwriting guidelines include systematic instructions for handling particular classes of commercial accounts, including pricing instructions. Such guidelines may identify specific hazards to evaluate, alternatives to consider, criteria to use when making the final decision, ways to implement the decision, and methods to monitor the decision. Other insurers use less comprehensive guidelines.

- Evaluating loss experience—Insurance products with greater-than-anticipated losses are usually targeted for analysis. Staff underwriters research loss data to determine the specific source of the excess losses. Part of this research includes analyzing—often augmented with big data—the insurance industry's loss experience, which may reveal trends affecting the insurer's products. Based on their evaluation, staff underwriters, usually with the agreement of other key departments, adjust the insurer's underwriting guidelines.

- Researching and developing coverage forms—When an insurer develops its own forms, staff underwriters collaborate with the insurer's actuarial and legal departments to meet changing consumer needs and competitive pressures. Additionally, insurers modify existing coverage forms so that the coverage provided will respond as anticipated.

- Reviewing and revising pricing plans—Staff underwriters review and update rates and rating plans continually, subject to regulatory constraints, to respond to changes in loss experience, competition, and inflation. Insurers and advisory organizations gather historical loss data to develop **prospective loss costs**. Each insurer then examines its own operational profit and expense requirements. Staff underwriters combine prospective loss costs with an insurer-developed profit and expense loading to create a final rate used in policy pricing. Insurers must develop their own rates for any coverage for which advisory organizations do not develop loss costs. In such situations, reviewing and revising rating plans become even more crucial to ensuring that the loss costs adequately reflect **loss development** and **trending**.

- Assisting others with complex accounts—Staff underwriters often serve as consultants to other underwriters. Generally, staff underwriters have significant first-hand experience in line underwriting. They regularly see complex and atypical accounts, unlike most line underwriters. Staff underwriters also function as referral underwriters, reviewing and approving the risk when an application exceeds a line underwriter's authority.

- Conducting underwriting audits—Staff underwriters are often responsible for monitoring line underwriters' activities and their adherence to **underwriting authority**, which can be evaluated by conducting **underwriting audits**. These audits focus on proper documentation; adherence to procedure, classification, and rating practices; and conformity of selection decisions to the underwriting guidelines. Staff underwriters also monitor underwriting activity by analyzing statistical results by type of insurance, class of business, size of loss exposure, and territory. Statistical data shows

Prospective loss costs

Loss data that are modified by loss development, trending, and credibility processes, but without considerations for profit and expenses.

Loss development

The increase or decrease of incurred losses over time.

Trending

A statistical technique for analyzing environmental changes and projecting such changes into the future.

Underwriting authority

The scope of decisions that an underwriter can make without receiving approval from someone at a higher level.

Underwriting audit

A review of underwriting files to ensure that individual underwriters are adhering to underwriting guidelines.

the extent to which underwriting goals are met, but it does not conclusively demonstrate whether the results are a product of the insurer's underwriting guidelines.

THE UNDERWRITING PROCESS

An underwriter engages in a series of tasks to help the insurer achieve its business goals.

The underwriting process incorporates these underlying concepts:

- The purpose of underwriting is to develop and maintain a profitable book of business.
- Underwriting includes line underwriting activities and staff underwriting activities.
- Levels of underwriting authority are based on experience and knowledge.
- Underwriting policy should support an insurer's mission.

Underwriter

An insurer employee who evaluates applicants for insurance, selects those that are acceptable to the insurer, prices coverage, and determines policy terms and conditions.

After a producer submits an application for insurance to an insurer, the insurer must qualify the application for acceptance. **Underwriters** perform this function by following the steps in the underwriting process. In addition to applications, insurers also apply the underwriting process to renewal policies and certain policy changes, such as a request to add a new location to a property policy. Applications, renewals, and policy changes to which the underwriting process is applied are generally referred to as underwriting submissions.

Although underwriters ultimately determine whether to accept or reject commercial lines submissions, their decision-making is often influenced by automated underwriting systems. Driven by the application of artificial intelligence to data collection and the ever-expanding universe of information about risk factors, pricing, and other crucial factors, these systems have accelerated the underwriting process by automating tasks traditionally performed manually while infusing them with more data and sophistication than would otherwise be possible. They've also increased the precision and consistency of underwriting decisions.

Although experienced underwriters do not always follow the steps in the underwriting process in strict order, the sequence of steps provides a sound framework within which underwriters can make decisions. See the exhibit "Steps in the Underwriting Process."

Loss exposure

Any condition or situation that presents a possibility of loss, whether or not an actual loss occurs.

Hazard

A condition that increases the frequency or severity of a loss.

Evaluate the Submission

The first step in the underwriting process is evaluating a submission's **loss exposures** and associated **hazards**. Hazards fall into four categories: physical, moral, morale, and legal. Underwriters must understand the activities, operations, and character of every applicant. To evaluate a submission, underwriters

> **Steps in the Underwriting Process**
> 1. Evaluate the submission
> 2. Develop underwriting alternatives
> 3. Select an underwriting alternative
> 4. Determine an appropriate premium
> 5. Implement the underwriting decision
> 6. Monitor the underwriting decision

[DA07556]

perform two tasks: weighing the need for information and gathering the necessary information.

Weigh the Need for Information

Underwriters apply **information efficiency** to weigh the need for information against the cost to obtain it. For example, an underwriter is likely to investigate a chemical manufacturer extensively but may require much less information to underwrite a gift shop. Sometimes, an account's premium size determines the amount of information gathered or the resources used to gather it; an account with a small premium volume may not justify expensive research. Underwriters may also categorize information as essential, desirable, or available when determining whether it should be obtained.

Information efficiency
The balance that underwriters must maintain between the hazards presented by the account and the information needed to underwrite it.

Gather the Necessary Information

Underwriters compile information from many sources to develop a profile of a submission and pay close attention to a submission's hazards to determine whether those hazards are typical of similarly classified accounts.

These are the principal sources of underwriting information:

- Producers—An underwriter relies more on the producer than on any other source because the producer has personal contact with an applicant, has firsthand knowledge of the applicant's business operations, knows the applicant's reputation in the community, and has determined the applicant's coverage needs.

- Applications—Insurance applications provide general information required to process, rate, and underwrite the applicant's loss exposures.

- Inspection reports—Independent inspections or risk control reports provide underwriting information about the property's physical condition, the business's safety record, and the policyholder's management.

- Government records—Some government records provide underwriting information, such as motor vehicle reports; criminal court records; and civil court records, including records of suits filed, mortgages and liens,

Loss run

A report detailing an insured's history of claims that have occurred over a specific period, valued as of a specific date.

Predictive analytics

Statistical and analytical techniques used to develop models that predict future events or behaviors.

Predictive modeling

A process in which historical data based on behaviors and events is blended with multiple variables and used to construct models of anticipated future outcomes.

Catastrophe model

A type of computer program that estimates losses from future potential catastrophic events.

Experience rating

A rating plan that adjusts the premium for the current policy period to recognize the loss experience of the insured organization during past policy periods.

Schedule rating

A rating plan that awards debits and credits based on specific categories, such as the care and condition of the premises or the training and selection of employees, to modify the final premium to reflect factors that the class rate does not include.

Retrospective rating plan

A rating plan that adjusts the insured's premium for the current policy period based on the insured's loss experience during the current period; paid losses or incurred losses may be used to determine loss experience.

business licenses, property tax records, United States Securities and Exchange Commission filings, and bankruptcy filings.

- Financial rating services—An applicant's financial status provides important underwriting information. Dun & Bradstreet, Standard & Poor's, and Experian are some of the major financial rating services that provide data on the credit ratings of individual businesses, together with industry averages for comparison.

- Loss data—Loss data, such as that contained in **loss runs**, is a significant underwriting tool for predicting future losses. The loss experience of a commercial policyholder might be extensive enough to be statistically significant on its own.

- Claims files— Claims representatives typically accumulate a significant amount of underwriting information during their investigations and record it in claims files. When renewing existing policies, an underwriter can obtain insights into the policyholder's character by reviewing relevant claims files.

Many tools are available to help underwriters evaluate, select, and price submissions. Examples of these tools include telematics, **predictive analytics**, **predictive modeling**, and **catastrophe modeling**. Underwriters consider the available tools and their costs when deciding which ones to use to make the decision, which requires a holistic understanding of all the information available.

Develop Underwriting Alternatives

The second step in the underwriting process is developing underwriting alternatives. The underwriter must consider each alternative carefully and choose the optimal one for the circumstances. The underwriter may accept a submission as is, reject it, or accept it subject to certain modifications. Determining the modification that best meets the needs of the insurer, producer, and applicant can be a challenge. An underwriter has four major ways to modify a submission through a counteroffer:

- Require implementation of additional risk control measures—Whether they are relatively inexpensive and simple to implement or require considerable capital investment (such as fire detection and suppression systems), an underwriter's risk control recommendations should be well-reasoned and convincing.

- Change insurance rates, rating plans, or policy limits—A rate increase compensates the insurer for potential increases in loss severity or frequency, while a decrease might prevent a desirable applicant from buying coverage from a competitor. Suggesting a change to an **experience rating**, a **schedule rating**, or a **retrospective rating plan** may also make a submission more acceptable. Changing policy limits may also make a borderline submission acceptable.

- Amend policy terms and conditions—Modifying a policy to exclude certain causes of loss, add or increase a deductible, or make another coverage change could ensure its acceptability. For example, increasing a deductible might make coverage more viable for a small commercial account with a large number of small losses that have caused unsatisfactory loss experience.
- Use facultative reinsurance—An underwriter may be able to transfer a portion of an otherwise unacceptable liability for an applicant's loss exposure to a facultative reinsurer. An alternative to purchasing facultative reinsurance is to ask the producer to divide the insurance among several insurers—an approach sometimes called agency reinsurance.

Select an Underwriting Alternative

The third step in the underwriting process is selecting an underwriting alternative that renders a submission acceptable. Selecting an alternative involves weighing a submission's positive and negative features, including loss exposures contemplated in the insurance rate, risk control measures, and management's commitment to loss prevention. Additional factors need to be considered before selecting an underwriting alternative:

- Underwriting authority—If the underwriter lacks the necessary authority to select an alternative, the submission must be referred to a higher underwriting authority.
- Supporting business—A submission that is marginal by itself might be acceptable if the other insurance components of the applicant's account—the supporting business—are desirable.
- Mix of business—The underwriting policy determined by management and specified in the underwriting guidelines frequently indicates the insurer's mix-of-business goals.
- Producer–underwriter relationships—The relationship between the underwriter and the producer should be based on mutually shared goals. Differences of opinion are common, particularly because some of the goals of producers and underwriters conflict when producers focus on production and underwriters focus on strict adherence to selection standards.
- Regulatory restrictions—An underwriter must be aware of state regulations that restrict underwriters' ability to accept or renew business. Additionally, federal and state privacy laws restrict the type and the amount of information about an applicant that an underwriter can obtain.

Determine an Appropriate Premium

The fourth step in the underwriting process is determining an appropriate premium. An underwriter must ensure that each loss exposure is properly classified so that it is properly rated.

Insurance loss costs are typically based on an elaborate classification system that groups similar loss exposures into the same rating classification. This enables the insurer to appropriately match potential loss costs with an applicant's particular loss exposures and develop an adequate premium to pay losses and operating expenses and to produce a profit.

For most types of personal insurance and some commercial insurance, proper classification automatically determines the premium. For some types of commercial insurance, such as general liability, an underwriter might have the option of adjusting the premium based on the characteristics of the account's loss exposures.

Implement the Underwriting Decision

The fifth step in the underwriting process is implementing the underwriting decision. It generally involves three tasks:

- Communicate the decision—If the decision is to accept the submission with modifications, the reasons must be clearly communicated to the producer and applicant, and the applicant must agree to accept or implement any modifications made as a counteroffer. If the underwriter decides to reject the application, he or she should communicate the rejection to the producer in a positive way to preserve their long-term relationship.

- Issue documents—In accepting a submission, an underwriter might need to issue a binder and prepare **certificates of insurance**.

- Record information—Information about the policy and the applicant is recorded for policy issuance, accounting, statistical, and monitoring purposes.

Certificate of insurance

A brief description of insurance coverage prepared by an insurer or its agent and commonly used by policyholders to provide evidence of insurance.

Monitor the Underwriting Decision

The sixth step in the underwriting process is monitoring the underwriting decision. After an underwriting decision has been made on a new submission or renewal, the underwriter must perform two tasks to ensure that satisfactory results are achieved: monitor activity for individual policies and monitor books of business.

Monitor Individual Policies

An underwriter must be alert to changes in insureds' loss exposures. Changes in the nature of an insured's business operation, for example, could significantly increase or decrease the policyholder's loss potential. Usually, existing policies are monitored in response to any of these triggering events:

- Substantive policy changes—Adding a new location to a property policy or a new driver to an auto policy can cause the underwriter to investigate whether the additions significantly change the loss exposures.

- Significant and unique losses—A notice of loss provides the underwriter with another opportunity to review the account and to determine whether that loss is the type the underwriter expected. Summary information about the claim or a review of the claim file provides valuable information about the nature of the loss and the insured's operations.

- Preparation for renewal—As a policy's expiration date approaches, an underwriter must determine whether any changes to the account have occurred and, if so, repeat the underwriting process.

- Risk control and safety inspections—A risk control and safety inspection might have contained recommendations that were requirements for policy issuance. A follow-up investigation could reveal whether they were met.

- Premium audits—Premium audits usually lag behind a renewal policy by several months. The audit report could disclose larger loss exposures than originally contemplated, unacceptable operations, new products, new operations, or financial problems.

Monitor Books of Business

Monitoring a book of business entails evaluating the quality and profitability of all the business written for any group of policies. The evaluation should identify specific problems for each type of insurance, which can be subdivided into class of business, territory, producer, and other policy subgroups. Additionally, insurers want to ensure that the premium volume covers fixed costs and overhead expenses for each book of business.

Underwriters use premium and loss statistics to identify aggregate problems in a deteriorating book of business. Reviewing the book of business can also help determine compliance with underwriting policy and detect changes in the type, volume, and quality of policies that may require corrective action.

Special attention is given to some books of business when they are defined by these characteristics:

- Class of business—A poor loss ratio in a particular class of business can indicate inadequate pricing or a disproportionate number of high-hazard policyholders relative to the average loss exposure in the classification.

- Territories or geographic areas—Monitoring territorial underwriting results can help the insurer target areas for future agency appointments in profitable regions. Poor results could indicate areas from which the insurer might withdraw or in which the insurer might raise rates, if permitted by regulators.

- Producers—The producer's premium volume, policy retention, and loss ratio are evaluated both on an overall basis and by type and class of business. That evaluation should include the balance or mix of business desired between personal and commercial insurance and the projected growth factor. Key considerations are the goals that the insurer and producer established and the progress made toward achieving them.

UNDERWRITING MANAGEMENT

To meet its goals, an insurer must adjust its underwriting rules and standards to respond to shifting business conditions. An insurer's underwriting management implements these adjustments.

The underwriting management role entails various responsibilities:

- Participating in the overall management of the insurer in making broad business decisions

- Arranging reinsurance, which can be either treaty reinsurance (on all eligible policies) or facultative reinsurance (involving a separate transaction for each reinsured policy)

- Delegating underwriting authority, which establishes the types of decisions an underwriter can make without receiving approval from someone at a higher level

- Developing and enforcing underwriting guidelines that reflect the insurer's overall underwriting objectives

- Monitoring underwriting results to determine whether the underwriting guidelines have had the desired effect

Participating in Insurer Management

An insurer's senior management generally includes officers responsible for marketing, product development, claims, finance, actuarial services, and other functions in addition to underwriting. The head of an insurer's underwriting department participates with other members of the insurer's management team in making broad business decisions about the insurer's goals, including annual written premium and loss ratio goals, and in devising plans to meet those goals.

Decisions at this level might determine what type of marketing system the insurer uses, office locations, the emphasis that will be placed on personal and commercial insurance, and so forth. Given senior management consensus on the insurer's broad goals and how the insurer's capacity should be allocated, underwriting management must decide how underwriting activities can contribute to these goals. An insurer's underwriting management must then develop underwriting goals that complement or support the organization's overall goals.

Arranging Reinsurance

One of underwriting management's responsibilities is purchasing reinsurance. Reinsurance (sometimes referred to as "insurance for insurers") serves several purposes, including stabilizing the insurer's loss experience, providing protection against catastrophic losses, and allowing an insurer to provide a large amount of insurance under a single policy. Reinsurers also can provide the insurer with additional underwriting information and expertise. There are two general types of reinsurance: treaty and facultative.

Treaty reinsurance is an arrangement in which a reinsurer agrees to automatically reinsure a portion of all eligible insurance of the primary insurer. The treaty is a contract that defines the eligible insurance. The primary insurer is required to reinsure—and the reinsurer must accept—all business covered by the treaty. Policies are not selected individually. Primary insurers and reinsurers periodically renegotiate the reinsurance treaty. Before entering into a treaty and agreeing on pricing, the reinsurer carefully evaluates the primary insurer's past performance and expected future underwriting results. Because the treaty is based on all eligible insurance written by the primary insurer, the reinsurer is more concerned with the group of insureds as a whole than with the individual accounts that compose the group.

Conversely, **facultative reinsurance** is not automatic but involves a separate transaction for each reinsured policy. That is, the reinsurer evaluates each policy it is asked to reinsure. Underwriters for the primary insurer decide which policies to submit for reinsurance, and underwriters for the reinsurer decide which policies to reinsure. Pricing, terms, and conditions of each policy are individually negotiated.

Delegating Underwriting Authority

In contrast with underwriters, who deal with individual applications for insurance, an insurer's underwriting management focuses on the entire group of insureds. Underwriting management must determine how much underwriting authority to grant to those underwriters. The authority given to an underwriter usually reflects the underwriter's experience and responsibilities and the types of insurance handled.

With some insurers, underwriting authority is highly decentralized; that is, underwriting management delegates extensive underwriting authority to field office personnel. Other insurers are highly centralized, with many or all final underwriting decisions made in the home office. For insurers with centralized underwriting authority, field offices serve as a point of contact where insurer personnel gather information, accept applications, and provide policyholder services. Many insurers are neither completely centralized nor completely

Treaty reinsurance

A reinsurance agreement that covers an entire class or portfolio of loss exposures and provides that the primary insurer's individual loss exposures that fall within the treaty are automatically reinsured.

Facultative reinsurance

Reinsurance of individual loss exposures in which the primary insurer chooses which loss exposures to submit to the reinsurer, and the reinsurer can accept or reject any loss exposures submitted.

decentralized; these insurers strive to maintain a balance between the underwriting authority given to underwriters in field offices and the underwriting authority reserved for home office underwriters.

Many insurers also grant some underwriting authority to the agents who represent them. These agents, known as front-line underwriters, make the initial underwriting decision about applications and then forward those applications that meet underwriting guidelines to the insurer's underwriter. Agents usually have the authority to accept applications and bind coverage for the insurer if the applicant clearly meets the guidelines and if the limit of insurance is within a predetermined amount. The extent of the authority granted to an agent generally depends on the agent's premium volume and loss experience with the insurer.

Developing and Enforcing Underwriting Guidelines

Underwriting management develops the guidelines that underwriters use in the underwriting process. Organization-wide rules guide underwriters toward consistent decisions that enable the insurer to meet its overall underwriting goals. Underwriting guidelines and bulletins explain how underwriters should approach each application. The guidelines list the factors that should be considered by the underwriter for each type of insurance, the desirable and undesirable characteristics of applicants relative to those factors, and the insurer's overall attitude toward applicants that exhibit those characteristics. Based on the guidelines, underwriters evaluate the applications they receive, decide how to handle the applications, and act on those decisions.

Underwriting management extends beyond the development of underwriting guidelines. The guidelines must be clearly communicated to all underwriters. This may require training programs. In addition, underwriting management must communicate guideline revisions whenever changes are made.

Monitoring Underwriting Results

Underwriting management must also monitor underwriting results to determine whether underwriting guidelines have produced the desired effect. Monitoring includes steps to ensure that underwriters are following underwriting guidelines and that underwriting goals are being met. If the guidelines are not followed, a determination of their effectiveness cannot be made. Periodically, underwriting management sends underwriting audit teams to visit field offices to perform an underwriting audit. If the audit reveals that guidelines are being followed, it is then necessary to determine whether they have produced the desired results.

For example, assume an insurer has broadened its homeowners insurance policies by adding extra coverages (such as an additional theft limit on jewelry) in an attempt to attract new customers. Monitoring would reveal the extent to which insured losses increase because of the coverage addition, whether sales have increased, and whether revenues from the increased sales more than offset the costs of claims.

Many factors affect an insurer's success. Constant monitoring of underwriting results enables underwriting management to adjust underwriting guidelines to accommodate changing conditions, goals, and results.

RATEMAKING

Many insurers have a separate department that is responsible for developing insurance rates, commonly called ratemaking.

Ratemaking is a complex process that requires analysis of both external and internal data. Most insurers employ **actuaries** who perform the analyses, usually as part of a separate actuarial department. Advances in technology have improved insurers' data-collection and data-storage capabilities and reduced costs related to collecting ratemaking data. Predictive modeling and **machine learning** applications have also improved ratemaking outcomes. Machine learning can be applied to reveal relationships and trends not found through traditional ratemaking analysis, which uses detailed linear models to model the data relationships.

Insurance rates, the basic price of insurance for each unit of exposure, are developed through insurance rating systems established by insurers and independent insurance advisory organizations. Typically, insurance rating systems are primarily based on insurers' **loss costs**. Insurance advisory organizations develop loss cost information by using either class or individual rating methodologies to analyze and categorize insureds.

In determining the final rate for a particular loss exposure, an insurer adds an allowance for expenses and profits to the basic rate that has been developed from loss costs. The insurer's underwriting department then determines the final premium by multiplying the final rate by the number of exposure units.

Insurance Advisory Organizations

Insurance advisory organizations work with insurers to develop insurance rating systems. The largest insurance advisory organization is Insurance Services Office, Inc., which provides analytical and decision-support products and services to the property-casualty industry. The National Council on Compensation Insurance is an insurance advisory organization that manages a database of workers compensation insurance information, analyzes industry trends, prepares recommendations for workers compensation rates, and assists in developing state-specific workers compensation forms and endorsements. Other insurance advisory organizations that operate on a countrywide basis include the American Association of Insurance Services and the Surety and Fidelity Association of America.

Ratemaking
The process insurers use to calculate insurance rates, which are a premium component.

Actuary
A person who uses mathematical methods to analyze insurance data for various purposes, such as to develop insurance rates or set claim reserves.

Machine learning
Artificial intelligence in which computers continually teach themselves to make better decisions based on previous results and new data.

Loss costs
The portion of the rate that covers projected claim payments and loss adjusting expenses.

Insurance advisory organization
An independent corporation that works with and on behalf of insurers that purchase or subscribe to their services, which include developing prospective loss costs and standard policy forms.

Insurance Rating Systems

Insurance advisory organizations help develop insurance rating systems by collecting reliable loss data that insurers use in establishing their rates and premiums. Insurance advisory organizations continually collect loss information from many insurers. For example, to assist insurers in determining an appropriate rate to charge for automobile insurance during a certain period, insurance advisory organizations may gather data on insurers' loss costs for automobile accidents involving certain types of vehicles during a particular year.

Insurance rating systems combine loss data from many insurers, an approach based on the law of large numbers. Including losses of a large number of exposure units makes the resulting loss data more reliable than an individual insurer's loss data.

Insurance advisory organizations then analyze the loss data to determine the average loss costs per exposure unit used in class rating. See the exhibit "Rate Development Process."

Loss Costs

Loss data reflects historical loss costs—costs incurred in the past. Insurers often adjust data on historical loss costs in anticipation of losses that can be expected in the future as a result of inflation or other measurable trends. These prospective loss costs indicate the amount of money an insurer can expect to pay for future claims for each exposure unit. However, it is not enough for insurers to collect money only to pay claims. An insurer must also cover its expenses and allow for profits and **contingencies**. Therefore, each insurer uses loss cost information to develop its own set of rates per exposure unit, determining how much to add to basic rates to arrive at the final rate it will charge.

Contingencies

A provision in an insurance rate for losses that could not be anticipated in the loss data.

Once determined, rates are published in an insurer's rating manual or stored in the insurer's rating system. These rates are also filed with the state insurance department where required. In many cases, the state insurance department might also reject, modify, or approve the rates that will be used.

Class Rating

Insurers develop loss costs for many different lines (or types) of business and many different groups or classes of insureds within those lines. Many kinds of insurance are priced using **class rating**. All members of a class are charged the same rate for insurance, although their premiums will be different if they have different numbers of exposure units. For example, a homeowner with a $400,000 home will pay more for homeowners insurance than a homeowner with a $200,000 home.

Class rating

A rating approach that uses rates reflecting the average probability of loss for businesses within large groups of similar risks; the predominant method used for rating commercial properties.

The basic premise of an insurance classification and rating system is that insureds with similar characteristics have similar potential loss frequency

Rate Development Process

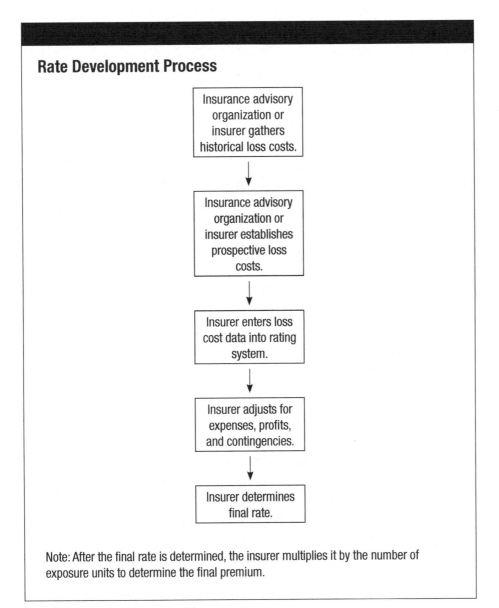

Note: After the final rate is determined, the insurer multiplies it by the number of exposure units to determine the final premium.

[DA00467]

and severity. Even though wide variation in actual losses may occur from one insured to the next, aggregate losses among all members of the class should be predictably different from the losses of all members of another class who have different characteristics. For example, an employer will pay more for workers compensation insurance for a construction worker than for a clerical worker because construction workers as a class are more likely to become injured or disabled on the job than clerical workers as a class.

While no two risks are identical, grouping them enables an insurer to take advantage of pooling. The groupings or classes should be big enough to reflect the law of large numbers but small enough that all members share characteristics related to frequency and severity of loss.

Individual Rating

Individual rate, or specific rate

A type of insurance rate that reflects the unique characteristics of an insured or the insured's property.

When insureds cannot be readily assigned to the same class, the insured loss exposure is rated individually. For example, an **individual rate, or specific rate**, might be developed for fire insurance on a large, unique factory building. The specific building is inspected by an underwriting professional using a point system that adds or subtracts points for such things as type of construction (masonry, wood, and so on), number and type of fire extinguishers, nature of the occupancy, capabilities of the local fire department, and the supply of water available at nearby hydrants. The number of points determines an insurance rate for that particular building. The rate is applied per $100 of insurance to determine the premium for fire insurance.

Sometimes it is necessary to insure an exposure for which there is no established premium-determining system. In such cases, underwriters have to rely heavily on their judgment, a practice that is referred to as **judgment rating**. Judgment rating is a type of individual rating.

Judgment rating

Rating used by underwriters to rate one-of-a-kind risks.

Judgment rating does not mean that an underwriter arbitrarily sets a rate for a particular exposure. The underwriter usually has experience with insurance covering comparable exposures and a resulting sense of what premium amount would be appropriate. For example, successful experience in insuring cross-country rail shipments of coal and iron ore might help an underwriter to decide the premium to charge for insuring the shipment of some other bulk cargo.

Final Rate and Premium Determination

Final rate

The price per exposure unit determined by adjusting the prospective loss costs for expenses, profits, and contingencies.

Final rates result from prospective loss costs that move through the rating system and are adjusted for expenses, profits, and contingencies. Insurance rating systems assist insurers in determining rates based on past and expected future losses. The rating systems also account for other factors that affect insurers' final rate determination.

To conduct business, insurers pay not only loss costs but also other expenses, such as underwriting and loss adjustment expenses, and plan for profits and contingencies. To set the final rates, they charge insureds for particular loss exposures. Individual insurers, therefore, add an allowance for factors such as expenses, profits, and contingencies to the basic insurance rates developed through insurance rating systems.

After the final rate has been calculated, it is multiplied by the number of exposure units to determine the final insurance premium.

PREMIUM DETERMINATION

One of the main activities performed by the underwriting department is pricing, or determining the policy premium, an activity commonly called "rating."

An insurance premium is a periodic payment by the insured to the insurer in exchange for insurance coverage. "Periodic" means that the payment must be made at certain time intervals. Each premium payment buys insurance protection for a particular time period, such as one year.

Although the terminology is different, insurance premiums are determined in much the same way as the prices of other products. For example, in many grocery stores, the "unit price" for each item is shown on the shelf. If an eighteen-ounce jar of peanut butter costs $2.34, the unit price is $0.13 per ounce and the final price is $2.34. In this case, one ounce is the unit.

In insurance, the premium (final price) is calculated by multiplying the insurance rate (unit price) by the number of exposure units. Depending on the type of coverage being rated, additional steps may be needed, such as adding charges for optional coverages.

Insurance Rates

An insurance **rate** is the "unit price" for insurance. Multiplying the rate by the number of exposure units determines the premium. Typically, an insurer has a separate rate in its **rate manual** for each of the rating classifications it uses. An insurer may have hundreds of rating classifications for a particular type of insurance. Rating classifications are based on characteristics of the insured and the loss exposures being insured.

The ISO *Commercial Lines Manual* (CLM) provides classification tables that contain hundreds of classifications of commercial business operations. When calculating the premium for commercial accounts, underwriters typically determine the insured's business operation and then find the appropriate rating classification in the applicable classification table. See the exhibit "Classification Table."

Rate

The price per exposure unit for insurance coverage.

Rate manual

A resource for classifying accounts and developing premiums for given types of insurance; includes necessary rules, factors, and guidelines to apply those rates.

Exposure Units

The fundamental measures of the loss exposures used in insurance rating are referred to as **exposure units**. Insurers use standardized exposure units for rating most types of insurance. For example, in homeowners insurance, exposure units are normally expressed as $1,000 of insured value. In the case of a home insured for $400,000, the number of exposure units is 400. In the case of a home insured for $200,000, the number of exposure units is 200. See the exhibit "Examples of Exposure Units."

Exposure unit (unit of exposure)

The unit of measure (for example, area, gross receipts, payroll) used to determine an insurance policy premium.

Calculation of Premium (Rate x Exposure Units)

After the insurance rate and number of exposure units are known, calculating the premium involves a relatively simple mathematical formula. This type of calculation is similar to that used in pricing many products that consumers purchase.

Classification Table

51300 Baby Food Mfg. – In glass containers

Class Code: 51300

Premium Base: Gross Sales

10100 Bakeries

Class Code: 10100

Premium Base: Gross Sales

Note: This classification includes baking operations at the same location as the store, if the products baked are sold principally in that store.

51315 Bakery Plants

Class Code: 51315

Premium Base: Gross Sales

Note: Risks shall be classified and rated as bakeries, if products baked are sold principally in the insured's own retail store at the same location.

10111 Barber or Beauty Shop Supplies Distributors

Class Code: 10111

Premium Base: Gross Sales

Used with permission of Insurance Services Office, Inc., and ISO Commercial Risk Services, Inc. [DA07509]

Consider the pricing structure at a produce stand. For example, assume two peaches are sold at the price (or rate) of $0.40 per peach. The cost is determined by multiplying the rate per peach by the number of peaches:

Rate per unit × Number of units = Price

$0.40 per peach × 2 peaches = $0.80

The same formula is used if five pounds of peaches are sold at the produce stand at a price of $0.98 per pound:

Rate per unit × Number of units = Price

$0.98 per pound × 5 pounds = $4.90

In both examples, the total cost is composed of a rate ($0.40 or $0.98) for some standard unit of purchase (peach or pound) multiplied by the number of units (two peaches and five pounds, respectively). The choice of standard units is a matter of convenience. For instance, peaches might be priced "per peach" or "by the pound"; gasoline in the United States is usually priced by the gallon, but in many other countries it is priced by the liter.

Underwriters who are calculating insurance premiums follow essentially the same process in determining premiums as is followed in calculating the price

Examples of Exposure Units

Type of Insurance	Typical Exposure Units
Auto	Each vehicle
Commercial Property	Each $100 of insured value
General Liability	Various exposure units are used, depending on the classification. Some examples are: Each $1,000 of gross sales (for example, a restaurant or retail store) Each 1,000 square feet of area (for example, a school) Each $1,000 of payroll (for example, a consulting firm) Each 1,000 admissions (for example, a movie theater)
Homeowners	Each $1,000 of insured value
Workers Compensation	Each $100 of payroll

[DA07494]

of commodities. Based on rates contained in the insurer's rating manuals, the final price of insurance (the premium) is determined by multiplying the rate per unit by the number of exposure units:

> Rate per unit × Number of exposure units = Premium

The formula is the same as before, except that in this instance, the word "premium" is substituted for the word "price." For example, if the insurance rating system shows a rate of $900 per auto to provide collision coverage for one year, this rate is multiplied by the number of autos to arrive at the annual premium. Consider a company with five autos to insure—the computation would be simple:

> Rate per unit × Number of exposure units = Premium
>
> $900 per auto × 5 autos = $4,500

Many insurance rating units are expressed in dollar amounts, such as "$100 of insured value" or "$1,000 of payroll."

A commercial property policy has a rate of $0.50 per $100 of building insurance, and the building is being insured for $600,000.

Insured value ÷ Unit size = Number of exposure units

$600,000 ÷ $100 = 6,000 units

Rate per unit × Number of exposure units = Premium

$0.50 × 6,000 = $3,000

Other Factors Affecting Premium Determination

Although a major part of establishing premiums is calculating rate times exposure units, other factors can affect premium determination. Manual or class rates usually serve as a standard for a type of insurance (such as homeowners or commercial auto) and are intended to represent the average risk in a class. However, there are many variations from the average.

Underwriters vary from the manual rate to reflect the reality of actual exposures to loss, the specific characteristics of those exposures, and competitive market influences. Underwriters can use experience or schedule rating plans to reflect the differences between the applicant and the average risk. Underwriters apply experience or scheduled rating credits to better-than-average risks and experience or scheduled debits to worse-than-average risks. For example, an underwriter might apply a 10 percent premium reduction to a better-than-average risk and a 5 percent premium increase to a worse-than-average risk.

Various other factors can affect final premiums, such as minimum premiums, increased limit factors for liability insurance, additional charges for certain coverage options, good-student discounts, and fire protection systems.

Apply Your Knowledge

ABC Company is a new business that provides Internet marketing services to commercial clients. ABC is applying for workers compensation insurance for its seven employees, who are classified as clerical employees. The manual rate is $0.30 per $100 of payroll. ABC's annual payroll is $500,000.

Calculate the basic premium that would be charged for ABC's seven employees, ignoring any additional rating factors that might apply.

a. $300
b. $3,000
c. $1,500
d. $10,500

Feedback: c. Rate × Exposure units = Premium. $0.30 × ($500,000 ÷ $100) = $1,500.

SUMMARY

Line underwriters evaluate new submissions and perform renewal underwriting, usually by working directly with insurance producers and applicants. Staff underwriters, meanwhile, manage risk selection by working with line underwriters and coordinating decisions about products, pricing, and guidelines.

The underwriting process consists of these steps:

- Evaluate the submission
- Develop underwriting alternatives
- Select an underwriting alternative
- Determine an appropriate premium
- Implement the underwriting decision
- Monitor the underwriting decision

An insurer's underwriting management has many responsibilities:

- Participating in the insurer's overall management
- Arranging reinsurance
- Delegating underwriting authority
- Developing and enforcing underwriting guidelines
- Monitoring underwriting results

Insurers and independent insurance advisory organizations develop insurance rates through insurance rating systems. Insurance advisory organizations gather historical loss costs from insurers to develop prospective loss costs. Some kinds of insurance are class rated by grouping insureds with similar characteristics into the same rating class to capture potential loss frequency and severity of the group. When an insured cannot be readily assigned to the same class, the insured loss exposure is rated individually.

Insurers add their allowance for their expenses, profits, and contingencies to the basic rate to arrive at the final rate they charge insureds for a particular loss exposure. After the final rate has been calculated, it is multiplied by the number of exposure units to determine the final insurance premium.

Insurers calculate premium by determining the insured's rate classification from a rate manual and multiplying the rate by the number of exposure units. Exposure units are based on the type of coverage and, for commercial insureds, the type of business. Various factors can either increase or decrease the standard rate for a particular insured.

Direct Your Learning ▶▶

6

Claims

Educational Objectives

After learning the content of this assignment, you should be able to:

▷ Illustrate how an insurer's claims function supports these primary goals:

- Keeping the insurer's promise

- Supporting the insurer's profit goal

▷ Examine how Claims Department results can be optimized by:

- Department structure

- The types and functions of claims personnel

- Claims performance measurements

▷ Describe the activities in the claims handling process.

▷ Explain how claims representatives handle these aspects of property insurance claims:

- Verifying coverage

- Determining the amount of loss

- Concluding the claim

▷ Explain how claims representatives handle these aspects of liability insurance claims:

- Verifying coverage

- Determining the cause of loss

- Determining the amount of damages

- Concluding the claim

▷ Examine the elements of good-faith claims handling.

Claims

6

GOALS OF THE CLAIMS FUNCTION

Claims representatives become more valuable and can provide better service to both the insurer and its customers when they understand the two primary goals of the Claims Department and know how to support those goals.

People purchase property-casualty insurance policies to protect against financial losses. When policyholders make claims under their insurance policies, the insurer is called on to honor the promise made in the policy—namely, to indemnify the policyholder for financial losses. This does not imply that the insurer should or will pay every claim that is presented; rather, it implies that the insurer's Claims Department will conduct a good-faith investigation of a claim and pay only legitimate claims that are covered by the policy.

An insurer's senior management establishes the goals for the claims function. In doing so, managers must equally consider the needs of the insurance customer (the policyholder) and the needs of the insurer. The claims function helps an insurer meet these two primary goals:

- Keeping the insurer's promise
- Supporting the insurer's profit goal

Keeping the Insurer's Promise

The first goal of the claims function is to satisfy the insurer's obligations to the policyholder as set forth in the insurance contract. In a property insurance policy, the insurer's promise is to pay for direct physical loss to covered property by a covered cause of loss. In a liability insurance policy, the insurer's promise is to pay on behalf of the insured any damages for which the insured is legally liable because of bodily injury, property damage, or other specified types of injury caused by an accident, up to the applicable limit of insurance. The insurer also agrees to defend the insured against claims or suits seeking damages covered by the policy.

The insurer fulfills its promise by providing fair, prompt, and equitable service to the policyholder either directly, when the loss involves a **first-party claim** made by the policyholder against the insurer, or indirectly, when the loss involves a **third-party claim** made against the policyholder by someone to whom the policyholder may be liable. See the exhibit "First-Party Insurance and Third-Party Insurance."

First-party claim

A demand by an insured person or organization seeking to recover from its insurer for a loss that its insurance policy may cover.

Third-party claim

A demand against an insured by a person or organization other than the insured or the insurer, seeking to recover damages that may be payable by the insured's liability insurance.

> ### First-Party Insurance and Third-Party Insurance
>
> Insurance coverage is often referred to as either first-party insurance or third-party insurance.
>
> Property insurance is considered first-party insurance because the insurer (second party) makes payment for covered losses directly to the policyholder. Liability insurance is considered third-party insurance because the insurer makes payments on behalf of the policyholder (first party) to a claimant (third party) who is injured or whose property is damaged by the policyholder.

[DA00038]

Claimant

A party that makes a claim and that can be either a first-party claimant or a third-party claimant.

Claims representative

A person responsible for investigating, evaluating, and settling claims.

The insurance contract is marketed not only as a financial mechanism to restore policyholders and other **claimants** to a pre-loss state, but also as a way for policyholders to achieve peace of mind. For a claimant, a loss occurrence and the consequences are not routine and can be overwhelming. A **claims representative** should handle claims in a way that promotes peace of mind for the policyholder who has suffered a loss and that quickly restores a claimant to his or her pre-loss condition.

Supporting the Insurer's Profit Goal

The second goal of the claims function is to support the insurer's profit goal. Achieving this goal is generally the responsibility of the marketing and underwriting departments; however, the claims function serves a role in generating underwriting profit by controlling expenses and paying only legitimate claims.

By managing all claims function expenses, setting appropriate spending policies, and using appropriately priced providers and services, claims managers can help maintain an insurer's underwriting profit. Similarly, claims staff can avoid overspending on costs of handling claims, claims operations, or other expenses. Finally, by ensuring fair claim settlement, claims representatives prevent any unnecessary increase in the cost of insurance and subsequent reduction in the insurer's underwriting profit.

Policyholders and other claimants are likely to accept an insurer's settlement offer if they believe they are receiving fair treatment. Parties who believe they have been treated unfairly may seek to settle their differences with the insurer by filing lawsuits. Litigation erodes goodwill between the parties and generates increased claims expenses, reducing the insurer's profitability. Additionally, dissatisfied policyholders or claimants may complain to their state Insurance Department, and, if the state regulatory authorities find fault, an insurer may be subjected to regulatory oversight or penalties. Costs associated with regulatory action can further erode an insurer's profits.

An insurer's success in achieving its profit goal is reflected in its reputation for providing the service promised. A reputation for resisting legitimate claims can undermine the effectiveness of an insurer's advertising. Consequently, the two goals of the claims function work together in support of a profitable insurance operation.

CLAIMS DEPARTMENT STRUCTURE, PERSONNEL, AND PERFORMANCE

Information generated by a Claims Department, including about loss payments and expenses, is essential to marketing, underwriting, and pricing insurance products. In this way, the claims function is crucial to fulfilling an insurer's promise to pay covered losses, creating an accompanying need for an insurer's Claims Department to operate efficiently.

The results of a Claims Department can be optimized by its structure, personnel, and performance measures. Let's look at all three.

Claims Department Structure

An insurer's Claims Department can be organized in several ways. Usually, a senior claims officer heads the Claims Department and reports to the chief executive officer (CEO), the chief financial officer, or the chief underwriting officer. The senior claims officer may have staff located in the same office. This staff often makes up the home office Claims Department. Within this area, any number of technical and management specialists can provide advice and assistance to remote claims offices and claims representatives.

The senior claims officer may have several claims offices or branches countrywide or even worldwide. Staff from remote claims offices can all report directly to the home office Claims Department, or regional/divisional claims officers may oversee the territory.

Regional claims officers may have one or more branch offices reporting to them—for example, in both Boston and New York City. And a branch office in New York City may have smaller offices in Albany, New York, and Erie, New York, reporting into it. Each branch office could have a claims manager, one or more claims supervisors, and a staff of claims representatives. Similar department structures are adopted by **third-party administrators (TPAs)**.

Third-party administrator (TPA)

An organization that provides administrative services associated with risk financing and insurance.

Claims Personnel

Claims personnel are among the most visible employees of an insurer and must therefore be able to interact well with a variety of people.

A claims representative fulfills the promise to either pay the insured or on behalf of the insured by handling claims when losses occur. People who handle claims may be staff claims representatives, independent adjusters, employees of TPAs, or producers who sell policies to insureds. Public adjusters also handle claims by representing the interests of insureds to the insurer.

Staff Claims Representatives

Staff claims representatives are employees of an insurer and handle most claims, usually while working from branch or regional offices rather than at the insurer's home office. They may include inside claims representatives, who handle claims exclusively from the insurer's office, and field claims representatives (also called outside claims representatives), who handle claims both inside and outside the office. Field claims representatives handle claims that require such tasks as investigating the scene of the loss; meeting with insureds, claimants, lawyers, and others involved in the loss; and inspecting damage. If the branch or region covers a large territory, the insurer may set up claims offices in areas away from the branch office to enable the claims representative to serve insureds more efficiently.

Independent Adjusters

Some insurers may find it economically impractical to establish claims offices in every state in which insureds reside. In such instances, insurers may contract with **independent adjusters** to handle claims in strategic locations.

Independent adjuster

An independent claims representative who handles claims for insurers for a fee.

Some insurers employ claims personnel in their home or branch offices to monitor claims progress and settle claims but use independent adjusters to handle all field work. Other insurers hire independent adjusters when their staff claims representatives are too busy to handle all claims themselves.

For example, if a disaster strikes, staff claims representatives may need assistance to handle the large number of claims quickly enough to satisfy the insurer and its insureds. Insurers may also use independent adjusters to meet desired service levels or when specialized skills are needed, such as to investigate aircraft accidents.

Some independent adjusters are self-employed, but many work for adjusting firms that range in size from one small office with a few adjusters to national firms with many offices employing hundreds of adjusters.

Third-Party Administrators

Businesses that choose to self-insure do not use agents, underwriters, or other typical insurer personnel. However, they do need personnel to handle losses that arise. Self-insured businesses can employ their own claims representatives or contract with TPAs, which handle claims, keep claims records, and perform statistical analyses. TPAs are often associated with large independent adjusting firms or with subsidiaries of insurers. Many property-casualty insurers have established subsidiary companies that serve as TPAs.

Producers

Producers can also function as claims representatives for certain claims. The term "producer" includes agents, brokers, sales representatives, and intermediaries who place insurance with insurers.

Insurers may allow producers to pay claims up to a certain amount, such as $2,500. Those producers can issue claim payments, called drafts, directly to insureds for covered claims, thus reducing an insured's wait time. In this capacity, producers function like inside claims representatives.

Public Adjusters

If a claim is complex, or if settlement negotiations are not progressing satisfactorily with the insurer, the insured may hire a **public adjuster** to protect his or her interests.

Some states have statutes that govern the services public adjusters can provide. But in general, the public adjuster prepares an insured's claim and negotiates the settlement with the staff claims representative or independent adjuster. The insured, in turn, pays the public adjuster's fee, which is usually a percentage of the settlement.

Public adjuster
An outside organization or person hired by an insured to represent the insured in a claim in exchange for a fee.

Apply Your Knowledge

A natural disaster just struck a large number of homes and businesses insured by Watkins Insurance Company. The company is receiving more claims than its staff claims representatives can handle in a timely manner. Which kind of professional would Watkins Insurance Company look to hire to make sure that it can satisfy its insureds?

a. Independent adjuster
b. Third-party administrator
c. Producer
d. Public adjuster

Feedback: *a.* Watkins Insurance Company would hire independent adjusters, which are independent claims representatives who handle claims for insurers for a fee. Some insurers hire independent adjusters when their staff claims representatives are too busy to handle all claims themselves.

Claims Performance Measures

Because Claims Department members have diverse roles and are spread over a wide geographic area, insurers face special issues when it comes to evaluating and measuring the performance of their Claims Department staff.

Insurers are businesses, so they must make a profit to survive. Claims departments play a crucial role in insurer profitability by paying fair amounts for legitimate claims and providing accurate, reliable, and consistent ratemaking data. Because paying claims fairly does not conflict with insurer profit goals, an insurer measures its claims and underwriting departments' performance using a loss ratio, which is a profitability measure.

In addition to reaching profit goals, an insurer strives to ensure that its Claims Department meets quality performance goals. Internally identified best practices, claims audits, and customer-satisfaction data are tools that provide measures of quality.

Profitability Measures

A loss ratio is one of the most commonly used measures for evaluating an insurer's financial well-being. It compares an insurer's losses and loss adjustment expenses (LAE) with its collected premiums and reveals the percentage of premiums being consumed by losses. An increasing loss ratio could indicate that the insurer is improperly performing the claims function. Increasing losses could also mean that the Underwriting Department elected to cover loss exposures that were more costly or occurred more frequently than it estimated or that the Actuarial Department failed to price the insurer's products correctly.

When an insurer's loss ratio increases, the Claims Department, along with other insurer functions, is pressured to reduce expenses. Claims representatives could quickly reduce LAE in the short term by offering the settlement payments insureds and claimants demand rather than spending resources on investigating claims and calculating and negotiating fair payments.

However, to reduce LAE in the long term, inflated settlement demands should be resisted; researched; negotiated; and, if necessary, litigated. LAE can also be reduced by making sure that claims procedures are always properly performed by claims representatives.

Apply Your Knowledge

An insurer's CEO is analyzing the organization's profitability. He sees that three years ago, the insurer's loss ratio was 0.67, while two years ago, the insurer's loss ratio was 0.70. Last year, the loss ratio was 0.75. Further analysis indicates that the Actuarial Department is pricing the insurer's products correctly and that the Underwriting Department was selecting appropriate loss exposures. This leads the CEO to focus on the Claims Department as potentially undermining the organization's profitability. Which of the following are measures the Claims Department could employ in an attempt to reduce LAE long term?

a.   Immediately offering the settlement payment insureds and claimants demand.

b.   Resisting; researching; negotiating; and, if necessary, litigating inflated settlement demands.

c.   Skipping claims procedures.

d.   None of these measures will reduce LAE long term.

Feedback: b. Resisting; researching; negotiating; and, if necessary, litigating inflated settlement demands reduces LAE long term.

Quality Measures

Three frequently used tools provide quality measures for evaluating a Claims Department's performance: best practices, claims audits, and customer-satisfaction data.

In a Claims Department, the term "best practices" generally refers to a system of identified internal practices that produce superior performance. Best practices are usually shared with every claims representative. An insurer can identify best practices by studying its own performance or the performance of similar successful insurers.

Claims Department best practices are often based on legal requirements specified by regulators, legislators, and courts. For example, a Claims Department may have a best practice stating that claims will be acknowledged within twenty-four hours of receipt. This time frame may have been selected because of a regulation, law, or court decision.

Insurers use claims audits to ensure compliance with best practices and to gather statistical information on claims. A claims audit is performed by evaluating information in a number of open and closed claims files. Claims audits can be performed by the claims staff who work on the files (called a self-audit), or they can be performed by claims representatives from other offices or by a team from the home office. Claims audits usually evaluate both quantitative and qualitative factors. See the exhibit "Quantitative and Qualitative Audit Factors."

The quality of a Claims Department's performance is also measured by customer satisfaction. Claims supervisors and managers monitor correspondence they receive about the performance of individual claims representatives. While compliments are usually acknowledged, supervisors or managers must respond to complaints. Claims Departments have procedures for responding to complaints, which can come directly from insureds, claimants, or vendors or be submitted on their behalf by a state insurance department.

No matter the source, complaints must be investigated by management and responded to in a timely manner. Complaints, such as not receiving a return phone call, may indicate legitimate service issues. Other complaints may simply indicate dissatisfaction with an otherwise valid claim settlement. Review of complaints received in a claims office can show whether problems exist with a particular claims representative, supervisor, or manager.

Quantitative and Qualitative Audit Factors

Quantitative	Qualitative
Timeliness of reports	Realistic reserving
Timeliness of reserving	Accurate evaluation of insured's liability
Timeliness of payments	Follow-up on subrogation opportunity
Number of files opened each month	Litigation cost management
Number of files closed each month	Proper releases taken
Number of files reopened each month	Correct coverage evaluation
Percentage of recovery from subrogation	Good negotiation skills
Average claim settlement value by claims type	Thorough investigations
Percentage of claims entering litigation	
Percentage of cases going to trial	
Accuracy of data entry	

[DA02267]

THE CLAIMS HANDLING PROCESS

To ensure that every claim is handled properly, the claims representative must follow a systematic claims handling process.

The claims handling process begins when the insured reports the loss to the producer or directly to the insurer's claim center. Losses can be reported using a loss notice form, which varies by type of loss, through a letter, or as part of a lawsuit. Once a loss notice has been received and the associated information has been entered into the insurer's claims information system, the insurer begins the claims handling process.

The claims handling process consists of a series of standard activities. The activities are not always sequential. Depending on the severity and complexity of the claim, the process may be completed quickly, or may take months or even years. These activities provide a framework for handling all types of property, liability, and workers compensation claims:

- Acknowledging and assigning the claim
- Identifying the policy
- Contacting the insured or the insured's representative
- Investigating and documenting the claim
- Determining the cause of loss, liability, and the loss amount
- Concluding the claim

Acknowledging and Assigning the Claim

Generally, the first activity of the insurer in the claims handling process involves two functions—acknowledging receipt of the claim and assigning the claim to a claim representative. The purpose of the acknowledgment is to advise the insured that the claim has been received. The acknowledgment also provides the name and contact information of the assigned claims representative and the claim number. Insurers acknowledge claims in a timely manner to comply with insurance regulations.

Insurers use different methods of assigning claims to claims representatives. Some assign claims based on territory, type of claim, extent of damage, workload, or other criteria contained in the insurer's claims information system. The goal is to assign the claim to a claims representative who possesses the appropriate skills to handle it. Some states require claims representatives who handle claims in the state to have an adjuster license. These licensing requirements must also be considered when assigning a claim to a claims representative.

After receiving the claim assignment, the claims representative contacts the insured, and possibly the claimant (if it is a third-party claim), to acknowledge the claim assignment and explain the claim process. For insurers that do not make contact immediately after receiving the loss notice, this contact serves as the claim acknowledgment. For some types of losses, the claims representative may give the insured instructions to prevent further loss, such as to cover roof damage with a tarp. If the claim involves property damage, the claim representative may arrange a time with the insured to inspect the damage or the damage scene. As an alternative, the claims representative may advise the insured or claimant that an appraiser or an independent adjuster will be in contact to inspect the property damage. If the claim involves bodily injury, the claims representative should get information about the nature and extent of the injury. See the exhibit "How Blockchain Can Assist in Processing Claims."

How Blockchain Can Assist in Processing Claims

Blockchain can make the claims handling process quicker and more cost efficient through the use of smart contracts. As an example, consider flight insurance that provides coverage for late or canceled flights. The insurance contract, which insures the on-time performance of a flight, is recorded on the blockchain. If the flight is late or canceled, data can be verified digitally by a trusted third party, which automatically triggers a claim payment.

Even when the entire insurance contract isn't recorded on the blockchain, smart contracts can help. For example, a smart contract tied to sensors or telematics in a car involved in an accident can provide the first report of loss to the insurer while simultaneously notifying recommended repair shops and alerting the insured of next steps. As with any new technology or process, care must be given that this process is used in compliance with applicable laws.

Identifying the Policy

Usually, the claims representative first identifies the policy under which the claim has been made upon receiving the assignment in order to determine what types of coverage apply to the loss. If it is apparent from the loss notice that coverage may not be available for the loss, the claims representative must notify the insured of this concern through a **nonwaiver agreement** or a **reservation of rights letter**.

Claims representatives may also establish claim or case (loss) reserves, often in conjunction with identifying the policy. This can occur at almost any point in the claim handling process. While the exact timing may differ among insurers, the setting of an initial reserve(s) usually occurs early in the claim handling process.

Setting accurate reserves is an important part of the claims representative's job. Establishing and maintaining adequate reserves is important for the insurer's financial stability because reserves affect the insurer's ability to maintain and increase business. See the exhibit "Setting Accurate Reserves Can Be Difficult."

Nonwaiver agreement

A signed agreement indicating that during the course of investigation, neither the insurer nor the insured waives rights under the policy.

Reservation of rights letter

An insurer's letter that specifies coverage issues and informs the insured that the insurer is handling a claim with the understanding that the insurer may later deny coverage should the facts warrant it.

Setting Accurate Reserves Can Be Difficult

After the claims representative receives notice of a loss, obtains initial information, and verifies coverage, a loss reserve (or case reserve) for that claim is established. Assume, for example, that an insured had a minor auto accident in which the insured's car hit a guardrail on a foggy night and that no injuries or other cars were involved. After obtaining initial information concerning the accident, verifying coverage, and receiving written estimates of the cost to repair the insured's car, the claims representative establishes a case reserve of $5,000. This figure is probably a very accurate estimate because a single-car collision loss is relatively easy to evaluate. Two weeks later, the repairs are made to the insured's car, and the insurer issues a check for $5,000. Once the loss is paid, the reserve is reduced to zero because no future loss payment is expected. Therefore, the $5,000 claim paid by the insurer equals the initial case reserve.

Conversely, complex claims are often difficult to estimate, especially liability claims. Assume, for example, that an insured was involved in a serious auto accident and that two persons in the other car were hospitalized with severe injuries. The cause of the accident is not immediately clear because of conflicting testimony of witnesses, and it is difficult to determine whether the insured is responsible for the accident. What case reserve should be established? The amount eventually paid because of this accident could range from almost nothing (if the insured is not found to be legally responsible) to hundreds of thousands of dollars (if the insured is responsible and the injured victims die or are permanently disabled). The eventual payment on this particular claim, which may not be made for several years, can vary significantly from the original reserve.

[DA07639]

Contacting the Insured or the Insured's Representative

Another activity in the claims handling process, which occurs soon after the loss is assigned to a claims representative and initial reserves are established, is contacting the insured or the insured's representative. For some insurers (or in certain claims as specified in the insurer's guidelines), this contact occurs at the same time as the claim acknowledgment. Generally, the claims representative reviews the initial loss report and policy and then contacts the insured and schedules a time to speak with the insured or a party representing the insured about the facts of the loss. This can be a face-to-face meeting at the insured's location or the loss location, or it can be a telephone discussion. If the loss involves a third-party claimant, then the claims representative also contacts the claimant and schedules a meeting with the claimant or a party representing the claimant (such as a public adjuster or an attorney) to discuss the facts of the loss. Once contact is made, the claims representative should take these actions:

- Inform the insured of what is required to protect damaged property and to document the claim.
- Describe the claims inspection, appraisal, and investigation process.
- Tell the insured what additional investigation is needed to resolve potential coverage issues.
- Explain potential coverage questions or policy limitations or exclusions, and obtain a nonwaiver agreement when necessary.
- If medical and wage loss information is part of the claim, obtain the necessary authorizations.
- Explain the amount of time it will take to process and conclude the claim.
- Supply the insured with a blank proof of loss form for property damage and any necessary written instructions so that the insured can document the claim.

Investigating the Claim

Claims representatives begin investigating a claim as soon as it is assigned. They can develop an outline or notes to logically organize the investigation and to ensure that information that may be available only for a short time is investigated first (such as accident scenes or damaged property that may be destroyed or discarded). Claims representatives should contact any third-party claimant early in the investigation. Doing so establishes rapport with claimants, facilitates the investigation, and contributes to a timely settlement.

Claims representatives must also know when they have sufficient information on which to base a decision. Investigations should be geared to obtain information that will help determine the cause of loss, the amount of loss, and liability. The insurer's claim handling guidelines help claims representatives determine the types and extent of investigation needed for a satisfactory claim settlement. Once sufficient information is obtained to make a reasoned determination, the claims representative does not need to continue the investigation, unless the determination is disputed.

During the course of an investigation, the claims representative may discover that the insured was not at fault and that a third party caused the accident. When an insurer pays a claim to an insured for a loss caused by a negligent third party, the insurer can recover that payment amount from the negligent third party through the right of **subrogation**. Subrogation rights are established by insurance policies and by law. Claims representatives investigate subrogation possibilities concurrently with other investigations.

Subrogation

The process by which an insurer can, after it has paid a loss under the policy, recover the amount paid from any party (other than the insured) who caused the loss or is otherwise legally liable for the loss.

Documenting the Claim

Along with the investigation, documentation of the claim must continue throughout the life of the claim. All aspects of a claim must be documented to create a complete claim file. Three crucial parts of the claims documentation are diary systems, file status notes, and file reports.

Because claims representatives simultaneously handle many claims, they must have a system for working on and reviewing each claim. Whether this system is called a diary system, a suspense system, or a pending system, the purpose is the same. The system allows the claims representative to work on a claim one day and then diary it or calendar it for review. For example, the claims representative may ask an insured to provide a repair estimate and then diary that file for review on a date two weeks in the future. During that time, the claims representative would expect to receive the requested estimate. If the estimate has not been received by then, the review would prompt the claims representative to follow up.

File status notes (or an activity log) must accurately reflect and document investigations, evaluations of claims, decisions to decline coverage, or decisions to settle the claims. Because lawyers and state regulators can obtain copies of claim files, the file status notes and other file documentation must reflect these elements:

- Clear, concise, and accurate information
- Timely claim handling
- A fair investigation considering the insured's and the insurer's interests
- Objective comments about the insurer, insured, or other parties associated with the claim
- A thorough good-faith investigation

File reports to various parties are developed by claims representatives to document claim activity. The reports include various types of internal and external reports:

- Internal reports—for parties within the insurance organization who have an interest in large losses or loss of a specific nature, such as death, disfigurement, or dismemberment

- Preliminary reports—acknowledge that the claims representative received the assignment, inform the insurer about initial activity on the claim, suggest reserves, note coverage issues, and request assistance, if needed

- Status reports—periodically report the progress of the claim, recommend reserve changes, and request assistance and settlement authority when necessary

- Summarized reports—detailed narratives that follow an established format with captioned headings that give them structure, usually filed within thirty days of the assignment date

- External reports containing information collected by claims representatives—inform producers, some states' advisory organizations, and others who have an interest in the claim about details of the losses, such as the amount paid and the amount in outstanding reserve

Determining the Cause of Loss, Liability, and the Loss Amount

Claims representatives use the information gained about a claim during their investigation to determine the cause of loss, liability, and the loss amount. The facts of the loss determine the cause of the loss. For example, in a fire loss, the claims representative may find that a toaster caused the fire. The claims representative also determines the liability for the loss based on the facts of the case. For example, in an auto accident, the claims representative applies statutory and case law on negligence to determine liability of the parties involved.

Concurrent to the determination of the cause of the loss and the liability for the loss, the claims representative may determine the amount of the loss. For a property claim, the claims representative investigates the amount of damage to the property and the cost to repair or replace it and may also investigate the amount of business income lost. To determine a loss amount in a bodily injury claim, the claims representative investigates the extent of the injury, the residual and lasting effects of the injury, and the amount of pain and suffering the individual has endured.

Concluding the Claim

When the investigation has been completed and all documentation has been received, the claims representative must decide whether to pay the claim or deny it.

Payments

When a covered claim is concluded through negotiation or other means, the claims representative or claims personnel must issue a claim payment. When issuing claim payments, claims personnel must ensure that the proper parties are paid. Other parties, such as mortgagees on homes and loss payees on autos and personal property, can have a financial interest in the property. Parties named in the policy have rights, described in the policy, to be included as a payee under certain circumstances, such as for property that has been destroyed. For third-party liability claim payments, the claims representative must determine whether an attorney or a lienholder, such as a medical service provider, should be named as an additional payee on the payment. The claims representative is responsible for including all required payees when issuing a claim payment.

Claim Denial

When claims investigations reveal that a policy does not provide coverage for a loss or when an insured fails to meet a policy condition, the claims representative must make a timely claim denial. Insurers often have strict guidelines that claims representatives must follow when denying claims, and some insurers require a claims manager's approval to issue a claims denial. Before denying a claim, the claims representative must analyze the coverage carefully, investigate the loss thoroughly, and evaluate the claim fairly and objectively. Courts often favor insureds when a claims denial fails to meet these requirements, and the insurer can be assessed penalties in addition to the loss amount.

Once claims management gives authority to deny a claim, the claims representative must prepare a denial letter as soon as possible. Insurers usually send denial letters by certified mail with a return receipt requested to be signed by the addressee. Some insurers also send a copy of the letter by regular mail, marked "personal and confidential," in case the certified mail is not claimed. These procedures help ensure that the denial letter reaches the correct party, and they provide documentation that it was received.

Alternative Dispute Resolution and Litigation

If an insurer and an insured or a claimant cannot agree on the claim value or claims coverage, they may resolve the disagreement in court. However, court costs and delays in the court system have encouraged insurers, insureds, and claimants to seek alternative dispute resolution (ADR) techniques for settling disputes outside the traditional court system, including these:

- **Mediation**
- **Arbitration**
- **Appraisals**
- **Mini-trials**
- **Summary jury trials**

Despite the variety of ADR methods available, many cases are concluded through litigation. Litigation can occur at almost any point during the life of a claim. However, it occurs most often when the parties to the claim are unable to reach an agreement by negotiation or ADR, or when a claim is denied. ADR reduces, but does not eliminate, the possibility that a claimant will sue and take a case to trial. Accordingly, insurers must be prepared to litigate some claims. Many insurance policies require insurers to defend their insureds at trial. The duty to defend usually ends when the amount the insurer has paid in settlements or judgments on the claim reaches the insurer's limit of liability.

When litigation cannot be avoided, claims representatives participate in developing a litigation strategy for the insured's defense and for litigation expense control. Claims representatives must carefully select and direct defense lawyers. The lawyer's role is to be the insured's advocate. To mitigate the claim against the insured and to encourage the claimant to settle out of court, the lawyer must address every aspect of the claimant's case, from liability to damages.

Closing Reports

When a claim is resolved, the claims representative may complete a closing or final report, which can include the claims representative's recommendations on subrogation, advice to underwriters, and other suggestions. In some instances, subrogation claims representatives use these reports to evaluate the likelihood of a successful subrogation action.

Claims supervisors and managers may use the reports to audit the claims representative's performance. These reports can also be submitted to reinsurers for reimbursement of loss payment. Claims representatives should be aware of claims that should be referred to reinsurers and must complete reports on those claims based on the insurer's internal guidelines and reinsurance agreements.

ASPECTS OF PROPERTY INSURANCE CLAIMS

When an insured files a claim under a property insurance policy, the claim negotiation process ultimately determines how the claim is resolved.

Mediation

An alternative dispute resolution (ADR) method by which disputing parties use a neutral outside party to examine the issues and develop a mutually agreeable settlement.

Arbitration

An alternative dispute resolution (ADR) method by which disputing parties use a neutral outside party to examine the issues and develop a settlement, which can be final and binding.

Appraisal

A method of resolving disputes between insurers and insureds over the amount owed on a covered loss.

Mini-trial

An alternative dispute resolution method by which a case undergoes an abbreviated version of a trial before a panel or an adviser who poses questions and offers opinions on the outcome of a trial, based on the evidence presented.

Summary jury trial

An alternative dispute resolution method by which disputing parties participate in an abbreviated trial, presenting the evidence of a few witnesses to a panel of mock jurors who decide the case.

In property insurance claims, two parties are usually involved in the claim negotiation process: the insured and the insurer. These are the three crucial components of the claim handling process for property insurance claims:

• Verifying coverage
• Determining the amount of loss
• Concluding the claim and exercising subrogation and salvage rights

Verifying Coverage

One of the claims representative's duties is to verify whether the claim is covered. If a question of coverage exists and the insurer plans to continue its investigation, the insurer might send a reservation of rights letter to the insured. After receiving the initial report of a claim, the claims representative must gather further information to verify coverage. The initial verification involves three steps:

1. Confirming that a valid policy was in effect
2. Determining that the date of the loss falls within the policy period
3. Establishing whether the damaged property is insured under the policy

The claims representative must determine whether the coverage provided by the policy will pay any or all of the claim submitted. For a property insurance claim, the claims representative must seek the answers to four questions to verify that the claim is covered:

• Does the insured have an insurable interest in the property?
• Is the damaged property covered by the policy?
• Is the cause of loss covered by the policy?
• Do any additional coverages, endorsements, or coverage limitations apply?

Insurable interest

An interest in the subject of an insurance policy that is not unduly remote and that would cause the interested party to suffer financial loss if an insured event occurred.

The first question determines whether the person or organization making a claim for the damaged property has an insurable interest in the property. In property insurance, an **insurable interest** exists if a person or another entity would suffer a financial loss if the property were damaged. In most property insurance losses, the insured is the property owner, so the question of insurable interest is easily answered. However, others may also have an insurable interest in the property. For example, a mortgagee (such as a bank that has provided a home mortgage loan) has an insurable interest in real property to the extent of the outstanding mortgage.

The second question that the claims representative must answer is whether the damaged property is covered by the policy. The answer, however, may not be as simple as it appears. For example, insurance coverage on a building usually includes any item permanently attached to the building and any outdoor equipment used to maintain the building. Although the building may be clearly insured, would a room air conditioner attached to a window frame be considered a part of the building? Would a toolshed connected to a dwelling by a fence be considered a part of the dwelling? These are the types of questions that the claim representative must answer according to the policy provisions.

The question of whether the damaged property is covered by the policy is equally important for personal property. Most property insurance policies exclude losses to certain types of property. For example, a homeowners policy generally does not cover losses to property of tenants or to most motorized vehicles.

The third question the claim representative must answer is whether the cause of loss is covered by the policy. Often, the cause of the loss, such as fire or lightning, is clearly covered under the policy. In such cases, disputes between the insured and the insurer are unlikely to occur. However, disagreements may arise when the cause of loss is less obvious. Disputes can occur, for example, if there is more than one possible cause of loss, as in a hurricane when damage may have been caused either by wind or by flooding.

The fourth question the claims representative must answer is whether any additional coverages, endorsements, or coverage limitations apply. In many insurance policies, additional coverages and limitations modify the basic coverage provided. The insured might also have purchased an additional coverage, selected one or more optional policy coverages, or modified coverage through an endorsement (policy amendment).

Insurance policies contain important limitations on coverage. For example, although a homeowners policy covers most types of personal property, certain types of property, such as jewelry and furs, are covered for only a specified dollar amount when the loss is because of theft.

The claims representative must also check to see whether a deductible applies to the loss, which would reduce the amount of the loss payment. For an especially large deductible or a small loss, application of the deductible may indicate that no payment can be made. Before determining whether a given loss is covered, the claim representative must confirm that the loss occurred during the time period and within the territory described in the policy.

Determining the Amount of Loss

For personal property, the most important information is what property was damaged or destroyed. Creating an inventory of damaged personal property can be an arduous task for some losses, such as serious fire losses. However, for the claims representative to determine the value of the loss, a detailed inventory is essential and specific information must be gathered.

The valuation of loss can be the most difficult aspect of settling property insurance claims. To indemnify the insured according to the policy provisions, the claims representative must be able to answer two questions:

- How does the policy specify that the property be valued?
- Based on that specification, what is the value of the damaged property?

Common Valuation Methods

All property insurance policies include a valuation provision that specifies how to value covered property at the time of the loss. The most common property valuation methods are actual cash value, replacement cost, and agreed value.

Actual cash value (ACV)
Cost to replace property with new property of like kind and quality less depreciation.

Depreciation
The reduction in value caused by the physical wear and tear or technological or economic obsolescence of property.

Actual cash value (ACV) is the cost to replace the property minus an allowance for the property's **depreciation**. For example, assume a fire completely destroys a new television and a four-year-old sofa. The television has a replacement cost of $600 (its cost when it was purchased a week earlier), and the sofa would cost $800 to replace with a comparable (of like kind and quality) new sofa.

Under these circumstances, an ACV settlement includes $600 for the television because it has not yet had time to depreciate. For the sofa, however, the claims representative has to place a value on the used property. The claims representative must determine the extent of depreciation that should be considered. This determination is usually made by estimating the property's expected useful life. If, under normal circumstances, a sofa might be used for ten years and it is now four years old, a good estimate of depreciation from normal wear and tear is 40 percent. Therefore, with a replacement cost of $800 and depreciation estimated at 40 percent, the ACV of the damaged sofa is $480. A payment of $480 would indemnify the insured for the loss of the four-year-old sofa.

Apply Your Knowledge

A covered cause of loss completely destroys a family's six-year-old pool table. The pool table would cost $2,500 to replace with a comparable (of like kind and quality) new pool table. A pool table is generally expected to be used for ten years. Explain how, as the claim representative, you would determine the covered pool table's ACV.

Feedback: You must place a value on the pool table by determining the extent of depreciation that should be considered. Because a pool table might be used for ten years and is now six years old, you estimate the depreciation from normal wear at 60 percent. Therefore, with a replacement cost of $2,500 and depreciation estimated at 60 percent, the ACV of the destroyed pool table is $1,500. A payment of $1,500 would indemnify the insured for the loss of the pool table.

Another valuation method specified in some property insurance policies allows for valuation on a **replacement cost** basis. In this case, deduction for depreciation is not part of the valuation, and the insured in the previous example would be paid $800 for the four-year-old sofa.

Still another method for valuing property losses is **agreed value**, which is used to insure property that is difficult to value, such as fine arts, antiques, and collections. This agreed value is often based on an appraisal, and that amount is stated in the policy declarations.

Valuation Process

Once the claims representative has verified coverage and identified the valuation method specified in the policy, the valuation process begins. Claims representatives use guidelines to determine both replacement cost and ACV. Personal property and real property present different valuation problems.

If the exact style and brand of the damaged personal property are available for purchase, obtaining the replacement cost is simple. If the particular item is no longer available, the claims representative identifies the closest substitute in style and quality and uses that substitute's value as the replacement cost. For ACV, however, depreciation must be estimated. While claims representatives have attempted to develop straightforward methods, such as the useful-life procedure described in the case of the damaged sofa, these procedures do not fit every circumstance.

For example, if a sofa has an expected life of ten years, the claims representative makes a reasonable estimate in considering the four-year-old sofa to be 40 percent depreciated. But what if the sofa is fifteen years old? Is it considered worthless? Therefore, he or she must use good judgment to determine depreciation.

The replacement cost of real property can usually be determined by using three factors:

- Square footage of the property
- Type and quality of construction
- Construction cost per square foot

The first factor is the square footage of the property. If the building has been badly damaged, its area can be determined from the original blueprints or by measuring the remains.

The second factor is the type and quality of construction. A one-family frame house with standard trim and fixtures costs far less to replace than a house of the same size built of stone with high-quality woodworking, skylights, and other features.

The final factor affecting replacement cost is the construction cost per square foot that is currently charged for the style and quality of the destroyed

Replacement cost

The cost to repair or replace property using new materials of like kind and quality with no deduction for depreciation.

Agreed value method

A method of valuing property in which the insurer and the insured agree, at the time the policy is written, on the maximum amount that will be paid in the event of a total loss.

building. Contractors who do business in the general location of the damaged building can quote costs per square foot in various quality-of-construction categories. Multiplying the square footage by the appropriate cost per square foot yields the building's replacement cost.

If the building is only partially damaged, the claims representative usually prepares a repair estimate or obtains repair estimates from one or more contractors. Replacing the property when a partial loss has occurred involves restoring the property to its previous state as closely as possible.

Concluding the Claim

After verifying coverage, determining the cause of loss, and determining the amount of damage or extent of loss, the claims representative must conclude the claim. This step usually requires that the claims representative and the insured discuss the details of the loss and the valuation of the damage to agree on an amount for the insurer to pay to settle the loss.

The negotiation phase of claims handling can be relatively simple, as in the example about the fire-damaged television. However, it may be complicated because of a large number of damaged items, property of high value, or disagreement between the insured and the claims representative regarding the value or circumstances of the loss.

After the claims representative and the insured agree on the amount of the settlement, two other factors can affect the insurer's cost for property claims: subrogation and **salvage rights**.

Salvage rights

The insurer's rights to recover and sell or otherwise dispose of insured property on which the insurer has paid a total loss or a constructive total loss.

Special Considerations for Property Catastrophe Claims

Most insurers cover properties that are subject to catastrophic events such as windstorms, floods, and wildfires. Insurers that have these exposures should be prepared to handle the large number of losses associated with a catastrophic event.

After a catastrophe, insureds and regulators expect an insurer to settle losses quickly, regardless of the volume of claims or any disruptions to the insurer's resources. Effective catastrophe response requires careful preparation. The exhibit presents some of the challenges involved in catastrophe response and illustrates how contingency planning can help an organization prepare to meet them. See the exhibit "Challenges Involved in Catastrophe Response."

Challenges Involved in Catastrophe Response

Area	Potential Problems	Possible Responses
Staffing	Insufficient claims staff to handle volume of incoming claims. Staff unavailable as they deal with their own property damage.	Identify and train staff from other areas to assist. Establish relationships with independent adjusters to help manage overflow. Bring in catastrophe teams of claims representatives from other regions.
Premises	The insurer's premises are damaged or must be evacuated.	Identify and arrange for the use of alternative premises. Secure existing premises.
Systems	Records are destroyed or computer systems are down.	Maintain current backup at a remote location where information can be accessed.
Communication	Communication links are destroyed.	Identify public broadcasting services that may be used. Arrange for wireless communication.
Transportation	Roads and bridges are damaged.	Identify alternative routes and resources to move staff and materials into damaged areas.
Utilities	Utilities are suspended.	Arrange for generator-powered electricity, water tank services, portable toilets, and showers.
Material and labor	Available construction materials and labor are insufficient.	Arrange sources of materials and labor from nearby communities.
Mass evacuation	Policyholders are evacuated from an area.	Identify and secure temporary housing, including motels, mobile homes, and other temporary buildings.
Policyholder needs	Policyholders are confused, stressed, and anxious.	Prepare catastrophe kits, including sources of information and assistance, for distribution to policyholders.
Community needs	Efficient claim settlement depends on restoring resources and community services.	Coordinate with other insurers and community disaster relief agencies.
Employee stress	Employees' stress levels during catastrophes are high.	Train employees in stress management, and have counselors available on site. Provide temporary daycare services and meals as other businesses are closed and employees work longer hours.
Security	Policyholders can become aggressive as they try to recover from their losses and payments are delayed. Insurers may become the target of violence when unfavorable rumors circulate. Criminals are attracted to post-catastrophe locations for temporary employment paid in cash.	Increase security at the insurer's premises and parking lots. Maintain visible security in lobby and public areas. Restrict access to work areas. In the event of a temporary curfew, arrange for travel passes for employees who work before or after curfew hours.

[DA02417]

ASPECTS OF LIABILITY INSURANCE CLAIMS

Because liability claims involve elements that property claims do not, claims representatives use different methods to settle them.

In liability claims, the claims representative's investigation focuses on whether the activity leading to liability comes within the scope of the policy and whether the insured could be legally responsible for the loss. If the claim goes to court, the insured could be held liable for compensatory damages (which include special damages and general damages) and possibly punitive damages.

These are four key aspects of liability insurance claims:

* Verifying coverage
* Determining the cause of loss
* Determining the amount of damages
* Concluding the claim

How Liability Claims Differ From Property Claims

Liability claims adjusting differs from and may be more difficult than property claims adjusting for three reasons. First, the claimant is a third party who has been injured or whose property has been damaged by the insured. The claimant may perceive the claims representative as an adversary, and this perception could cause the claimant to act in a hostile or unfriendly manner.

Second, a liability claim may involve bodily injury. While it is not always easy to determine the amount of the loss in property damage liability claims, determining the amount of loss is often even more difficult and complex when the claim seeks damages for bodily injury or death.

Third, liability claim settlement sometimes involves a claim for damage to the property of others that the insured has allegedly caused. The claims handling process for property damage liability claims resembles that of property insurance claims, with the added difficulty of determining whether the insured is legally responsible for the property damage that has occurred.

Verifying Coverage

As in a property claim, the claims representative must gather information to verify coverage. The process includes checking whether a valid policy was in effect and, if so, determining whether the date of the loss falls within the policy period and whether any additional coverages, endorsements, or coverage limitations apply. When handling a liability claim, the key difference from a property claim is that the claims representative must determine whether the insured is legally responsible for the loss; if not, liability coverage does not apply.

Determining the Cause of Loss

After receiving the first report of injury or damage and verifying coverage, the claims representative must gather detailed information relating to the liability claim. Because the amount of the loss is relevant only if the loss is covered under the insured's policy and if the insured is legally responsible for the loss, the question of how much damage occurred may be secondary in importance. Therefore, the claims representative must first determine how and why the loss occurred and whether the insured appears to be responsible.

In investigating a liability claim, the claims representative often inspects the scene of the occurrence or accident. This inspection is particularly useful if a traumatic event has occurred, such as an auto accident, a building collapse, or a fire. By studying the scene and interviewing the insured, the claimant, and any witnesses, the claims representative attempts to reconstruct the events that led to the loss. This reconstruction helps determine, as closely as possible, how the loss occurred and who is responsible. Additional details are needed to determine the extent of the bodily injury or property damage. At this point, the claims representative collects enough information to help determine whether the liability policy covers the loss and, if so, whether the insured may be legally responsible.

As soon as possible, the claims representative speaks directly with the injured party or the injured party's legal representative to hear that side of the story and to assess what bodily injury or property damage has been sustained. Many times, the events surrounding an accident are difficult to reconstruct, and the injured party and the insured may give the claims representative different accounts of the events. The claims representative seeks to resolve these discrepancies by taking statements from the claimant, the insured, and any available witnesses.

The injured party has the option of suing the insured, and the ensuing legal process could end in a legal decision determining whether the insured is legally liable and, if so, to what extent. Because of the time, expense, and uncertainty involved in a lawsuit, insurers often prefer to settle claims out of court. If the claim does go to court, the insurer is obligated to provide and pay for the insured's defense for a covered claim (until the insurer has paid the full policy limit for the occurrence involved).

Liability policies usually cover the insured's liability arising from certain specified activities, such as owning or using an automobile or operating a business, subject to certain exclusions. Coverage depends on whether the activity leading to the claim is within the scope of the policy's coverage and whether any exclusions in the policy apply to the specific case. Based on the information gathered, the claims representative must determine whether coverage applies.

If the claims representative's investigation finds that coverage does not apply, the insurer will deny the claim. For example, if the policy excludes injury intended by the insured and the insured purposely injures someone with a baseball bat, there would be no coverage unless the insured has evidence that the injury was careless but not intentional. If coverage does exist, the valuation aspect of liability claims settlement then becomes very important.

Determining the Amount of Damages

Damages are money claimed by or a monetary award to a party who has suffered bodily injury or property damage for which another party is legally responsible. When bodily injury occurs, determining the amount of damages often depends on medical records and the reports and opinions of physicians. Properly evaluating medical information is important in determining the amount of damages and is a distinguishing factor in the loss settlement process for bodily injury liability claims. This aspect of bodily injury claims requires experience and skill.

Legal liability cases may involve these types of damages:

- Compensatory damages
- Punitive damages

Compensatory Damages

Compensatory damages are intended to compensate a victim for harm actually suffered. They include special damages and general damages.

Specific, out-of-pocket expenses are called **special damages**. In bodily injury cases, these damages usually include hospital expenses, doctor and miscellaneous medical expenses, ambulance charges, prescriptions, and lost wages for time spent away from the job during recovery. Because they are specific and identifiable, special damages are easier to calculate than general damages.

General damages are compensatory damages awarded for losses that do not have a specific economic value. Examples of general damages include compensation for pain and suffering; disfigurement; loss of limbs, sight, or hearing; and the loss of the ability to bear children. Because these losses do not involve specific and measurable expenses, estimating their dollar value requires considerable expertise. To arrive at an estimate, claims representatives usually analyze past cases that are similar to the case currently under investigation. The claims representative may also use supervisor guidance, roundtable discussions with other claims representatives, or computer software to estimate bodily injury valuation.

There is usually no direct relationship between the amount of general damages and the amount of special damages. In some cases, such as when a claimant loses an eye, the amount of special damages may be relatively low but the general damages quite high because of pain and suffering and the change in the claimant's quality of life. In other cases, such as for whiplash injuries, general damages may be minimal but special damages considerable because the claimant requires physical therapy or other medical treatment.

Damages
Money claimed by, or a monetary award to, a party who has suffered bodily injury or property damage for which another party is legally responsible.

Compensatory damages
A payment awarded by a court to reimburse a victim for actual harm.

Special damages
A form of compensatory damages that awards a sum of money for specific, identifiable expenses associated with the injured person's loss, such as medical expenses or lost wages.

General damages
A monetary award to compensate a victim for losses, such as pain and suffering, that does not involve specific, measurable expenses.

Punitive Damages

When a court finds the defendant's conduct particularly malicious or outrageous, it might award **punitive damages**. The purpose of punitive damages is to punish the wrongdoer and to deter others from committing similar acts. In some states, insurer's cannot pay awards for punitive damages because the insured would thereby avoid punishment. Some policies expressly exclude coverage for punitive damages.

Concluding the Claim

A large percentage of liability cases are settled out of court through negotiations between the claims representative and the claimant or the claimant's attorney. In most instances, neither party wishes to become involved in a formal legal action and the accompanying costs and delays.

When negotiations do not result in a settlement, however, the claimant has the option of suing for the alleged damages. A court then decides who is responsible and determines the value of the bodily injury or property damage.

Even if a claimant initiates a lawsuit, however, the claims negotiations usually continue. Many out-of-court settlements have resulted after some or all of the courtroom testimony had been given. Negotiating with the claimant while simultaneously preparing for proceedings in court requires a great deal of skill, patience, and understanding on the part of the claims representative.

GOOD-FAITH CLAIMS HANDLING

Because insurance policies require utmost good faith between parties, good-faith claims handling is essential to an insurer's ability to fulfill its legal duties to insureds.

A primary function of insurers is to pay valid insurance claims. Claims representatives should strive to handle claims with utmost good faith and in an ethical and professional manner. Because interactions with claims representatives are often the only personal contacts that the general public has with an insurer, claims representatives' actions may be closely scrutinized and are often criticized. These criticisms, whether or not legitimate, can result in bad-faith allegations against an insurer. Throughout the claims handling process, the claims representative must remember that a loss often produces strong emotions from an insured or a claimant who has been through a trying, or possibly traumatic, experience. Effective interpersonal and communication skills are vital. Good-faith claims handling consists of several elements.

Law of Bad Faith

To avoid bad-faith allegations, claims representatives must understand the law of bad-faith claims. No single widely accepted definition of bad faith exists.

Punitive damages (exemplary damages)
A payment awarded by a court to punish a defendant for a reckless, malicious, or deceitful act to deter similar conduct; the award need not bear any relation to a party's actual damages.

Black's Law Dictionary (eighth edition, 2004) defines "bad faith" in insurance as this:

> An insurance company's unreasonable and unfounded (though not necessarily fraudulent) refusal to provide coverage in violation of the duties of good faith and fair dealing owed to an insured. Bad faith often involves an insurer's failure to pay the insured's claim or a claim brought by a third party.

While some state laws define bad faith differently or more specifically, the *Black's* definition is broad enough to encompass actions that courts nation-wide have determined to constitute bad faith.

Although the standard of conduct for proving bad faith continues to evolve, most bad-faith claims for breach of the implied duty of good faith and fair dealing arise under insurance-related contracts rather than other types of contracts. This is because, in insurance contracts, the insurer not only dictates the terms of the contract (the policy), but also usually controls the claims investigation, evaluation, negotiation, and settlement and therefore has more "bargaining power" than the insured. Because insurers control how claims are resolved, courts reason that insurers should be responsible for the outcome of their claims handling if they have acted in bad faith. Thus, courts hold insurers to a higher standard of conduct to discourage them from abusing their position of power.

To conclude that an insurer has acted in bad faith, courts must determine the standard of conduct to which the insurer should be held. Some courts use a negligence (sometimes called due care) standard in determining whether a claims representative's (and, by extension, the insurer's) actions constitute bad faith. Some courts may use negligence as a basis to award compensatory damages but award punitive damages only when the insurer has exhibited gross misconduct.

When applying a gross misconduct standard, courts generally focus on whether a claims representative acted on purpose or had a dishonest intent in his or her actions. Bad faith may fall somewhere between simple error and outright fraud. Other courts focus on the claims representative's lack of concern for a party's interests to describe bad-faith behaviors. Because these behaviors are judged on a subjective basis, courts attempt to determine the claims representative's state of mind at the time that bad-faith acts are alleged to have occurred. Claims representatives should understand the subjective interpretation of negligence and gross misconduct. The difference between negligence and gross misconduct is determined by the court's or jury's inter-pretation of the facts.

Elements of Good-Faith Claims Handling

Good-faith claims handling consists of these elements:

- Thorough, timely, and unbiased investigation
- Complete and accurate documentation

- Fair evaluation
- Good-faith negotiation
- Regular and prompt communication
- Competent legal advice
- Effective claim management

Thorough, Timely, and Unbiased Investigation

Investigations that are thorough, timely, and unbiased are the foundation of good-faith claims handling. Claims representatives should collect all relevant and necessary evidence, develop the information and documentation necessary to determine liability and damages, and make decisions when they believe they have sufficient information to do so. In a thorough investigation, the claims representative is alert for new information that may change the course of the claim.

In addition to being thorough, an investigation should be timely. An insured who makes a claim expects prompt contact from the claims representative. Most insurers have guidelines requiring the claims representative to contact the insured and the claimant within a specific period, such as twenty-four hours after the claim has been submitted. Documentation of timely contact in the claims file can help prove an insurer's use of good-faith claims handling procedures.

Finally, investigations should seek to discover the facts and consider all aspects of the claim to reach an impartial decision. Claims representatives should pursue all relevant evidence, especially evidence that establishes the claim's legitimacy, without bias. While striving for impartiality, claims representatives must still be alert to indicators of possible fraud and investigate them thoroughly. Insurers must also make a good-faith effort to find experts who are reputable within their profession and who will provide unbiased evaluations. Insurers may face bad-faith claims for failing to consider an expert's opinion in denying a claim or for failing to ascertain the unreliability of an expert's opinion and acting on it.

Complete and Accurate Documentation

A claim file must provide a complete and accurate account of all the activities of and actions taken by the claims representative. Claims representatives should be aware that many people, each with a different purpose, may read a claim file, including, for example, supervisors, a home-office examiner or an auditor, claims department peers, an underwriter, an agent or a broker, a state insurance department representative, and so forth. Claims files should provide complete information for all of their purposes.

Fair Evaluation

Fair evaluations are based on facts, not opinions. Claims representatives determine a range of claim amounts based on the facts of the claim, the credibility of the evidence, and applicable laws. Fair evaluations result from thorough, timely, and unbiased investigation and from an understanding of the laws of the jurisdiction in which the claim is brought. For assistance in making evaluations, claims representatives can consult with sources inside and outside the insurance company, including co-workers, supervisors and managers, defense lawyers, people who represent a typical jury, and jury verdict research companies.

File documentation showing that the claims representative used best practices to evaluate a claim is evidence of good-faith claims handling. Fair evaluation is particularly important in liability claims, which may result in damages that exceed policy limits. By evaluating liability claims as if no coverage limit existed, claims representatives can avoid the mistake of unfairly attempting to settle a claim for less than the policy limit when it may be worth more.

A crucial element of fair claim evaluation is promptness. Compliance with statutory time limits for completion of evaluations of coverage and damages can help reduce the insurer's exposure to bad-faith claims. Promptness is also important in responding to the claimant, the insured, or their respective lawyers' demands. Promptness is particularly important when there is a demand for settlement that is at or near the policy limits.

Good-Faith Negotiation

Claims representatives should respond to exaggerated demands from lawyers by offering and documenting a settlement that is consistent with the evidence and documentation in the claim file. An increasing number of bad-faith claims arise from insurers' failure to settle liability claims against the insurer within policy limits. In many such cases, the insured has demanded that the insurer settle the case within policy limits and has made it clear that the insurer is expected to pay the entire amount of the damages if settlement does not occur. If a verdict in excess of policy limits is delivered and the insurer refuses to pay the insured, a bad-faith lawsuit ensues.

To resolve disputes over settlement amounts, claims representatives should use policy provisions, such as arbitration clauses, when applicable. An insurer that adheres to policy provisions and pays the amount determined through arbitration is in a better position to defend a bad-faith lawsuit. Claims representatives should consider all possible forms of voluntary alternative dispute resolution, including mediation or a series of face-to-face negotiations, to resolve claims.

Regular and Prompt Communication

Communicating with all parties to a claim (for example, the insured, the defense attorney, and the excess insurer) is a crucial aspect of good-faith claims handling and resolving claims. Keeping insureds informed is especially important because they expect it, they are most likely to make a bad-faith claim, and they may have the most important information about an accident. The claims representative has a duty to inform the insured of policy provisions that apply to the claim, rights under the policy, and steps to be taken to get maximum benefits. Additional questions from the insured should be answered clearly and promptly. The duty to inform stems from the insurer's duty of utmost good faith under the insurance contract and is also required under many states' unfair claims practices acts.

Competent Legal Advice

Following the advice of competent lawyers can be considered evidence that an insurer acted in good faith. Claims representatives should provide lawyers with all information and documentation necessary to reach a complete and accurate opinion and should avoid any attempts to influence the lawyer's independent judgment.

When resolving a coverage question, insurers should avoid conflicts of interest by using lawyers other than the defense lawyers hired to defend an insured. Asking a lawyer who defends an insured a coverage question creates an ethical dilemma for that lawyer because the answer may not be in the insured's best interest. Insurers that use in-house or staff lawyers to defend insureds should be especially sensitive to the possibility of a conflict of interest and, if any appearance of such a conflict exists, should use outside lawyers.

Effective Claims Management

An insurer's claims management directly affects a claims representative's ability to handle claims in good faith. Claims management in this context refers to how claims departments are managed by claims supervisors and claims managers. Especially crucial to good-faith claims handling are consistent supervision, thorough training, and manageable caseloads.

SUMMARY

Two primary goals of the claims function are keeping the insurer's promise and supporting the insurer's profit goal. Claims personnel help meet these goals by using the claims handling process to promptly, fairly, and equitably pay all legitimate first- and third-party claims and by managing operational and claims handling expenses. Policyholders' satisfaction that the insurer's contractual promises have been upheld promotes goodwill and supports an insurer's profit goals.

Insurers and other insurance organizations have claims departments, which can be structured in various ways. Claims personnel may be staff claims representatives, independent adjusters, employees of TPAs, or producers. Public adjusters can also handle claims by representing the insured's interests to the insurer. Claims Department performance can be measured by a loss ratio and the use of internally identified best practices, claim audits, and customer-satisfaction data.

Claims representatives must be able to apply the information contained in the policy to the activities in the claim handling process. This process creates consistency in claims handling and helps ensure that claims are handled in a manner that conforms with legal and ethical standards. These activities are performed on every claim, to some degree:

- Acknowledging and assigning the claim
- Identifying the policy
- Contacting the insured or the insured's representative
- Investigating and documenting the claim
- Determining the cause of loss, liability, and the loss amount
- Concluding the claim

There are three crucial components of the claims handling process for property insurance claims. The first is verifying whether the claim is covered. Next is determining the amount of loss. Finally, the claims representative concludes the claim. Catastrophic events, such as floods or wildfires, can result in a large number of losses. Effective catastrophe response requires careful preparations by insurers' claims departments.

Claims representatives must handle liability claims differently than property claims. These are four key aspects of liability insurance claims:

- Verifying coverage
- Determining the cause of loss
- Determining the amount of damages
- Concluding the claim

Good-faith claims handling is essential to an insurer's ability to fulfill its legal duties to insureds. Good-faith claims handling consists of several elements:

- Thorough, timely, and unbiased investigation
- Complete and accurate documentation
- Fair evaluation
- Good-faith negotiation
- Regular and prompt communication
- Competent legal advice
- Effective claims management

Segment C

Direct Your Learning ▶▶

Risk Management

Educational Objectives

After learning the content of this assignment, you should be able to:

▷ Describe the basic purpose and scope of risk management.

▷ Explain how to identify and analyze loss exposures.

▷ Appraise the various risk control and risk financing techniques.

▷ Explain how to select and implement the appropriate risk management techniques, and monitor a risk management program.

▷ Explain how risk management benefits businesses, individuals, families, society, and insurers.

▷ Applying the risk management process, recommend appropriate risk management techniques for handling loss exposures of an individual, a family, or a business.

Risk Management

7

BASIC PURPOSE AND SCOPE OF RISK MANAGEMENT

Risk management involves the efforts of individuals or organizations to efficiently and effectively assess, control, and finance risk in order to minimize the adverse effects of losses or missed opportunities.

Individuals practice risk management to protect their limited assets from losses and to help meet personal goals. For an organization, sound risk management adds value and helps to ensure that losses or missed opportunities do not prevent it from meeting its goals. While many organizations have traditionally focused their risk management efforts on **pure risk**, the emerging discipline of enterprise-wide risk management is focused on managing all of an organization's pure and **speculative risks**.

Risk Management for Individuals and Organizations

In its simplest form, **risk management** includes any effort to economically deal with uncertainty of outcomes (risk). For individuals, risk management is usually an informal series of efforts, not a formalized process. Individual or personal risk management may be viewed as part of the financial planning process that encompasses broader matters such as capital accumulation, retirement planning, and estate planning.

Individuals and families often practice risk management informally without explicitly following a risk management process. For example, individuals purchase insurance policies to cover accidental or unexpected losses, or they contribute to savings plans so that they have money available to cover unforeseen events.

In smaller organizations, risk management is not usually a dedicated function, but one of many tasks carried out by the owner or senior manager. In many larger organizations, the risk management function is conducted as part of a formalized risk management program. A risk management program is a system for planning, organizing, leading, and controlling the resources and activities that an organization needs to protect itself from the adverse effects of accidental losses.

Pure risk
A chance of loss or no loss, but no chance of gain.

Speculative risk
A chance of loss, no loss, or gain.

Risk management
The process of making and implementing decisions that will minimize the adverse effects of accidental losses on an organization.

Most risk management programs are built around the risk management process. The risk management process is the method of making, implementing, and monitoring decisions that minimize the adverse effects of risk on an organization. Although the exact steps in an organization's risk management process may differ from the process discussed in this section, all risk management processes are designed to assess, control, and finance risk.

Traditional Risk Management and Enterprise-Wide Risk Management

Traditionally, the risk management professional's role has been associated with loss exposures related mainly to pure, as opposed to speculative, risks. This view excludes from the scope of risk management all loss exposures that arise from speculative risk, also referred to as business risk. Therefore, organizational risk management has focused on managing safety, purchasing insurance, and controlling financial recovery from losses generated by hazard risk.

Enterprise-wide risk management (ERM) is the term commonly used to describe the broader view of risk management that encompasses all types of risk. ERM is an approach to managing all of an organization's key risks and opportunities with the intent of maximizing the organization's value.

An ERM approach allows an organization to integrate all of its risk management activities so that the risk management process occurs at the enterprise level, rather than at the departmental or business unit level. How ERM is implemented in practice varies significantly among organizations, depending on their size, nature, and complexity.

IDENTIFYING AND ANALYZING LOSS EXPOSURES

The risk management process, which enables businesses and individuals to effectively manage the risk of accidental loss, begins with an examination of loss exposures.

To help ensure the success of a business or household, a risk manager must identify and analyze any loss exposures. The risk management process helps risk managers find and deal with loss exposures efficiently and effectively. In this discussion, the term "risk manager" refers to anyone who is responsible for risk management within an organization or a family.

Insurance professionals who know the risk management process can better understand why individuals and entities purchase insurance products. They are also able to better help prospective policyholders identify risks that can be effectively managed using insurance products.

The risk management process has six steps. The first two are identifying loss exposures and analyzing loss exposures. See the exhibit "The Risk Management Process."

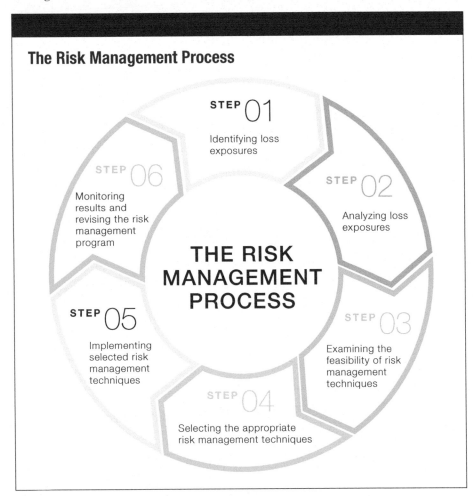

The Risk Management Process

STEP 01
Identifying loss exposures

STEP 02
Analyzing loss exposures

STEP 03
Examining the feasibility of risk management techniques

STEP 04
Selecting the appropriate risk management techniques

STEP 05
Implementing selected risk management techniques

STEP 06
Monitoring results and revising the risk management program

THE RISK MANAGEMENT PROCESS

[DA02595]

Identifying Loss Exposures

Identifying loss exposures involves developing a thorough list of accidental losses that could affect a household or organization. To do this, the risk manager must understand how the household or organization operates.

A physical inspection of the premises is a starting point. From there, the risk manager can use other techniques, such as financial statement analysis, flowchart development, interviews, loss exposure surveys, and loss history analysis.

Technology can also play a big role in identifying loss exposures. Smart devices and sensors can provide real-time loss exposure identification and assessment and quickly explore a vast number of potential outcomes and responses using collected data. See the exhibit "Step 1: The Risk Management Process."

Step 1: The Risk Management Process

STEP 01
Identifying loss exposures

STEP 06
Monitoring results and revising the risk management program

STEP 02
Analyzing loss exposures

THE RISK MANAGEMENT PROCESS

STEP 05
Implementing selected risk management techniques

Examining the feasibility of risk management techniques

Selecting the appropriate risk management techniques

[DA02595_1]

Physical Inspection

A risk manager generally cannot gain a complete picture of possible loss exposures by sitting at a desk away from the source of risk. The most straightforward method of identifying loss exposures is to physically inspect all locations, operations, maintenance routines, safety practices, work processes, and other activities in which a household or organization is involved. For example, a risk manager for an industrial operation may observe that the safety guards have been removed from machines or that boxes of parts are stacked high on a storage shelf, creating an exposure for injury if the parts fall.

However, physical inspection alone may not be enough, because the risk manager may not have sufficient knowledge of the household or operations to identify all exposures or to ask the right questions to uncover all loss exposures. That is where technology can be extremely valuable. Smart devices and sensors complement and enhance the physical inspection process by supplying large amounts of relevant data a risk manager may not be able to gather alone. When connected to wireless networks, smart devices and sensors can capture and report many types of vital information that can be used to identify and mitigate risks. For example, sensors can capture and report environmental conditions, worker health and safety markers, air quality, shipment inventories, temperatures (and sudden temperature changes), and humidity levels.

Loss Exposure Surveys

Loss exposure surveys, or checklists, are documents listing potential loss exposures that a household or an organization may face—and that a risk manager should look for. Such surveys are often designed to be comprehensive enough to apply to almost any household or organization, even though a given household or organization is unlikely to face all of the loss exposures detailed. These surveys usually group similar exposures together, like those from manufacturing operations or the use of vehicles. See the exhibit "Sample of Questions Frequently Asked on Loss Exposure Surveys."

For businesses, the risk manager usually discusses the items on the survey with managers, supervisors, and other employees familiar with the identified exposures. But because surveys may omit an important exposure, especially if the organization has unique operations not included on a standard survey, risk managers cannot depend solely on them. So risk managers should use surveys as guides when developing a comprehensive picture of the organization's operations and loss exposures.

Loss History Analysis

Loss history analyses deal with an organization's past losses and can assist a risk manager in identifying the organization's exposures to future losses. A high-quality loss history is complete, organized, and relevant.

Past events or conditions that were not recorded, inaccurately recorded, or made irrelevant by changing environments have little, if any, value for forecasting future events. For example, data quality is reduced when an item of information normally collected about losses (such as where or when they occur) is omitted.

Predictive modeling may be used during this stage. Advanced software can take raw data obtained from the insured (like loss history) and turn it into indicators that can help predict future outcomes. This information can be valuable not only in identifying loss exposures but also in finding ways to prevent losses.

Sample of Questions Frequently Asked on Loss Exposure Surveys

Yes No

❏ ❏ 1. Do you have a brochure or other written material that describes your business operations or products?

❏ ❏ 2. Is your business confined to one industry?

❏ ❏ 3. Is your business confined to one product?

❏ ❏ 4. Do you own buildings?

❏ ❏ 5. Do you lease buildings from others?

❏ ❏ 6. Do you lease buildings to others?

❏ ❏ 7. Do you plan any new construction?

❏ ❏ 8. Are your fixed asset values established by certified property appraisers?

❏ ❏ 9. Do you own any vacant land?

❏ ❏ 10. Are any properties located in potential riot or civil disturbance areas?

❏ ❏ 11. Are any properties located in potential flood or earthquake areas?

❏ ❏ 12. Do your properties have security alarm systems (fire-sprinkler discharge, burglary, smoke detection, and so forth)?

❏ ❏ 13. Are there any unusual fire or explosion hazards in your business operation (welding, painting, woodworking, steam boilers or pressurized machinery, and so forth)?

❏ ❏ 14. Do you take a physical count of inventory at least once a year?

❏ ❏ 15. Do you lease machinery or equipment other than automotive?

❏ ❏ 16. Do you stockpile inventory, either raw or finished?

❏ ❏ 17. Could you conveniently report inventory values on a monthly basis?

❏ ❏ 18. Do you buy, sell, or have custody of goods or equipment of extremely high value (radium, gold, and so forth)?

❏ ❏ 19. Do you use any raw stock, inventory, or equipment that requires substantial lead time to reproduce?

❏ ❏ 20. Do you export or import?

[DA02673]

Apply Your Knowledge

An insurer wants to identify all of the potential loss exposures at a customer's business. Which one of the following is the most straightforward method of identifying the business's loss exposures?

a.   Analyzing data sent to the insurer through smart devices and sensors

b.   Physically inspecting the operation

c.   Conducting a loss exposure survey of the operation

d.   Performing a loss history analysis

Feedback: b. The most straightforward method of identifying loss exposures is to physically inspect all locations, operations, maintenance routines, safety practices, work processes, and other activities in which a household or an organization is involved.

Analyzing Loss Exposures

Analyzing a loss exposure requires estimating how large a possible loss could be and how often it might occur. Such an analysis helps determine how losses may interfere with the activities and objectives of the household or organization and what their financial effects may be.

By analyzing the probable frequency and severity of possible losses, the risk manager can prioritize the most significant loss exposures. Predictive modeling can help with making these determinations. See the exhibit "Step 2: The Risk Management Process."

Loss Frequency

Loss frequency indicates the number of losses that occur within a specified period. Examples of frequent losses include employees' abrasions and minor lacerations at a manufacturing plant, minor accidents involving autos from an organization's fleet, and spoilage of produce at a supermarket.

Accurate measurement of loss frequency is important because the proper treatment of the loss exposure often depends on how frequently the loss is expected to occur. If a particular type of loss occurs frequently, or if its frequency has been increasing in recent years, the risk manager may decide that it is time to implement procedures for controlling the risk. Alternatively, if the loss occurs rarely or its frequency has dropped, corrective procedures may not be cost-effective.

Loss Severity

Loss severity is the amount of loss, typically measured monetarily, for a loss that has occurred. It's much easier to gauge the potential severity of property

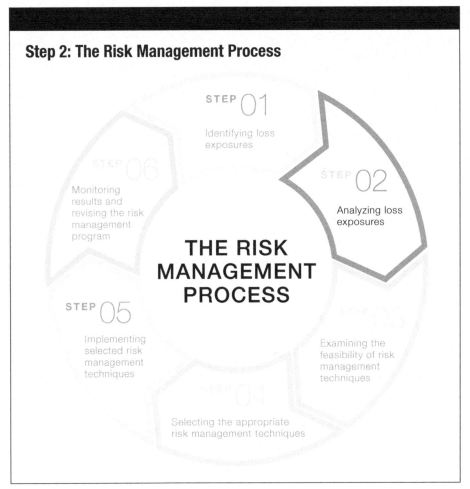

Step 2: The Risk Management Process

STEP 01

Identifying loss exposures

STEP 02

Analyzing loss exposures

STEP 06

Monitoring results and revising the risk management program

THE RISK MANAGEMENT PROCESS

STEP 05

Implementing selected risk management techniques

STEP 03

Examining the feasibility of risk management techniques

STEP 04

Selecting the appropriate risk management techniques

[DA02595_2]

losses than liability losses. Most property losses have a finite value. Whether the property is partially or completely destroyed, the severity of the loss is usually calculable.

On the other hand, the severity of liability exposures can be almost impossible to calculate. For example, if a popular paint manufacturer's top-selling paint produces toxic fumes when applied, the severity of this potential liability loss is almost unlimited.

Another example: The severity of property loss from an airplane crash may equal several million dollars, but it's still a calculable amount. But if a commercial passenger aircraft crashed in a densely populated area, the potential severity of the liability loss would be difficult, if not impossible, to estimate accurately.

Still, properly estimating loss severity is essential in treating the loss exposure, as the potential severity of losses is a major consideration in determining whether the household or organization should insure a particular exposure or retain all or part of the financial consequences of the loss.

EXAMINING THE FEASIBILITY OF RISK MANAGEMENT TECHNIQUES

Understanding the various techniques for managing risk is essential for any individual, family, or organization that uses the risk management process.

Once loss exposures have been identified and analyzed, the next step in the risk management process is to examine all possible techniques for handling the exposures. These techniques are grouped into two broad categories—risk control and risk financing. An overview of some of the more common risk management techniques will help insurance professionals understand options to control and finance risk. See the exhibit "Step 3: The Risk Management Process."

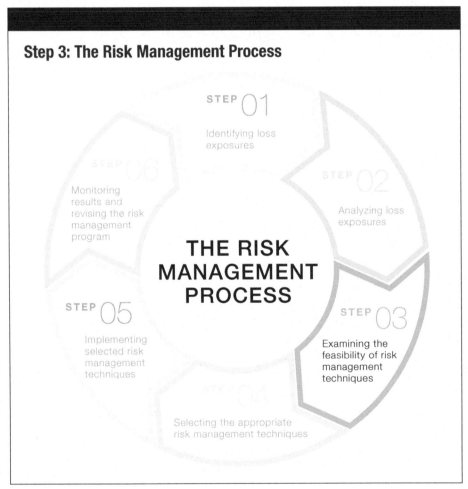

[DA02595_3]

Risk Control

Risk control is a risk management technique that attempts to decrease the frequency and/or severity of losses or make them more predictable. These are some common risk control techniques:

- Avoidance
- Loss prevention
- Loss reduction
- Separation
- Duplication

Avoidance

Avoidance
A risk control technique that involves ceasing or never undertaking an activity so that the possibility of a future loss occurring from that activity is eliminated.

Avoidance eliminates a loss exposure and reduces the chance of loss to zero. For example, a manufacturer of sports equipment may decide not to sell football helmets to avoid the possibility of large lawsuits from head injuries. Likewise, a family may decide not to purchase a motor boat to avoid the potential property and liability exposures that accompany boat ownership.

The advantage of avoidance as a risk control technique is that the probability of loss equals zero—there is no doubt or uncertainty about the loss exposure because a loss is not possible. Avoidance has the disadvantage of sometimes being impractical and is often difficult, if not impossible, to accomplish.

For example, suppose Priya is contemplating the purchase of her first automobile, but she is worried about the exposures inherent in automobile ownership. She may believe the chance of damage to the car is too great. Further, Priya may be unwilling to assume the chance of liability imposed by law, or perhaps she cannot afford automobile insurance.

In Priya's case, however, avoidance of these exposures may pose additional problems for Priya. Does she need a car for commuting to work or for other activities? If so, she will have to exchange the exposures of automobile ownership for the exposures inherent in some other type of transportation. Renting or leasing a car may be more expensive than auto ownership, and Priya would still be liable for any accidents she may cause.

Loss Prevention

Loss prevention
A risk control technique that reduces the frequency of a particular loss.

Loss prevention seeks to lower the frequency of losses from a particular loss exposure. Some common examples of loss prevention are keeping doors and windows locked to prevent burglaries, and maintaining a regular program of vehicle maintenance to prevent accidents caused by faulty equipment.

Loss Reduction

Loss reduction
A risk control technique that reduces the severity of a particular loss.

Loss reduction seeks to lower the severity of losses from a particular loss exposure. Some common loss reduction measures include installing a sprinkler system, which does not usually prevent fires, but can limit damage should a fire occur, and installing a restrictive money safe that a store clerk cannot open.

Many insurers have a risk control department that includes risk management professionals who attempt to reduce an insured's frequency and severity of losses. Insureds often use risk control measures because the insurer has recommended them. Insurers direct much risk control effort to commercial insurance accounts. The risk control programs recommended by insurers are generally based on inspection reports prepared by the insurers' risk control representatives. An inspection report is one of the best sources of underwriting information, and it supplements the application.

An inspection report usually has these two main objectives:

- To provide a thorough description of the applicant's operation so that the underwriter can make an accurate assessment when deciding whether to accept the application for insurance.

- To provide an evaluation of the applicant's current risk control measures and recommend improvements in risk control efforts. The underwriter may require that the applicant implement the risk control recommendations for the application to be accepted.

Separation

Separation is a risk control technique that isolates loss exposures from one another to minimize the adverse effect of a single loss. For example, an organization may store inventory in several warehouses for valid business reasons, as well as for risk control. Another example of separation is using several suppliers for raw material purchases, which might also provide competitive pricing.

Duplication

Duplication is a risk control technique that uses backups, spares, or copies of critical property, information, or capabilities and keeps them in reserve. For example, an organization may store copies of key documents or information at another location and may maintain an inventory of spare parts for critical equipment. Risk control techniques are rarely used alone and are most often effective when used in conjunction with risk financing techniques.

Risk Financing

Risk financing is an effective risk management technique that includes steps to pay for or transfer the cost of losses. The most common risk financing techniques include retention and transfer (noninsurance risk transfer and insurance).

Retention

Retention

A risk financing technique by which losses are retained by generating funds within the organization to pay for the losses.

The financial consequences of any loss exposure that has not been avoided or transferred are retained. **Retention** involves acceptance of the costs associated with all or part of a particular loss exposure. Retention can be intentional or unintentional. After thoroughly analyzing the alternatives, a risk manager may decide that retention is the best way to handle a given exposure, perhaps because insurance is not available or is too expensive. For example, a risk manager may decide that purchasing collision coverage on a fleet of older vehicles is not worth the premium and may thus decide to retain the organization's exposure by paying for any collision losses from the company's operating funds.

Unintentional retention may result from inadequate exposure identification and analysis or from incomplete evaluation of risk management techniques. For example, a restaurant may not identify its liability exposure for serving too much alcohol to a customer and therefore may fail to purchase liquor liability insurance to cover this exposure.

Retention can be partial or total. For example, a $10,000 per building deductible on a commercial property insurance policy is a partial retention. An example of total retention would be a husband and wife choosing not to purchase flood insurance on their lakeside home because they believe it is too expensive—they are effectively retaining their entire exposure to flood losses.

Retention is usually used in combination with other risk management techniques, particularly risk control and insurance. A deductible in a business auto policy is an example of the combination of retention and insurance. If the risk manager also implements a driver safety program to lower the frequency of corporate auto accidents, the combination of risk control, retention, and insurance can handle the exposure economically.

Transfer

Businesses often treat loss exposures by noninsurance risk transfer, a risk financing technique in which one party transfers the potential financial consequences of a particular loss exposure to another party that is not an insurer. For example, the landlord of a commercial building may wish to transfer the financial consequences of a liability exposure arising out of activities of a tenant. The landlord accomplishes this transfer by having the tenant sign a hold-harmless agreement. The agreement can be a separate contract, but it is usually a provision included in the lease. In this case, the hold-harmless agreement might state that the tenant agrees to indemnify the landlord for any damages the landlord becomes legally obligated to pay because of injury or damage occurring on the premises occupied by the tenant.

In addition to other techniques for handling loss exposures, households and small businesses depend heavily on insurance—another transfer technique—which transfers the potential financial consequences of certain specified loss exposures from the insured to the insurer. Most medium-sized and large businesses also rely on insurance as a major component of their risk management programs, but they may be less dependent on insurance and employ other risk management techniques more systematically than households and small businesses.

Even large businesses face loss exposures that they can handle most economically by purchasing insurance. No viable alternative exists for highly unpredictable loss exposures that could result in catastrophic financial consequences. Such businesses may use large retention amounts (deductibles or self-insurance) and purchase insurance policies to provide coverage above these amounts to protect them against large losses.

By working closely with the organization's insurance producer, a risk manager can develop an insurance program tailored to the company's needs and coordinate an insurance program with risk control and other risk financing to develop a complete risk management program. See the exhibit "Risk Management Techniques."

Apply Your Knowledge

Dorian has followed the auto manufacturers' scheduled maintenance recommendations on her new Kia and five-year-old Honda to avoid any accidents caused by mechanical malfunctions. Her sixteen-year-old son, Marvin, has just received his driver's license. Dorian decides that Marvin will drive the Honda, which has dual front and side airbags installed. Dorian adds Marvin to her auto insurance policy and asks her insurer to increase the comprehensive and collision deductibles for the Honda to $1,000 to reduce the cost of the insurance coverage. At Dorian's insistence, Marvin completed a safe-driver education program, which included thirty hours of driving time with a certified driver education instructor, before obtaining his driver's license.

Identify the risk management techniques that Dorian has used to manage her auto loss exposures.

Feedback: Dorian used these techniques to manage her auto loss exposures:

- Dorian's auto maintenance practice is a loss prevention technique.
- Dorian's decision for Marvin to drive the older auto with dual airbags is a loss reduction technique because the value of the older Honda is less than that of the newer Kia, and the airbags could minimize or prevent injury to Marvin and his passenger in an accident.
- Adding Marvin to her insurance policy is an insurance risk transfer technique.
- Increasing the auto deductibles on the Honda is a retention technique.
- The safe-driver education program that Marvin completed is both a loss reduction technique and a loss prevention technique because Marvin's knowledge of safe-driving practices can help prevent accidents (losses) and his knowledge of how to react in an accident might help him reduce the amount of damage incurred if he has an accident.

Risk Management Techniques

Risk Control Techniques

Technique	What the Technique Does	Example
Avoidance	Eliminates the chance of a particular type of loss by either disposing of an existing loss exposure or by not assuming a new exposure.	A family decides not to purchase a boat and therefore avoids the loss exposures associated with boat ownership.
Loss prevention	Lowers loss frequency (number of losses).	A business installs bars on windows and door deadbolts to prevent burglaries.
Loss reduction	Lowers loss severity (dollar amount of losses).	A business installs a sprinkler system to reduce the amount of fire damage from potential fires.
Separation	Lowers loss severity.	A business buys multiple small warehouses to contain the effects of a single loss.
Duplication	Lowers loss frequency.	A taxi firm maintains a few spare vehicles to keep all drivers on the road even if one vehicle needs repair.

Risk Financing Techniques

Technique	What the Technique Does	Example
Retention	Retains all or part of a loss exposure (intentionally or unintentionally), which means that losses must be paid for with available funds or other assets.	A business decides not to purchase collision coverage for its fleet of vehicles and sets aside its own funds to pay for possible collision losses.
Noninsurance transfer	Transfers potential financial consequences of a loss exposure from one party to another party that is not an insurer.	In a lease, a landlord transfers the liability exposures of a rented building to the tenant.
Insurance	Transfers financial consequences of specified losses from one party (the insured) to another party (the insurer) in exchange for a specified fee (premium).	A family purchases homeowners and personal auto policies from an insurer.

[DA02674]

SELECTING, IMPLEMENTING, AND MONITORING RISK MANAGEMENT TECHNIQUES

After identifying and analyzing loss exposures and considering the feasibility of the available risk management techniques, the risk manager must select appropriate risk management techniques. Selected techniques are then implemented and monitored.

The fourth step in the risk management process is to select the most appropriate risk management technique(s) based on financial criteria and guidelines. The fifth step is implementation of the selected techniques. The final step involves monitoring the results and revising the program as needed. An understanding of these steps helps insurance professionals guide customers through the risk management process and provides a deeper understanding of the issues a customer might face in developing and implementing a risk management program.

Selecting the Appropriate Risk Management Techniques

Organizations and households select risk management techniques based on financial criteria or informal guidelines. For example, organizations that are accustomed to reaching decisions based on expected profits or other financial criteria will probably use these same financial standards to select the most promising risk management techniques. In contrast, organizations that are less financially oriented are more likely to apply informal guidelines in choosing risk management techniques. See the exhibit "Step 4: The Risk Management Process."

Selection Based on Financial Criteria

Financial management decisions are typically made with the objective of increasing profits and/or operating efficiency. Selection of risk management techniques can be based on the same objectives. When an organization undertakes an activity to achieve profit goals or other objectives, it also assumes the exposures to accidental loss that are inherent in that activity. How the organization deals with those loss exposures affects the profits or output from the activity. By forecasting how selection of a particular risk management technique will affect profits or output, an organization can choose the risk management technique that is likely to be the most financially beneficial.

For example, a corporation may analyze its financial position and decide that it does not want any retained loss exposures to affect annual corporate earnings by more than five cents per share of stock. If the corporation has 100 million shares outstanding, the risk management department can retain up to $5 million for all exposures in a fiscal year. The risk management department makes its retention decisions for the coming year based on this strategy of protecting corporate earnings.

Selection Based on Informal Guidelines

Most households and small organizations follow informal guidelines in selecting risk management techniques. Four guidelines might be used to select techniques.

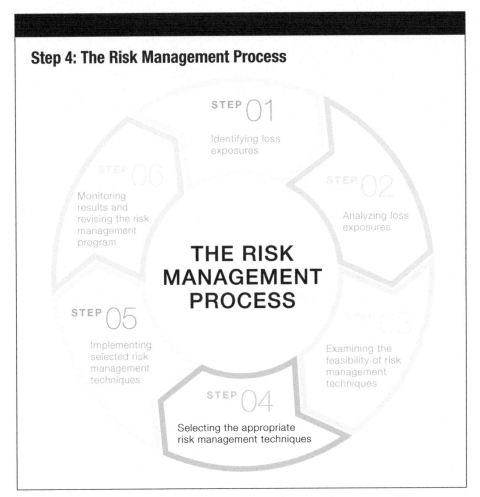

[DA02595_4]

The first guideline: do not to retain more than you can afford to lose. Setting an upper limit on the proper retention level is an important guideline. The amount that a household or an organization can afford to lose depends on its financial situation. For example, if a family has only $500 in its savings account and has little remaining from each paycheck after paying expenses, it may not be feasible for the family to carry a $1,000 deductible on either its homeowners or personal automobile policies.

The second guideline: do not retain large exposures to save a little premium. A risk manager should not retain a loss exposure with high potential severity, such as auto liability, to save a small amount of insurance premium. Depending on market conditions, certain types of liability insurance coverage, such as some umbrella policies (designed to cover large liability losses), can cost relatively little because the potential frequency of large liability losses is low. However, such coverage can be priced much higher given different market conditions.

Exposures with the potential of low frequency but high severity should generally be insured because they are highly unpredictable. For example, the probability of a building's suffering a total fire loss is low because total fire losses happen infrequently; however, if a family's residence does burn to the ground, the severity of the loss would be great. One such loss would cost the family many times an annual insurance premium, so the family should fully insure the residence but use an appropriate deductible to decrease the policy premium.

The third guideline: do not spend a lot of money for a little protection. Risk managers should spend insurance dollars where they will do the most good. If the exposure is almost certain to lead to a loss during the policy period, the insurer must charge a premium close to the expected cost of the loss plus a portion of the insurer's overhead, premium taxes, and profit. It is better to retain exposures of this type because the household or organization could absorb the cost of a loss almost as easily as the cost of the insurance. For loss exposures with high frequency and low severity, retention and risk control are usually the best alternatives. For example, a family may choose a higher deductible on auto physical damage coverage and use that savings to buy umbrella insurance to provide coverage for the infrequent but severe liability losses exceeding their homeowners or auto policy liability limits.

The fourth guideline: do not consider insurance a substitute for risk control. A company's risk manager may evaluate a particular exposure, such as automobile collisions, and discover that the frequency of accidents has been increasing in recent years. If the company has a $1,000 collision deductible for each accident, the risk manager may consider reducing the company's total annual retention for auto accidents. However, lowering the deductible to $500 so that the company retains less of the loss exposure on each accident would not solve the real problem, which is the increase in loss frequency. The insurance cost increases with the lower deductible, and the loss frequency is likely to remain high. In this case, the risk manager would be using the purchase of insurance in lieu of risk control.

A better option would be for the company to implement a risk control program to prevent accidents from occurring. This program could include more careful screening of company drivers, periodically reviewing drivers' motor vehicle records, training employees in safe driving practices, ensuring vehicle safety through regular vehicle maintenance, and implementing other risk control activities to reduce the frequency of collisions.

Implementing the Selected Risk Management Techniques

Implementing the risk management techniques that an organization has selected requires the risk manager to make these decisions: See the exhibit "Step 5: The Risk Management Process."

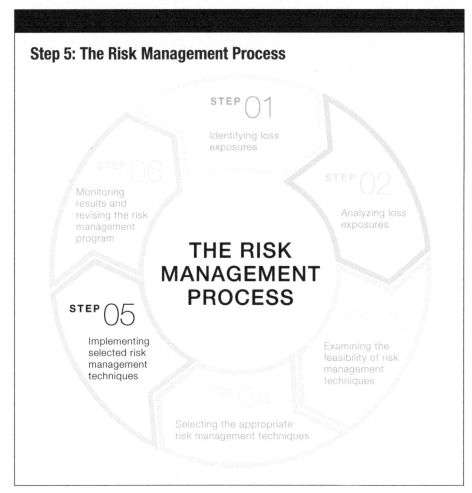

Step 5: The Risk Management Process

STEP 01 Identifying loss exposures

STEP 02 Analyzing loss exposures

STEP 06 Monitoring results and revising the risk management program

THE RISK MANAGEMENT PROCESS

STEP 05 Implementing selected risk management techniques

Examining the feasibility of risk management techniques

Selecting the appropriate risk management techniques

[DA02595_5]

- What should be done
- Who should be responsible
- How to communicate the risk management information
- How to allocate the costs of the risk management program

Once these decisions have been made, the risk management program will be effectively implemented.

Deciding What Should Be Done

Once the risk manager has decided which risk management techniques to use, he or she must implement them. For example, Helen, the risk manager of a supermarket, has decided that the store needs a sprinkler system. She must now decide how much the supermarket can afford to spend on the system, what kind of system should be installed, and which contractor should install it. She might also need to check on the local water supply and building permits and decide what is necessary to comply with local ordinances. Because the store executives will want to minimize customer disruption, Helen must decide how to accomplish this objective. She must also consult with the store's insurance agent to make sure that appropriate property and liability coverages are in place during and after the installation and that the insurer gives an insurance credit for the sprinkler system. Helen must take into account these considerations and many others before deciding exactly how to implement the risk control technique she has selected.

Deciding Who Should Be Responsible

The risk manager usually does not have complete authority to implement risk management techniques and must depend on others to implement the program based on the risk manager's advice. Larger organizations may have a written risk management statement and a risk management manual outlining guidelines, procedures, and authority for implementing risk management techniques. In smaller organizations and in households, the person making risk management decisions is often the person implementing the program because that person is the organization's owner or the household's primary wage earner.

Communicating Risk Management Information

A risk management program must include a communications plan. Risk management departments of large organizations generally rely on a manual to inform others of how to identify new exposures, which risk management techniques are currently in place, how to report insurance claims, and other important information. Management and other employees must communicate information to the risk manager so that the program can be modified for new exposures and evaluated for effectiveness.

Allocating Costs of the Risk Management Program

Allocating the costs of the risk management program also requires consideration. In large organizations, the costs of risk control, retention, noninsurance risk transfers, and insurance, as well as the expenses of the risk management department, must be spread appropriately across all departments and locations.

In smaller organizations or within households, allocating costs is also feasible. For example, an employee of a small business may be required to pay the deductible arising from damage she caused to a company car, or a teenager may have to pay to fix a neighbor's window that he accidentally broke.

Monitoring Results and Revising the Risk Management Program

Monitoring the results of the risk management program is an ongoing activity that a risk manager must carefully perform. Because the needs of all households and organizations change over time, a risk management program should not be allowed to become outdated. Monitoring the program ranges from handling routine matters, such as updating fleets of vehicles by replacing those less roadworthy, to making complex decisions concerning new activities to initiate or avoid. See the exhibit "Step 6: The Risk Management Process."

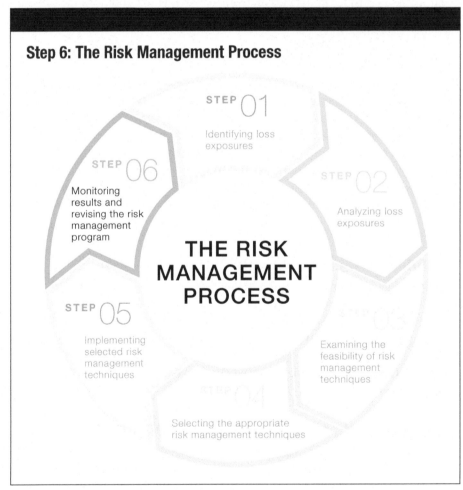

Step 6: The Risk Management Process

STEP 01
Identifying loss exposures

STEP 02
Analyzing loss exposures

Examining the feasibility of risk management techniques

Selecting the appropriate risk management techniques

STEP 05
Implementing selected risk management techniques

STEP 06
Monitoring results and revising the risk management program

THE RISK MANAGEMENT PROCESS

[DA02595_6]

A household or an organization should review its insurance program with its agent or broker each year. Because decisions regarding insurance are usually associated with other risk management techniques, any change in insurance will affect the other areas.

The last step in the risk management process is actually a return to the first. To monitor and modify the risk management program, the risk manager must periodically identify and analyze new and existing loss exposures and then reexamine, select, and implement appropriate risk management techniques. Thus, the process of monitoring and modifying the risk management program begins the risk management process once again.

 Reality Check

Construction Company Uses Electronic Tracking Equipment to Recover Stolen Property

Zachry Construction earned an award for Innovative Construction Project Planning Process at an International Risk Management Institute, Inc., conference. Zachry implemented use of a global tracking system as part of its risk management program and later found that it met that need even more completely than it originally expected. When an unauthorized move of a thirty-ton crane was noted, Zachry's equipment superintendent was able to quickly confirm that the crane, a truck, and a trailer were all missing; he used a tracking device to pinpoint the geographic location of the equipment. He notified police, who recovered the unit and released it back to Zachry. Zachry noted cost benefits of using the tracking device in this manner. The company avoided filing an insurance claim, losing time and paying rental fees to temporarily replace the equipment, and paying storage and retrieval fees to the police department because the police could immediately and definitively confirm that the equipment belonged to the construction firm.

[DA07679]

BENEFITS OF RISK MANAGEMENT

A sound risk management program benefits businesses, individuals, and families, enabling them to better manage their loss exposures. Additionally, risk management can benefit society and insurers.

Risk management's benefits to businesses, individuals, and families can include peace-of-mind, improved access to affordable insurance, cost-effective achievement of goals, and the ability to take on more risk and explore greater opportunities. Society and insurers also benefit when businesses and individuals practice risk management.

Benefits of Risk Management to Businesses

Making insurance part of an overall risk management program rather than relying solely on insurance improves access to affordable coverage. Insurers are more receptive to organizations that practice good risk management than those that rely solely on insurance for protection against the financial consequences of accidental losses. An insured that combines insurance with the risk management techniques of avoidance, risk control, retention, and noninsurance risk transfer usually has fewer and smaller losses than do other insureds. Therefore, insurers are likely to generate better loss ratios and underwriting results by insuring policyholders having sound risk management programs. Consequently, such insureds are often able to obtain broader coverage at lower premiums than insureds who do not practice risk management.

By diminishing uncertainty of future losses from new business activities, risk management increases opportunities for the insured. The possibility of future losses tends to make many business owners and executives reluctant to undertake activities they consider to be risky. This reluctance deprives the business of the benefits that undertaking such activities could bring. A business that has an effective risk management program is better prepared to seek opportunities that could increase its profits. For example, if a business is confident it has appropriately managed its present property and liability loss exposures, it may consider proposals to manufacture a new product or expand its present sales territory that it otherwise would not.

Risk management also leads to achievement of business goals through better management of large loss exposures, and it helps organizations achieve their business and financial goals in a cost-effective manner. Risk management techniques help minimize the chance that a business would face a disruption or would have to absorb a large loss caused by a loss exposure. As a result, profits could be increased because of the reduced expenses. For example, a firm may reduce its insurance costs because the risk manager chooses to retain a loss exposure instead of insuring it.

Benefits of Risk Management to Individuals and Families

Like businesses, individuals and families benefit from effective risk management.

Risk management helps individuals and families cope more effectively with financial disasters that may otherwise cause a greatly reduced standard of living, personal bankruptcy, or family discord. Additionally, it helps them continue their activities following an accident or other loss, reducing inconvenience.

Risk management provides individuals and families greater peace of mind because they know that their loss exposures are under control. It also reduces expenses by handling loss exposures in the most economical fashion.

Risk management enables individuals and families to take more chances and make more aggressive decisions on ventures with the potential for profit, such as investing in the stock market, changing careers, or starting a part-time business. Though this may seem inconsistent with the purpose of risk management, such decisions can have long-term value when made with a full knowledge of costs and potential benefits.

Benefits of Risk Management to Society

By helping themselves through effective risk management, businesses, individuals, and families also benefit society.

Risk management can help reduce the number of persons dependent on society for support, because businesses and families plan for financial crises. For example, families who buy flood insurance need less help from charitable agencies or the government for federal flood relief after a flood event.

Risk management also results in fewer disruptions in the economic and social environment. Organizations and families that practice risk management are not subject to the big and sudden expense of bearing the cost of a loss.

In addition, economic growth can be stimulated by effective risk management. Because fewer and less costly losses result, funds are available for other uses, such as investment.

Benefits of Risk Management to Insurers

From an insurer's point of view, risk management is beneficial in many ways. Risk management creates a positive effect on an insurer's underwriting results, loss ratio, and overall profitability because insureds who practice sound risk management tend to experience fewer or less severe insured losses than those who do not.

Consumers of insurance who practice risk management are generally more knowledgeable about handling loss exposures than consumers who don't practice risk management. They are likely to combine insurance with other techniques for handling loss exposures, and therefore may incur and submit fewer claims.

Risk management also stimulates insurers to create innovative insurance products and maintain competitive prices and services. Professional risk managers seek to get the most for their insurance dollars and are often willing to pay higher premiums in exchange for greater insurance value. As a result, these risk managers may encourage insurers to be more innovative and competitive in the products and services they provide.

APPLYING THE RISK MANAGEMENT PROCESS

By applying the risk management process, insurance professionals can recommend the most appropriate risk management techniques for their customers to use.

Risk management programs for organizations can be quite sophisticated. These programs become more complex as organizations increase in size and their loss exposures become more extensive and complicated. However, even typical households face many loss exposures, such as various property and liability exposures from home and automobile ownership. A family scenario, including the loss exposures to be treated, facilitates an uncomplicated application of the risk management process.

Tony and Maria

Tony and Maria both work outside their home, and they have three school-aged children. They own two automobiles and a home with a pool, have a modest savings account, and have invested in the stock market. After attending a seminar at his company on risk management, Tony decided that the family should initiate a risk management program of its own. To do so, Tony knew that the family must follow these steps in the risk management process:

- Identify the family's loss exposures
- Analyze the loss exposures
- Examine the feasibility of risk management techniques
- Select risk management techniques that are appropriate for the family
- Implement the selected techniques
- Monitor and revise the family's risk management program

Identifying and Analyzing Loss Exposures

Tony and Maria identified loss exposures by listing the exposures they could think of and then inspecting their home, looking for other exposures they had not yet considered. For example, when Tony spotted his son's hockey stick, he realized that they have a liability exposure arising from the children's various athletic activities. His daughter's saxophone in her bedroom reminded Tony that the saxophone was not specifically insured and that they did not have the funds readily available to replace it if it were stolen or damaged. As Tony viewed their swimming pool full of neighborhood children, he realized that they needed higher liability limits than their current homeowners policy provided.

After physically inspecting their home and property, Maria called their insurance agent and obtained a household inventory form that they used to inventory their household contents and other possessions to determine their property loss exposures. The agent also sent them a survey to complete, which they used to list potential liability exposures for the family.

Maria and Tony then analyzed all the loss exposures they had identified and attempted to determine which ones could cause the most frequent or most severe losses.

Examining, Selecting, and Implementing Risk Management Techniques

After identifying and analyzing their property and liability exposures, Tony and Maria's third step was to examine risk management techniques. Tony knew from the seminar that the possible techniques include avoidance, risk control, noninsurance risk transfer, and retention, as well as insurance.

In an attempt to practice sound risk control, Tony and Maria installed deadbolt locks on all their doors and locks on all their windows. They also installed smoke detectors in several places in their home, and they are contemplating installing a burglar alarm system if they can find one that is both effective and affordable.

Tony and Maria explored noninsurance risk transfer by considering leasing a car, but they found that they would still be responsible for all liability connected with the use of the auto and would therefore still have to purchase insurance. They decided noninsurance risk transfer was not a good risk management technique.

Because Tony and Maria do not have much disposable income after they pay their mortgage, car payments, and other household bills each month, they know that they must rely heavily on insurance to cover their loss exposures. Although they cannot afford to retain a large amount of their loss exposure, they did raise the deductibles on both their homeowners and personal auto policies from $250 to $500, thereby reducing their premiums.

They decided not to specifically insure their daughter's saxophone because their homeowners policy already covered it for fire, theft, lightning, and other causes of loss. They also decided to apply the retention technique if their daughter simply lost or damaged the saxophone; in other words, they would replace the saxophone from their personal funds, make their daughter earn money to replace it, or choose not to buy a new one.

Furthermore, they decided to purchase an umbrella policy to cover large liability losses such as those that might arise from use of autos, the children's sporting activities, or the pool exposure. The increased deductibles and retention of the property loss exposures for the saxophone were about all the retention Tony and Maria thought they could handle. Thus, as in most households, insurance will play a dominant role in treating loss exposures for the Garcia family.

By installing locks and smoke detectors, purchasing umbrella insurance, and deciding to retain some loss exposures, the Garcias effectively completed the fourth and fifth steps in the risk management process: selecting and implementing their risk management techniques.

Monitoring Results and Revising the Risk Management Program

The last step in Tony and Maria's risk management process is to periodically monitor and modify their program. For a family, an annual review of the program is probably sufficient unless the family's circumstances change significantly.

An ideal time for Tony and Maria to do another physical inspection and inventory would be at the renewal of their homeowners policy or if either Tony or Maria changes jobs, receives a large bonus, receives a salary increase, or purchases any type of high-value property.

When Tony first began to monitor their risk management program, he realized that they had neglected to consider their net income loss exposures, such as death, illness, injury, or unemployment. Tony and Maria immediately took steps to modify their risk management program to include their net income loss exposures and thus began the risk management process with exposure identification and analysis all over again.

Apply Your Knowledge

Six months after implementing their risk management program, Tony and Maria considered building a new house in a neighborhood that is next to a river. Maria's elderly mother lives in that neighborhood, and moving there would allow them to help her more readily should an emergency or another need arise. However, Tony and Maria are concerned because this new neighborhood has a history of flooding in the spring and late summer.

Evaluate each of these risk management techniques, and explain how each technique could apply to Tony and Maria's potential flood loss exposure:

- Avoidance
- Loss prevention or loss reduction
- Insurance
- Retention

Feedback: These answers provide examples of how these techniques could apply, but other answers may be acceptable as well:

Avoidance—Tony and Maria could decide not to build a house in that location. Instead, they might build in a neighborhood that is not subject to flooding but is still reasonably near Maria's mother's home.

Loss prevention or reduction—Tony and Maria might consider building the house on a built-up lot or building it according to a plan with an elevated first floor and no basement to prevent or reduce flood damage.

Insurance—Tony and Maria could buy federal flood insurance and accept the possibility that their property may flood, knowing that the insurance would pay most of their loss.

Retention—Choosing to retain the entire flood risk would be a poor risk management decision, as Tony and Maria could lose the entire value of their home and personal property. However, Tony and Maria could buy flood insurance subject to a larger deductible (compared with their deductible for other perils) to enable them to save money on the cost of insurance. To improve their risk management program, Tony and Maria could create a special savings account and have money deducted from their paychecks until they have sufficient savings to fund the uninsured portion of their flood loss exposure.

SUMMARY

Risk management can differ markedly for individuals, small organizations, and large organizations. At whatever level it is practiced, risk management is aimed at dealing economically with risk, whether through an individual's informal efforts or through an organizations's formalized risk management program. Traditionally, risk management has been concerned almost exclusively with pure risk, while enterprise-wide risk management is concerned with all risks, pure and speculative, that an organization faces.

The risk management process can be used to help organizations and families deal with loss exposures efficiently and effectively. Physical inspections, loss exposure surveys, and loss history analyses can be used to identify loss exposures—the first step in the risk management process. To analyze loss exposures, the second step in the process, probable frequency and severity of the losses and the effect on the activities, objectives, and finances of the organization or household must be determined.

The third step in the risk management process is examining the feasibility of risk management techniques. These techniques are categorized as risk control and risk financing. Risk control includes avoidance, loss prevention, loss reduction, separation, and duplication. Risk financing includes retention and transfer (both insurance and noninsurance).

The fourth step in the risk management process is to select the most appropriate risk management technique(s) based on financial criteria and guidelines. The fifth step is implementation of the selected techniques and includes the decisions to be made and by whom, communication of the information, and cost allocation of the program. The final step involves monitoring the results and revising the program as needed by restarting the entire process.

Risk management's numerous benefits to businesses, individuals, and families include peace-of-mind, improved access to affordable insurance, cost-effective achievement of goals, and the ability to take more risk and explore greater opportunities. When individuals, families, and organizations practice risk management, society benefits from the reduced need for social services after losses, improved social/economic environment, and encouragement of economic growth. Insurers benefit from improved profitability, more knowledgeable insurance consumers, and being stimulated to innovate and create competitive products and services.

Although businesses are the primary users of formal risk management programs, individuals and families can also benefit from applying risk management to their loss exposures. A risk management program for a large business can be complex, but one for a family can be simple and is well worth the time and effort to implement.

8

Loss Exposures

Educational Objectives

After learning the content of this assignment, you should be able to:

▷ Describe property loss exposures in terms of assets exposed to loss, causes of loss, financial consequences of loss, and parties affected by loss.

▷ Explain how legal liability to pay damages can be based on torts, contracts, or statutes.

▷ Describe liability loss exposures in terms of assets exposed to loss, causes of loss, and financial consequences of loss.

▷ Describe personnel loss exposures in terms of assets exposed to loss, causes of loss, and financial consequences of loss.

▷ Describe net income loss exposures in terms of assets exposed to loss, causes of loss, and financial consequences of loss.

▷ Describe the characteristics of an ideally insurable loss exposure.

Loss Exposures

8

PROPERTY LOSS EXPOSURES

The elements of a property loss exposure are important to an insurance professional because they provide a framework for analyzing loss exposures that may be handled through appropriate risk management techniques.

There are three important elements of property loss exposures:

- Assets exposed to property loss—The types of property that may be exposed to loss, damage, or destruction.
- Causes of loss—Those that may result in property being lost, damaged, or destroyed.
- Financial consequences—Those consequences that may result from a property loss. A property loss can be the cause of a net income loss; however, that is considered a separate loss exposure.

In addition to describing these elements of property loss exposures, this section discusses the parties who may be affected when property is lost, damaged, or destroyed.

Assets Exposed to Property Loss

An asset is property, which is any item with value. Individuals, families, and businesses own and use property, depend on it as a source of income or services, and rely on its value. Property can decline in value—or even become worthless—if it is lost, damaged, or destroyed. Different kinds of property have different qualities that affect the owner's or user's exposure to loss.

Two basic types of property are real property and personal property. Insurance practitioners further divide these kinds of property into several categories:

- Buildings
- Personal property contained in buildings
- Money and securities
- Vehicles and watercraft
- Property in transit

These categories overlap to some extent. For example, vehicles, when carried on trucks, can be property in transit. These categories are listed separately here because they represent types of property for which specific forms of insurance have been developed.

8.3

Buildings

Buildings are more than bricks and mortar. Most buildings also contain plumbing, wiring, and heating and air conditioning equipment, which can lead to leaks, electrical fires, and explosions. Most buildings also contain basic portable equipment, such as fire extinguishers and lawn mowers, that is required to service the building and surrounding land. Under most insurance policies, such equipment is considered part of the building. Property that is permanently attached to the structure, such as wall-to-wall carpeting, built-in appliances, or boilers and machinery, is generally considered part of the building as well.

Boilers and machinery constitute a special class of property. They are often affixed to a building in such a manner that they become a permanent part of the building and are considered to be **fixtures**. This class of property includes any of these types of equipment:

Fixture

Any personal property affixed to real property in such a way as to become part of the real property.

- Steam boilers (large water tanks heated by burning gas, oil, or coal to produce steam for heating or to produce power)
- Unfired pressure vessels, such as air tanks
- Refrigerating and air conditioning systems
- Mechanical equipment, such as compressors and turbines
- Production equipment
- Electrical equipment

Boilers and machinery share these two characteristics:

- They are susceptible to explosion or breakdown that can result in serious losses to the unit and to persons and property nearby.
- They are less likely to have explosions or breakdowns if they are periodically inspected and properly maintained.

Personal Property Contained in Buildings

The contents of a typical home include personal property such as furniture, clothing, electronic equipment, jewelry, paintings, and other personal possessions. The contents of a commercial building may include these items:

- Furniture, such as desks or file cabinets in an office
- Machinery and equipment, such as cash registers in a supermarket
- Stock, such as groceries in a store

Although most policies use the term "personal property" (which is all property other than land and property attached to the land, such as buildings) to refer to the contents of a building, many insurance practitioners and policyholders use the term "contents" as a matter of convenience and common practice. Property insurance policies refer to personal property, rather than contents, because the property is often covered even when it is not literally contained in the building. When the contents of a commercial building are involved, policies generally use the term "business personal property."

Money and Securities

For insurance purposes, money and securities are separate from other types of contents because their characteristics present special problems. **Money** and **securities** are highly susceptible to loss by theft. Cash is particularly difficult to trace because it can be readily spent. In contrast, other types of property must be sold for cash before the thief can make a profit. Money and securities are also lightweight, easily concealed, and easy to transport.

In addition to being susceptible to theft, money and securities can be quickly destroyed in the event of a fire. For example, unless a store owner makes a bank deposit every night after the store closes, the store owner could lose a considerable amount of currency and checks in a fire.

Money

Currency, coins, bank notes, and sometimes traveler's checks, credit card slips, and money orders held for sale to the public.

Securities

Written instruments representing either money or other property, such as stocks and bonds.

Vehicles and Watercraft

The primary purpose of most vehicles and watercraft is to move people or property, and this movement exposes vehicles and watercraft to several causes of loss. Vehicles may be grouped by vehicle type, by operator type, by typical usage, or by a combination of these characteristics. No matter which classifications are used, some vehicles (such as snowmobiles or utility vehicles) fit into more than one category, depending on the purpose for which they are owned and used. However, these categories are useful in identifying property loss exposures:

- Autos and other highway vehicles
- Mobile equipment
- Recreational vehicles

In insurance terminology, the word "**auto**" can also include such diverse vehicles as fire engines, ambulances, motorcycles, and camping trailers. **Mobile equipment** may be damaged in a highway collision, but the most frequent exposures to loss involve off-road situations. In some cases, the owners of **recreational vehicles** face exposures to loss both on and off the road.

Watercraft are exposed to special perils not encountered in other means of transit. Those perils include extreme weather conditions that can create rougher seas than the craft can handle; poor navigation, resulting in striking the ground or another obstacle; and, depending on the shipping route, piracy.

Auto

As defined in commercial general liability and auto forms, a land motor vehicle, trailer, or semitrailer designed for travel on public roads, including attached machinery or equipment; or any other land vehicle that is subject to a compulsory or financial responsibility law or other motor vehicle insurance law in the state where it is licensed or principally garaged.

Mobile equipment

Various types of vehicles designed for use principally off public roads, such as bulldozers and cranes.

Property in Transit

A great deal of property is transported by truck, but property is also moved in cars, buses, trains, airplanes, and watercraft. When a conveyance containing cargo overturns or is involved in a collision, the cargo can also be damaged. In addition, cargo can be destroyed without damage to the transporting vehicle

Recreational vehicle

A vehicle used for sports and recreational activities, such as a dune buggy, all-terrain vehicle, or dirt bike.

or watercraft. Liquids can leak out, fragile articles can be jostled during transit, and perishables can melt or spoil.

When property is damaged or lost in transit, it must be replaced. Delays often result, because replacement property may have to be shipped from the location of the original shipment. The property owner may also incur expense to move damaged property.

Property being transported by watercraft could be lost entirely if the watercraft were to sink. Even more so than other property, ocean cargoes fluctuate in value according to their location. If the watercraft cannot reach its intended destination and the cargo must be sold in a different port, the price received for the cargo might be less than the price expected at the original destination.

Causes of Property Loss

Peril
The cause of a loss.

Causes of loss (or **perils**) include fire, lightning, windstorm, hail, and theft. Most causes of loss adversely affect property and leave it in an altered state. A fire can reduce a building to a heap of rubble. A collision can change a car into twisted scrap. Some causes of loss do not alter the property itself, but they affect a person's ability to possess or use the property. For example, property lost or stolen can still be usable, but not by its rightful owner.

The terms "peril" and "hazard" are often confused. As stated, a peril is a cause of loss. Fire, theft, collision, and flood are examples of perils that cause property losses. (Many property insurance policies use the term "cause of loss" instead of peril.)

A hazard is anything that increases the frequency or the severity of a loss. These are two examples:

- Careless smoking practices are a fire hazard because they increase the frequency of fires.
- Keeping large amounts of money in a cash register overnight is a theft hazard affecting both the frequency and the severity of loss.

Financial Consequences of Property Losses

When a property loss occurs, the property is reduced in value. The reduction in value can be measured in different ways, sometimes with differing results. If the property can be repaired or restored, the reduction in value can be measured by the cost of the repair or the restoration. Property that must be replaced has no remaining worth, unless some salvageable items can be sold. Consider these examples:

- A fence worth $7,000 was damaged by a car, and the fence owner has to pay $2,000 to have the damage repaired. The fence owner has incurred a partial loss that reduced the fence's value by $2,000.
- A camera worth $400 is run over by a truck. The camera owner has incurred a total loss that reduced the camera's value by $400.

If property is lost, is stolen, or otherwise disappears, its value to the owner is reduced just as though it had been destroyed and retained no salvage value. A further reduction in value might occur if repaired property is worth less than it would have been if it had never been damaged. This is true for items such as fine paintings and other art objects. Many collectibles are valuable largely because they are in mint or original condition. An object that has been repaired after damage from a tear, a scratch, or fire is no longer in that unspoiled condition, and its value will decline. The owner faces loss in the form of the cost to repair the object, as well as a reduction in value because of the altered condition.

Property may have different values, depending on the method by which the value is determined. The most common valuation measures used in insurance policies are replacement cost and actual cash value (ACV). In certain situations, however, other valuation measures are used, such as agreed value.

Parties Affected by Property Losses

Parties that may be affected by a property loss include these:

- Property owners
- Secured lenders of money to the property owner
- Property holders

Property Owners

The party that is affected most when property is lost, damaged, or destroyed is usually the owner of the property. If the property has some value, the owner of the property incurs a financial loss to repair or replace it. In a supermarket fire, for example, the store's owner could incur a considerable financial loss because it had to rebuild the store and restock the shelves.

Secured Lenders

When money is borrowed to finance the purchase of a car, the lender usually acquires some conditional rights to the car, such as the right to repossess the car if the car's owner (the borrower) fails to make loan payments. This right gives the lender security. Such a lender is therefore called a secured lender or a secured creditor. When a person or business borrows money to buy a home or a building and the property serves as security for the loan, the secured

Mortgagee

A lender in a mortgage arrangement, such as a bank or another financing institution.

Mortgagor

The person or organization that borrows money from a mortgagee to finance the purchase of real property.

lender is called a **mortgagee** (or mortgageholder), and the borrower is called a **mortgagor**.

When property is used to secure a loan, the lender is exposed to loss. Returning to the supermarket fire example, if the store owner had a mortgage on its supermarket building, the mortgagee would lose the security for the mortgage loan if the building burned. Similarly, if a financed car is destroyed in an accident, no vehicle would be available for the lender to repossess in the event that the owner defaulted on the loan. Property insurance policies generally protect the secured lender's interest in the financed property by naming the lender on the insurance policy and by giving the lender certain rights under the policy.

Property Holders

Bailee

The party temporarily possessing the personal property in a bailment.

Bailees are responsible for safekeeping property they do not own. Dry cleaners, repair shops, common carriers, and many other businesses temporarily hold property belonging to others. To estimate its property loss exposures, such a business has to consider not only its own property, but also the property held for others.

Apply Your Knowledge

Sam rents retail space in a strip mall, in which he operates a florist shop. His employees make deliveries with two vans owned by the shop. How should an insurance professional analyze each of the three elements of the florist shop's property loss exposures?

Feedback:

- Assets exposed to property loss—Sam has exposure in each of the property types, except for a building. Because he rents the retail space from which his store operates, he does not have the exposure of a building being damaged. However, he does have personal property contained in the rented space of the building. Specifically, he is likely to have equipment to run his business, such as refrigerated display cabinets, telephones, file cabinets, computer equipment, a cash register, and an inventory of flowers and the tools and supplies to arrange and display them. Sam also has exposure with money and securities, as he collects payments from customers. He has exposure related to the vehicles used to deliver flowers as well. The vehicles have a high value and could be expensive to repair or replace. Finally, he has exposure connected to property in transit. The flowers are valuable inventory, and if they are damaged in transit to a customer, Sam will probably have to replace them at his expense.

- Causes of loss—Some of the perils include fire, theft, and collision. Fire could damage or destroy all the types of property at the store or in a van. Theft could also involve all of the individual types of property, including money and securities in particular, personal property in the building, vehicles, and property in transit. Another peril is collision of a van with another object, which could damage both the vehicle and the property in transit in the same accident.

- Financial consequences—Each type of property, if damaged or destroyed, could incur a reduction in value. If property is damaged, the cost to repair or restore it is often the amount of reduction in value. For example, if Sam's van were involved in a collision while making a delivery, it may be possible to have it repaired for a cost that is less than the value of the van; therefore, it would not be a total loss. The value of the van after the collision would be reduced until repairs were completed. The flower arrangements in the van at the time of the collision may be difficult to repair. Consequently, it may be more cost effective to consider them destroyed and replace them. The damaged flowers would have lost all value.

THE BASIS FOR LEGAL LIABILITY

An understanding of legal liability is essential to recognizing liability loss exposures. Although complex legal questions require the professional expertise of an attorney, knowledge of some fundamental legal terms and concepts is essential for anyone dealing with liability loss exposures or liability insurance.

Legal liability can arise based on torts, contracts, and statutes. Before examining torts, contracts, and statutes, it is necessary to understand these legal foundations: the general sources of law, the distinction between civil and criminal law, and the concept of damages. See the exhibit "Legal Basis of a Liability Claim."

Legal liability
The legally enforceable obligation of a person or an organization to pay a sum of money (called damages) to another person or organization.

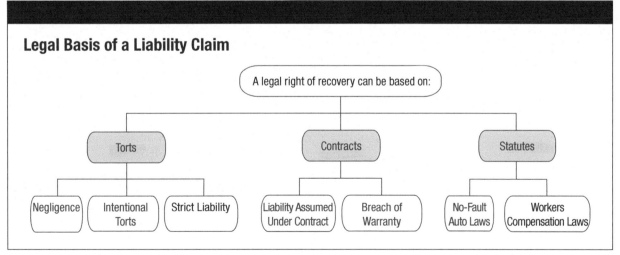

Legal Basis of a Liability Claim

A legal right of recovery can be based on:

- Torts
  - Negligence
  - Intentional Torts
  - Strict Liability
- Contracts
  - Liability Assumed Under Contract
  - Breach of Warranty
- Statutes
  - No-Fault Auto Laws
  - Workers Compensation Laws

[DA02531]

Legal Foundations

Laws exist in a civilized society to enforce certain standards of conduct. Laws generally require conduct that makes the world safer and more secure. Laws accomplish this objective by holding people responsible for their actions. The legal foundations of sources of law, criminal law, civil law, and damages explain, in part, how laws enforce responsibility.

Sources of Law

The legal system in the United States derives essentially from the Constitution, which is the source of constitutional law; legislative bodies, which are the source of statutory law; and court decisions, which are the source of common law.

Constitutional law

The Constitution itself and all the decisions of the Supreme Court that involve the Constitution.

The Constitution is the supreme law in the U.S., and it outlines the respective powers of its legislative, executive, and judicial branches. With its amendments, the Constitution guarantees to all citizens certain fundamental rights, such as freedom of speech and freedom from unreasonable searches and seizure. All other laws must conform to **constitutional law**. The courts interpret the Constitution to decide constitutional issues. If the U.S. Supreme Court decides that a particular law conflicts with the Constitution, that law is invalidated. Each state also has a constitution and some type of supreme court to hear appeals on matters of state law. States must ultimately follow the U.S. Constitution.

Statute

A written law passed by a legislative body at either the federal or state level.

National, state, and local legislatures enact **statutes** to deal with perceived problems. At the national level, any member of the U.S. Senate or House of Representatives may introduce a bill. If the bill receives a majority vote in both the Senate and the House and the president signs it, the bill becomes law. State legislatures also make new laws in similar fashion. Laws made by local governments are often called ordinances. Collectively, these formal enactments are referred to as **statutory law**.

Statutory law

The formal laws, or statutes, enacted by federal, state, or local legislative bodies.

Some federal, state, and local government agencies have regulatory powers derived from authority granted by legislative bodies. These regulatory agencies issue detailed rules and regulations covering a particular public concern. They also render decisions on the application of these rules and regulations in certain cases.

Common law (case law)

Laws that develop out of court decisions in particular cases and establish precedents for future cases.

In contrast to statutory law, common law has evolved in the courts. When the king's judges began hearing disputes in medieval England, they had little basis for their decisions except common sense. However, each decision became a precedent for similar cases that followed it. Gradually, certain principles evolved over time that became known as **common law (case law)**. These common-law principles guided judges in the English colonies in America as well. When neither constitutional nor statutory law applies, judges still rely on precedents of previous cases to reach their decisions.

Criminal Law and Civil Law

The U.S. legal system makes an important distinction between criminal law and civil law. Legal cases related to insurance usually involve civil law.

Criminal law applies to wrongful acts that society deems so harmful to the public welfare that the government takes the responsibility for prosecuting and punishing the wrongdoers. For example, criminal laws prohibit robbery, arson, and driving while intoxicated. Crimes are punishable by fines, imprisonment, or, in some states, death. When a crime occurs, the police investigate and, if sufficient evidence is found, criminal charges are brought on behalf of the state against the accused wrongdoer.

Civil law deals with the rights and responsibilities of citizens with respect to one another. Civil law proceedings provide a forum for hearing disputes between private parties and rendering a decision binding on all parties. This procedure enables individuals to protect themselves against infringement of their rights by others. Civil law also protects contract rights. People and businesses are more willing to make agreements or contracts with one another when they know that the contracts will be enforceable. If a party does not honor its contract with another party, the other party can ask the court to enforce compliance or assess damages.

An act can have both criminal and civil law consequences. For example, Carole was returning from a business trip when her car was broadsided by another vehicle. Beyond the damage to her car, her injuries required medical care costing thousands of dollars, and she missed two weeks of work. Following the accident investigation, the other driver was criminally charged and convicted of driving while intoxicated. Carole's auto insurer paid most of her medical and auto physical damage bills. However, she also brought a civil suit against the other driver for her lost wages. Based on the merits of the case, the jury decided in her favor, and the court ordered the other driver to pay an amount equal to the income she had lost.

Damages

A person must sustain actual harm for a liability loss to result in a valid claim. For example, passengers injured in an auto accident can collect damages from the driver only if they can prove they actually suffered some harm as a result of the driver's actions. Perhaps they had to be treated in the hospital emergency room, their clothing was ruined, or they could not go to their jobs and thus lost a day's pay. To those who can show that actual harm or injury was suffered because of the driver's actions, the court may award damages that the driver will have to pay.

There are two main categories of damages: compensatory damages and punitive damages. Compensatory damages are intended to compensate the victim for the harm actually suffered. An award of compensatory damages is the amount of money that has been judged to equal the victim's loss, and it is the amount the party responsible for the loss will have to pay. Compensatory

Criminal law

The branch of the law that imposes penalties for wrongs against society.

Civil law

A classification of law that applies to legal matters not governed by criminal law and that protects rights and provides remedies for breaches of duties owed to others.

damages include both special damages and general damages. In addition, the court could award punitive damages (exemplary damages).

Torts

Tort

A wrongful act or an omission, other than a crime or a breach of contract, that invades a legally protected right.

Tort law

The branch of civil law that deals with civil wrongs other than breaches of contract.

A **tort** is any wrongful act, other than a crime or breach of contract, committed by one party against another. Crimes differ from torts, because criminal law allows the state to prosecute and civil law does not. Tort law is enforced by the injured party bringing a private lawsuit against the alleged wrongdoer. The central concern of **tort law**, which deals with civil wrongs other than breaches of contract, is determining responsibility for injury or damage. Although largely modified or restated in statutes, tort law is still based mainly on common law.

A person who is legally responsible for an injury may be compelled to compensate the victim only if there is some standard for assigning that responsibility. Under tort law, an individual or organization can face a claim for legal liability on the basis of negligence, intentional torts, or strict liability. See the exhibit "Types of Torts."

Types of Torts

	Description	Element(s)	Examples
Negligence	Failure to act in a prudent manner	• Duty owed to another • Breach of that duty • Breach of duty is proximate cause of injury or damage • Injury or damage	• Driving while intoxicated and causing an accident • Allowing a pet dog to run loose and bite a child
Intentional Torts	Deliberate acts that cause harm	Deliberate act (other than a breach of contract) that causes harm to another person	• Assault • Battery • Libel • Slander • False arrest • Invasion of privacy
Strict Liability	Inherently dangerous activities	Inherently dangerous activities or dangerously defective products that result in injury or harm	• Owning a wild animal • Blasting operations

[DA02532]

Negligence

Negligence occurs when a person or an organization fails to exercise the level of care that a reasonably prudent person would have exercised under similar circumstances. The greatest number of liability cases arise from negligence. Tort law gives injured parties the right to seek compensation if they can demonstrate that someone else's negligence led to their injuries. The party seeking compensation is referred to as the plaintiff, and the party from whom the plaintiff is seeking damages is referred to as the defendant.

A liability judgment based on negligence requires proof of four elements. If any one of these elements is missing, the plaintiff cannot prove that the defendant was negligent:

- The defendant owed a legal duty of care to the plaintiff—The first element of negligence is that a person or an organization must have a duty to act (or not to act) that constitutes a responsibility to another party. For example, the driver of a car has a duty to operate the car safely.

- The defendant breached the duty of care owed to the plaintiff—A breach of duty is the failure to exercise a reasonable degree of care expected in a particular situation. For example, if a tank explodes, the fact that a storage tank had been filled beyond its listed capacity could indicate that a defendant failed to act reasonably and breached its duty to provide safe conditions.

- The defendant's negligent act was the **proximate cause** of the plaintiff's injury or damage—A finding of negligence also requires that the breach of duty initiate an unbroken chain of events leading to the injury. The breach of the duty must be the proximate cause of the injury. For example, patrons of a night club were injured by other patrons' panicking when part of a stage caught fire. The injured patrons would have to prove that the club owner's breach of its duty to provide safe conditions was the proximate cause of their injuries.

- The plaintiff suffered actual injury or damage—The fourth element of negligence requires that the claimant must suffer definite injury or harm. For example, passengers may claim a driver negligently caused an accident, but unless they actually suffered an injury, such as medical expenses, lost wages, or pain and suffering, they will not have a valid claim.

A person or an organization whose conduct is proved to be negligent is generally responsible for the consequences. This party is called the **tortfeasor**, the wrongdoer, or the negligent party. All of these terms refer to a party who does something that a reasonable person would not do (or fails to do something that a reasonable person would do) under similar circumstances.

In addition to the person who actually commits the act, other persons or organizations may be held responsible for the tortfeasor's action. This responsibility is called **vicarious liability**. Vicarious liability often arises in business situations from the relationship between employer and employee. An employee performing work-related activities is generally acting on behalf of

Negligence

The failure to exercise the degree of care that a reasonable person in a similar situation would exercise to avoid harming others.

Proximate cause

A cause that, in a natural and continuous sequence unbroken by any new and independent cause, produces an event and without which the event would not have happened.

Tortfeasor

A person or an organization that has committed a tort.

Vicarious liability

A legal responsibility that occurs when one party is held liable for the actions of a subordinate or an associate because of the relationship between the two parties.

Intentional tort

A tort committed by a person who foresees (or should be able to foresee) that his or her act will harm another person.

Assault

The threat of force against another person that creates a well-founded fear of imminent harmful or offensive contact.

Battery

Intentional harmful or offensive physical contact with another person without legal justification.

Defamation

A false written or oral statement that harms another's reputation.

Slander

A defamatory statement expressed by speech.

Libel

A defamatory statement expressed in writing.

False arrest

The seizure or forcible restraint of a person without legal authority.

Invasion of privacy

An encroachment on another person's right to be left alone.

Strict liability (absolute liability)

Liability imposed by a court or by a statute in the absence of fault when harm results from activities or conditions that are extremely dangerous, unnatural, ultrahazardous, extraordinary, abnormal, or inappropriate.

the employer. Therefore, the employer can be vicariously liable for the actions of the employee. If, for example, an employee drives a customer to a meeting and negligently causes an accident in which the customer is injured, both the employee and the employer could be held liable for the customer's injuries. Responsibility would not shift from the employee to the employer but rather could extend to include the employer.

Intentional Torts

An **intentional tort** is a deliberate act (other than a breach of contract) that causes harm to another person, regardless of whether the harm is intended. Assault and battery are common examples of intentional torts. **Assault** is an intentional threat of bodily harm under circumstances that create a fear of imminent harm. **Battery** is any unlawful and unprivileged touching of another person.

Another common example of an intentional tort is defamation. **Defamation** includes both slander and libel. **Slander** is a spoken, untrue statement about another person. **Libel** most often occurs when someone prints and distributes an untrue statement about another person that damages the person's reputation. However, libel can take place through any medium, such as radio, television, film, or the Internet. As a rule, the law affords public figures less protection against libel and slander than ordinary persons except when a false statement is also malicious. For defamation to occur, someone other than the defamed person must read or hear the false statement. Moreover, true statements are not defamatory.

The intentional tort of **false arrest** presents a potential problem for retail stores. False arrest can occur when a store employee detains a customer suspected of shoplifting. If it is later determined that the customer had not stolen any merchandise, the detainment is a false arrest that inconveniences and embarrasses the customer.

Liability for the intentional tort of **invasion of privacy** can arise from the unauthorized release of confidential information, the illegal use of hidden microphones or other surveillance equipment, an unauthorized search, or the public disclosure of private facts.

Strict Liability

Strict liability (absolute liability) is the legal liability arising from inherently dangerous activities or dangerously defective products that result in injury or harm to another, regardless of how much care was used in the activity.

Although most liability cases arise from negligence and some arise from intentional torts, liability under tort law is not entirely limited to cases of injury caused by negligent or deliberate conduct. In situations involving inherently dangerous activities, tort law can give an injured person a right of recovery without having to prove negligence or intent. Such inherently dangerous activities can give rise to strict liability for any injury regardless of the intent or the carefulness of the person held liable. The situation itself, rather than the person's conduct, becomes the standard for determining liability.

For example, the owner of a wild animal is liable for any injury the animal inflicts, regardless of the precautions the owner may have taken. Blasting operations present an exposure to strict liability for businesses. The mere fact that the business conducts blasting operations is enough to make the owners of the business liable for any injuries or damage that results.

Contracts

Contract law enables an injured party to seek recovery because another party has breached a duty voluntarily accepted in a contract. A contract is a legally enforceable agreement between two or more parties. If one party fails to honor the contract, the other may sue to enforce it. In such a case, it is the specific contract, rather than the law in general, that the court interprets. Two areas of contract law that are often the basis of legal liability for bodily injury or property damage to another are liability assumed under contract and breach of warranty.

Parties to a contract sometimes find it convenient for one party to assume the financial consequences of certain types of liability faced by the other. For example, the owner of a building and a contractor make a contract in which the contractor accepts responsibility for certain actions of a subcontractor. If one of the specified actions of the subcontractor injures a customer and the customer sues the owner, then the contractor will pay any damages owed to the customer because of the subcontractor's action. Such arrangements, called **hold-harmless agreements**, are common in construction and service businesses. They are called hold-harmless agreements because they require one party to "hold harmless and indemnify" the other party against liability specified in the contract.

Hold-harmless agreement (or indemnity agreement)
A contractual provision that obligates one of the parties to assume the legal liability of another party.

The law of contracts also governs claims arising from breach of warranty. Contracts for sales of goods include **warranties**, or promises made by the seller. The law also implies certain warranties. A seller warrants, for example, that an item is fit for a particular purpose. If Juanita buys the hair conditioner recommended and sold by her beautician, she relies on the warranty that the conditioner will be good for her hair. If the conditioner damages her hair instead, the beautician (as well as the manufacturer) could be held liable for a breach of warranty. The buyer does not have to prove negligence on the part of the seller. The fact that the product did not work shows that the contract was not fulfilled.

Warranty
A written or an oral statement in a contract that certain facts are true.

Statutes

Statutory liability is legal liability imposed by a statutory law. Although common law may cover a particular situation, statutory law may extend,

Statutory liability
Legal liability imposed by a specific statute or law.

restrict, or clarify the rights of injured parties in that situation. One reason for such legislation is to ensure adequate compensation for injuries without lengthy disputes over who is at fault. Examples of this kind of statutory liability involve no-fault auto laws and workers compensation laws. In these legal areas, a specific statute (rather than the common-law principles of torts) gives one party the right of recovery from another or restricts that right of recovery.

To reduce the number of lawsuits resulting from auto accidents, some states have enacted "no-fault" laws. These laws recognize the inevitability of auto accidents and restrict or eliminate the right to sue the other party in an accident, except in the more serious cases defined by that state's law. Victims with less serious injuries collect their out-of-pocket expenses from their own insurers without the need for expensive legal proceedings.

A similar concept of liability without regard to fault applies to workplace injuries. Each of the fifty states has a workers compensation statute. Such a statute eliminates an employee's right to sue the employer for most work-related injuries and also imposes on the employer automatic (strict) liability to pay specified benefits. In place of the right to sue for negligence, workers compensation laws create a system in which injured employees receive benefits specified in these laws. As long as the injury is work-related, the employer pays the specified benefits (such as medical, disability, and rehabilitation benefits) regardless of who is at fault.

Apply Your Knowledge

The Smiths were having an anniversary party at their home. They served beer and wine to their guests, including Barry, who drank too much wine. He missed a patio chair he was trying to sit in. He broke his wrist in his fall. He incurred thousands of dollars in medical bills and lost wages because of his injury. When he discovered the chair in question was rotten and would have fallen apart had he sat in it, he sued the Smiths, alleging negligence. Applying the four elements of negligence, are the Smiths likely to be found legally liable for Barry's injuries?

Feedback:

The Smiths did owe a legal duty of care to Barry because he was their guest at their party and on their premises. So Barry would likely be able to satisfy the requirements of the first element.

The second element requires the Smiths to have breached a duty of care to Barry. This may have occurred in two ways. First, the Smiths provided the wine Barry became intoxicated with. As the hosts for the party, the Smiths may be found to have failed to accurately monitor Barry's drinking and allowed him to become a danger to himself. Second, the chair was rotten because of poor maintenance and presented a dangerous condition. Both of these breached duties could be found to be failures to exercise the reasonable degree of care expected in this situation. So Barry would likely be able to satisfy the second element.

However, the third element requires that the breach of duty initiate an unbroken chain of events leading to the injury. That is, the breach of either duty owed must be the proximate cause of Barry's injury. Regarding the first duty, Barry is an adult and presumably capable of acting responsibly enough to avoid getting so intoxicated he is unable to perform the simple act of safely sitting down. Further, Barry drank the wine voluntarily and therefore his own negligence may break the chain of events of the first duty. Regarding the second duty, the chair may have been rotten and unable to support Barry's weight, but that is not what caused his injuries as he missed the chair in his fall. Barry may have difficulty proving the requirements of the third element have been met.

The fourth element requires Barry to have actually suffered damages. He has incurred thousands of dollars in medical expenses and lost wages because of his fall. Barry will likely be able to prove the fourth element is satisfied. Because Barry has to prevail on all four elements and the third element will likely not be found in his favor, he will probably not be able to prove that the Smiths were negligent.

LIABILITY LOSS EXPOSURES

Understanding the elements of liability loss exposures provides an essential foundation for managing them.

These are the three elements of liability loss exposures:

- Assets exposed to liability loss
- Causes of liability loss
- Financial consequences of liability loss

Assets Exposed to Liability Loss

The first element of liability loss exposures consists of assets exposed to liability losses. The asset can be anything of value an individual or organization owns. However, the asset that plaintiffs claim most frequently is money. Money can be used, for example, to make a payment of damages to a plaintiff or to pay attorneys' fees and other costs of defending against claims. Assets owned by an individual or organization, such as property (including buildings, automobiles, and furniture) and investments, can be sold and converted to money that can be used to make a payment to a plaintiff. Furthermore, a plaintiff can claim income that a defendant will receive in the future.

Causes of Liability Loss

The second element of liability loss exposures consists of the causes of liability losses. The cause of a liability loss is the initiation of a claim or lawsuit against an individual or organization by another party seeking damages or some other legal remedy. Even the threat of another party's initiating such a claim or suit can cause a liability loss in the form of costs an individual or organization incurs to investigate and, if necessary, settle the threatened liability claim or suit. Liability claims can arise from various activities. Common examples of such activities include these:

- Autos, watercraft, and other vehicles
- Premises
- Personal activities
- Business operations
- Completed operations
- Products
- Advertising
- Pollution
- Liquor
- Professional activities

Autos, Watercraft, and Other Vehicles

A significant liability loss exposure for almost all persons and businesses comes from the ownership, maintenance, and use of automobiles. In the United States, auto accidents produce the greatest number of liability claims. Even people or businesses that do not own an auto can be held vicariously liable for the operation of an auto by others. For example, an employer could be held liable for an auto accident caused by its employee making a sales call on a customer, whether the employee was driving his own vehicle or one owned by the employer.

Liability loss exposures are also created by owning and operating other conveyances, such as watercraft, aircraft, and recreational vehicles.

Premises

Anyone who owns or occupies real property has a premises liability loss exposure. If a visitor slips on an icy front porch and is injured, the homeowner may be held liable for the injury. A business has a similar loss exposure arising from its premises. For example, a grocery store will probably be held liable if a customer is injured after slipping and falling on a wet floor in the store.

Personal Activities

Individuals can become liable to others when engaged in a personal activity not business related and away from the defendant's premises. For example, a person could hit a golf ball off a tee at a golf course and strike and injure another golfer with the ball. The activity need not be recreational; it could involve, for instance, owning a dog that escapes from the owner's premises and bites a neighbor.

Business Operations

In terms of liability loss exposures, businesses must be concerned not only about the condition of their premises but also about their business operations. Whatever activity the business performs has the potential to cause harm to someone else. Many business operations occur away from the organization's premises. A plumbing contractor, for example, may start a fire in a customer's house while soldering a copper pipe. Similarly, a roofing contractor may drop debris from a ladder and injure a member of the customer's family. In both cases, the customer could make a liability claim against the contractor.

Completed Operations

Even after a plumber, an electrician, a painter, or another contractor completes a job and leaves the work site, a liability loss exposure remains. If faulty wiring or toxic paint leads to an injury, the person or business that performed the work may be liable. Considerable time could pass in the interim, but the person or business may still be held liable if faulty work created the condition that eventually caused the injury. If, for example, a homeowner could prove that a natural-gas explosion in her house was caused by the negligence of the contractor who installed her new furnace, the contractor may be liable for the resulting damage to the house.

Products

Liability resulting from products that cause bodily injury or property damage is a significant exposure for manufacturers. This exposure begins with the design of the product and might not end until the consumer properly disposes of the product. Millions of customers use or consume mass-produced products, foods, and pharmaceuticals. A prescription drug may be dangerous, but the danger might not be known for several years, after which it is too late to help those who have taken the drug.

Advertising

Businesses often include photographs of people using their products in their advertisements. If a local retailer cannot afford professional models, it might use pictures of people using its products or shopping in its store. Unless the retailer obtains proper permission, publishing the pictures could lead to a lawsuit alleging invasion of privacy. Using another company's trademarked slogan or advertisement can also generate a liability claim.

Pollution

Many types of products pollute the environment when they are discarded. In addition, the manufacture of some products creates contaminants that, if not disposed of properly, can cause environmental impairment, or pollution. If an explosion at an oil refinery polluted a nearby body of water, the refinery owner might have a liability loss. The Love Canal case in New York State remains a good example of how industrial products or wastes can have serious detrimental effects on the environment. Toxic wastes in the Love Canal area polluted the ground water and made the surrounding community a dangerous place to live. Cleanup costs and expenses to relocate persons living in the contaminated area can be enormous in such cases.

Liquor

The consumption, serving, and sale of alcohol can present liability loss exposures. Intoxicated persons can pose a threat to themselves as well as to others. Providers of alcohol can be held responsible for customers or guests who become intoxicated and injure someone while driving drunk. Both the drunk driver and the person who served the alcohol can be held legally liable. A business that sells or serves alcoholic beverages, therefore, has a significant liability loss exposure.

Professional Activities

Negligence involves a failure to exercise the degree of care that is reasonable under given circumstances. It is reasonable to expect that professionals with special competence in a particular field or occupation will exercise a higher standard of care in performing their duties than someone without special competence. Attorneys, physicians, architects, engineers, and other professionals are considered experts in their field and are expected to perform accordingly. Professional liability arises if injury or damage can be attributed to a professional's failure to exercise the appropriate standard of care. For insurance professionals and others, this failure is sometimes called errors and omissions (E&O). For medical professionals, it is often called malpractice. For example, a physician who prescribes a drug but ignores the possible side effects may be held liable for any resulting harm to the patient, because accepted medical practice requires the doctor to consider possible side effects. When professionals make errors, the injured party usually expects to be compensated.

Financial Consequences of Liability Loss

The third element of liability loss exposures consists of the financial consequences of such losses. In theory, the financial consequences of a liability loss exposure are limitless. In practice, financial consequences are limited to the total wealth of the person or organization. Although some jurisdictions limit the amounts that can be taken in a claim, liability claims can result in the loss of most or all of a person's or organization's assets. For a person or an organization that has been held legally liable for injury or damage, the financial consequences can be the payment of damages, the payment of defense costs, and damage to the person's or organization's reputation.

Damages

The damages of a liability loss can be more difficult to determine than those involved with other types of losses. For example, the ultimate value of liability claims resulting from a hotel fire injuring hundreds of guests may be hard to predict because each claim is different and it may take years for all of them to reach settlement or be tried in court to a final judgment.

Defense Costs

In addition to damages, the financial consequences of a liability loss may include costs to defend the alleged wrongdoer in court. These defense costs include not only the fees paid to lawyers but also all the other expenses associated with defending a liability claim. Such expenses can include investigation expenses, expert witness fees, premiums for necessary bonds, and other expenses incurred to prepare for and conduct a trial. Even in the unlikely event that all the possible lawsuits against a defendant are ultimately found groundless, defendants and their liability insurers will probably incur substantial defense costs.

Damage to Reputation

A third financial consequence of liability loss may be the defendant's loss of reputation. Such consequences are often difficult to quantify, but they do exist. For example, in 2000, a tire manufacturer recalled more than six million tires after they were alleged to be a factor in rollover crashes. In addition to damages paid and defense costs for the lawsuits that followed, the manufacturer suffered a damaged reputation and resultant loss of sales.

Apply Your Knowledge

Robert and Lillian are married and own a home with a pool in the backyard. Robert frequently goes hunting for sport. Joey, their son, plays Little League baseball. Their daughter, Sally, plays soccer on a team in an organized league. Lillian frequently drives Sally and several of her teammates to and from games. Lillian also serves on the local YMCA board. Describe the family's liability loss exposures in terms of these three elements:

- Assets exposed to a liability loss
- Causes of liability loss
- Financial consequences of liability loss

Feedback:

- Assets exposed to liability loss—Robert and Lillian's cash accounts, home, furniture, autos, future income, and other personal property are exposed to the risk of being liquidated to pay damages to a plaintiff.

- Causes of liability loss—Claims and suits by plaintiffs could result from any of the activities described. The swimming pool in the backyard is a premises loss exposure that could attract neighborhood children. If a child were to drown while swimming in the pool, his or her parents could accuse Robert and Lillian of negligence. Robert's hunting is a personal activity that could result in a claim for accidently shooting a person. Joey's playing baseball is a personal activity that could result in a claim that Joey hit someone with a ball or bat. Sally's playing soccer is a personal activity that probably has the least significant liability exposure, but other players could claim she injured them by running into or tripping them. Lillian's driving Sally and her teammates to and from games is an auto-related activity that could result in an auto accident and claims that she negligently injured the teammates. Lillian's board service could be considered a professional activity, which could in turn result in a claim alleging that she failed to exercise the standard of care expected of a board member.

- Financial consequences of liability loss—Each of these activities could result in a claim or suit whose value is limited only by the wealth of the family. Even if the claim or suit is without merit, the defense costs and damage to the family members' reputation may be substantial.

PERSONNEL LOSS EXPOSURES

For many organizations, their most valuable assets are their employees because they add to the value of the organization through their physical and mental labor. Understanding the elements of personnel loss exposures provides an essential foundation for managing these exposures and protecting these assets.

A **personnel loss exposure** is composed of these elements:

- Assets exposed to a personnel loss
- Causes of a personnel loss
- Financial consequences of a personnel loss

Assets Exposed to Personnel Loss

While everyone in an organization has value, some people are more easily replaced than others. Valuable employees (**key employees**) present a critical loss exposure to an organization. Similarly, groups of employees who perform crucial functions, if they are all lost simultaneously, can cause a crisis for an organization.

Personnel loss exposure

A condition that presents the possibility of loss caused by a person's death, disability, retirement, or resignation that deprives an organization of the person's special skill or knowledge that the organization cannot readily replace.

Key employee

An employee whose loss to a firm through death or disability before retirement would have economic effects on the company.

Personnel loss exposures can include several categories of key personnel:

* Individual employees
* Owners, officers, and managers
* Groups of employees

Individual Employees

The category of individual employees includes employees with unique talents, creativity, or special skills vital to the organization's ability to meet its goals. These employees do not own, manage, or oversee the organization, but they add value to it. They could be high-performing sales representatives or systems engineers who help focus a firm's efforts on customer needs during a complex engineering project.

Owners, Officers, and Managers

Owners, officers, and managers are responsible for making decisions essential to the organization, as well as managing and motivating others. In organizations in which the owner is a key person, that person's activities, health, and managerial competence all influence the organization's value. A sole proprietorship literally ceases to exist as a legal entity when its owner dies or retires. Similarly, partnerships may legally terminate when a partner dies or retires. The same is true in close corporations, in which ownership is typically concentrated in just a few major shareholders, most of whom are also managers.

☑ Reality Check

Example of Losing a Key Person

Steve Jobs of Apple, Inc., is an example of how one visionary key person can have a major influence on the success of even a large corporation. The company, which relied on Jobs for its run of successes, was shaken by his health concerns that started when he was diagnosed with pancreatic cancer in 2003. As part of Apple's succession plan to replace Jobs' contributions, the company has hired high-profile academics to provide training for its executives.

[DA07696]

Groups of Employees

Sometimes a group of employees is critically important to an organization, even if an individual employee in that group is not. An organization may be unable to function without the contributions of an important group. With the exception of layoffs, group departure is rare, and when an entire group is laid off, it is usually because it is considered expendable. However, over a short time period, an entire group may leave because of common dissatisfaction (such as poor management), may follow a manager to a new organization, or may be lost because of a catastrophic event.

Causes of Personnel Loss

The causes of personnel losses are the actual means by which an employee is removed from the service of an employer. Each cause of loss varies considerably in frequency and severity. These are some of the major causes of loss:

- Death
- Disability
- Resignation, layoffs, and firing
- Retirement
- Kidnapping

Causes of loss could occur inside or outside the workplace; however, the personnel loss remains the same in both instances.

Death

The death of an employee results in the complete, permanent loss of the employee's services. Unless a disaster occurs, most losses from death are low frequency, and the severity of impact on the employer depends on the employee's value to the organization. The risk of death varies widely according to the nature of the organization's business (for example, financial services versus oil exploration and extraction). Numerous events, accidental or natural, can cause death of key employees. Risk control efforts can focus on events that can result in the death of large numbers of employees at once, such as fire, explosion, severe windstorm, and terrorist attacks.

Disability

Although death as a cause of loss often attracts more media attention than disability, overall disability occurs far more frequently than death. The severity of personnel losses resulting from **disability** can be equal to those resulting from death if the disability is permanent and total. However, temporary disability is more common than permanent disability, and partial disability is more common than total disability.

As with death, numerous accidental or natural events can cause disability of key employees. Risk control efforts can focus on events that can disable large numbers of employees at once and on events that disable many employees over time, such as workplace injuries.

Disability

The inability (because of impairment) of a person to meet his or her personal, social, or occupational demands; other activities of daily living; or statutory or other legal requirements.

Workplace injuries are often related to companies' failing to take adequate safety measures. Examples include these:

- Failing to apply ergonomics to prevent injuries, such as carpal tunnel syndrome, from repetitive motions
- Not allowing workers performing physical labor to take periodic breaks
- Operating an assembly process too quickly, thereby encouraging workers to take chances assembling products and increasing their exposure to potential injury

Resignation, Layoffs, and Firing

Employees may leave an employer voluntarily (for example, by resignation) or involuntarily (for example, by a layoff or firing). Resignation (voluntary separation) is an expected part of doing business. The frequency of resignations depends, in part, on the type of industry. Some organizations, such as fast-food restaurants or construction companies, could expect very high turnover rates, while others, such as accounting firms or governments, could expect a low turnover rate. The severity of a resignation depends on who is resigning. If a key person leaves or if a group of employees sharing a similar function departs simultaneously, the severity of the personnel losses may be high.

Involuntary employee separations generally are not considered a personnel loss because the organization has determined that it is better off without the employees. If, for example, a layoff is the result of a change in the organization's goals—meaning that the laid-off employees are no longer needed for the organization to operate efficiently—their departure will have a minimal effect on the organization's success. Employees are typically fired for cause—that is, for not performing their jobs effectively or behaving in an unacceptable manner. Usually, organizations rationally consider all the costs and benefits of retaining an employee before firing him or her.

Retirement

While death and voluntary resignation often occur suddenly, retirement is usually planned. With plenty of notice, an organization can usually prepare for the retirement of even key personnel by locating and training replacements. However, as with resignation or death, when a key person decides to retire suddenly, the losses can be severe.

Kidnapping

Kidnapping of a key employee can be a significant cause of loss for employers, especially for those with operations outside the United States. Some kidnappings result from political unrest, but employers are more likely to face financially motivated kidnappings, such as kidnapping for ransom.

Kidnapping is a fairly low-frequency event that tends to occur mostly in high-risk locations. The most obvious loss to an employer is the absence of a key employee. In this sense, kidnapping losses are similar to death and disability losses; the severity depends on the importance of the employee and the cost of temporarily or permanently replacing him or her.

Financial Consequences of Personnel Losses

Because employees are assets of an organization, the financial effect of the loss of these assets (personnel losses) on an organization is similar to the effect of property and liability losses in that they reduce the value of the organization. The major difference is that personnel losses typically manifest themselves as net income losses. These are some of the financial consequences of personnel losses:

- Loss of the value the employee contributed to the organization. (In cases in which a key person is lost, this may be severe, with the organization's value lowered at least for the short term.)
- Replacement costs (recruitment, interviewing, and training of replacement personnel).
- Losses to the organization's value caused by negative publicity.
- Losses caused by low morale, such as reduced productivity and increased illness.

Apply Your Knowledge

Roger and Susan are realtors and employees of the same real estate agency. Roger has been with the agency for thirty years and plans to retire next month. He has an excellent reputation and almost more referral business than he can service. Susan has been with the agency for a year and is considering a job offer from another agency. She is a hard worker but is still learning how to best serve her clients and has few referrals. Roger and Susan were traveling to a sales convention in Susan's car when they were broadsided by a driver who failed to stop at a red light. Both Roger and Susan were injured and taken to a hospital. The doctors estimate both Roger and Susan will be totally disabled for four months. Describe the real estate agency's personnel loss exposures in terms of the three elements of personnel loss exposures:

Feedback:

- Assets exposed to personnel loss—Roger and Susan are valuable assets of the agency because they add to the value of the organization through their physical and mental labor. While both Roger and Susan have value, Susan can be replaced more easily than Roger. Roger is a key employee of the agency because of his referral business, which provides substantial income to the agency.
- Causes of personnel loss—The four-month disability resulting from the auto accident is an immediate cause of loss for the agency. Roger's planned retirement is another cause of loss. By the time Roger recovers from the accident, it will be past his retirement date. So, in effect, the

agency might as well consider Roger's disability to be permanent. Susan's potential resignation to go work for another agency once she recovers from her disability is another possible cause of loss.

- Financial consequences of personnel loss—The referral business may not continue if Roger is not working at the agency. However, Roger's employer probably knows about his planned retirement date. Therefore, his replacement has likely been hired and trained and may have met with Roger's clients to assure them that the same excellent level of service will continue after Roger's departure. The costs to replace Roger were probably incurred before the auto accident, and Roger's loss of value to the agency minimized. Furthermore, the accident may generate sympathy in the market that may result in more business for the agency. Susan has few referrals, and her absence will not be as much of a loss to the agency economically whether she comes back in four months or decides to work for another agency.

NET INCOME LOSS EXPOSURES

Understanding the elements of net income loss exposures and how they result from other causes of loss provides an essential foundation for managing such exposures.

A net income loss exposure is a condition that presents the possibility of loss caused by a reduction in net income. These are the three elements of net income loss exposures:

- Assets exposed to net income loss
- Causes of net income loss
- Financial consequences of net income loss

Assets Exposed to Net Income Loss

The asset exposed to loss in a net income loss exposure is the future stream of net income of the individual or organization. The future stream of net income includes revenues minus expenses and income taxes in a given time period. If income taxes are considered to be part of an organization's expenses, a net income loss is a reduction in revenue, an increase in expenses, or a combination of the two.

For example, a fire at an organization's production facilities could not only destroy the facilities (a property loss exposure), but also force the organization to stop operations for a few weeks, resulting in a loss of sales revenue (a net income loss exposure). Similarly, if a tornado damaged the retail store of a self-employed business owner, the inability to earn income while the store is being repaired represents a net income loss exposure.

Net income losses are often the result of a property, liability, or personnel loss (all of which are direct losses). Therefore, net income losses are considered to be indirect losses. A direct loss is a loss that occurs immediately as the result of a particular cause of loss, such as the reduction in the value of a building that has been damaged by fire.

An indirect loss is a loss that results from, but is not directly caused by, a particular cause of loss. For example, the reduction in revenue that an organization suffers as a result of fire damage to one of its buildings is an indirect loss. Estimating indirect losses is often challenging because of the difficulty in projecting the effects that a direct loss will have on revenues and expenses. For instance, a litigation manager working for a restaurant chain may be able to project with some certainty the amount needed to settle a lawsuit brought by a customer accusing the restaurant of food poisoning (a direct liability loss). However, projecting the effect on future restaurant sales (an indirect loss) of any negative publicity relating to the lawsuit would be more difficult.

In the insurance industry, the term "net income losses" is usually associated with property losses, and some insurance policies provide coverage for net income losses related to property losses. However, there are many other causes of net income losses.

Causes of Net Income Loss

Various circumstances can lead to a net income loss. For many of these causes of loss, it can often be difficult to discern when the direct property loss, liability loss, personnel loss, or business risk loss ends and when the indirect net income loss begins.

Property Loss

A property loss is a loss sustained by a person or an organization resulting from damage to property in which that person or organization has a financial interest. Damage to property can cause a reduction in that property's value, sometimes to zero. For example, when a car is stolen, the owner suffers a total loss of that property because the owner no longer has use of it. As a result of the theft, the owner could incur a net income loss by renting a replacement vehicle. The owner's expenses will increase, but the added expense may be necessary in order to allow the owner to continue commuting to and from work.

Similarly, a nuclear power plant that just endured an earthquake may incur a net income loss when it pays the extra expense of immediately shipping in a replacement water pump. By incurring the additional shipping costs to receive the pump more quickly, the plant may be able to prevent a larger direct loss of radiation contamination and resume operations sooner. This action would also avoid a larger loss of income and, consequently, a larger net income loss.

Liability Loss

Liability losses are caused by a claim of legal liability from someone who is usually seeking monetary damages against a person or an organization. The direct costs that a person or an organization can incur as a result of a liability claim include damages and defense costs. In addition, a liability loss can result in a net income loss. For example, if a driver of a car develops a history of poor driving and injures multiple parties in a series of accidents who claim liability against the driver, the costs of renewing the driver's personal auto policy, if available, will likely be substantially higher. Many doctors also incur an increase in net income losses when their professional liability insurance coverage renews at a higher rate as a consequence of successful claims of professional malpractice made against them.

Another example of increased net income losses can occur when two organizations merge or one organization acquires another. Part of the negotiations associated with drafting the agreement joining the organizations involves whether either of them is facing pending or expected litigation. If so, the organization being sued will often have to sacrifice some form of net income.

Personnel Loss

A personnel loss is often caused by a key person's death, disability, retirement, or resignation. Such a loss deprives those dependent on that person of a special skill or knowledge that cannot be readily replaced. As an example, a family incurs a net income loss as a result of a personnel loss when a homemaker is temporarily disabled because of an auto accident and the family must pay someone else to perform many of the essential services needed to maintain the household while the homemaker is recovering. The wages paid to the worker to perform these services constitute a net income loss. If the homemaker were also a wage earner outside the home, the loss of income while he or she recovers from the disability would also be a net income loss.

An example of personnel losses that cause organizations to incur net income losses involves contractors recruiting employees to work in areas of the world where hostile military conflicts are ongoing. The frequent personnel losses caused by death or disability of the contractors' current employees force the contractors to pay higher salaries to attract new employees and retain existing ones.

Business Risks

Business risk refers to risk that is inherent in the operation of a particular organization. These are examples of potential net income losses from business risk that may affect individuals or organizations:

- Loss of goodwill—Organizations are concerned with maintaining goodwill among customers and other stakeholders. Goodwill can be lost in many ways, including providing poor service, offering obsolete products, or mismanaging operations. For a not-for-profit organization, goodwill is equivalent to reputation. Goodwill has broader implications than just reputation in for-profit organizations, because goodwill may have a monetary value. To maintain goodwill, many organizations choose to pay for certain accidents for which they are not legally responsible. For example, if a guest sustains an injury on an organization's premises and the organization did not cause or contribute to the injury, that organization might still choose to pay any medical bills in order to maintain goodwill and avoid adverse publicity.

- Failure to perform—Net income losses may occur as a result of some type of failure to perform, including a product's failure to perform as promised, a contractor's failure to complete a construction project as scheduled, or a debtor's failure to make scheduled payments.

- Missed opportunities—An organization may suffer a net income loss as a result of a missed opportunity for profit. For example, an organization that delays a decision to modify its product in response to market demand might lose market share and profit that it could have made on that updated product.

Financial Consequences of Net Income Losses

The financial consequences of a net income loss are a reduction in revenues, an increase in expenses, or a combination of the two. To determine the severity of a net income loss, it is sometimes necessary to project what revenue and expenses would have been had no loss occurred. Once a loss occurs, the difference between the projected net income and the actual net income earned after the accident is the net income loss. The worst-case scenario for a net income loss is a decrease in revenues to zero and a significant increase in expenses for a prolonged period.

Apply Your Knowledge

Sally is a single parent of two boys. She owns the house they live in and rents an apartment above their garage to a young married couple. The rent pays half of Sally's monthly mortgage payment. The rest of Sally's income comes from her job as a reporter for a newspaper whose advertising income has been declining for years. Describe a significant net income loss exposure, based on the facts presented, that could result from each of the following: a property loss, a liability loss, and a personnel loss.

Feedback:

- Property loss—The house that Sally and her boys live in could become uninhabitable because of fire, flood, or another disaster. If that happened, the value of their home would decrease sharply—a direct property loss. Furthermore, the family would incur the indirect, consequential loss of paying for another place to live. Costs to rent a hotel room or an apartment would be incurred until the house was repaired, which could take months. If the apartment over the garage also became uninhabitable, the young couple would move out, and the monthly rent they paid would stop. Without the rental income, Sally may not be able to pay the full amount of the mortgage herself, which could result in the bank declaring her mortgage in default and foreclosing on the property. Sally and her boys would then lose their home.

- Liability loss—If the husband of the young couple slipped on the outdoor stairs going down to his car and injured his knee, he may decide to sue Sally. He could claim the stairs were not properly maintained and presented a hazardous condition that she should have prevented. Sally would incur the direct costs of her defense but may also incur the indirect costs of repairing the steps and losing income for being off work on the days she must attend trial of the lawsuit. The indirect costs would increase Sally's expenses and thereby lower her net income.

- Personnel loss—The newspaper for which Sally works has been losing advertising income for years. If its management decides it must cut expenses, it may decide to do so by laying off workers, including Sally. She will probably be able to find other employment eventually, but until she does, her family will lose the income she would have earned.

IDEALLY INSURABLE LOSS EXPOSURES

Although insurers insure many loss exposures, not all loss exposures are ideally insurable. To be insurable, a loss exposure should have certain characteristics.

Most insured loss exposures do not completely embody all of the characteristics of an ideally insurable loss exposure. However, the criteria are useful to an insurer when deciding to offer new coverages or to continue offering existing coverages. See the exhibit "Six Characteristics of an Ideally Insurable Loss Exposure."

Pure Risk

The first characteristic of an ideally insurable loss exposure is that it should be associated with pure risk, not speculative risk. Pure risk entails a chance of loss or no loss, but no chance of gain. Conversely, a speculative risk presents the possibility of loss, no loss, or gain. Insurance is not designed to finance speculative risks. A purpose of insurance is to indemnify the insured for a loss, not to enable the insured to profit from the loss. Indemnification is the process of restoring the insured to a pre-loss financial condition. Limiting insurance coverage to only pure risks reduces the complexity of the loss exposures insured by the policy to two situations: having a loss or not having a loss.

Six Characteristics of an Ideally Insurable Loss Exposure

1. Pure risk—involves pure risk, not speculative risk
2. Fortuitous losses—subject to fortuitous loss from the insured's standpoint
3. Definite and measurable—subject to losses that are definite in time, cause, and location and that are measurable
4. Large number of similar exposure units—one of a large number of similar exposure units
5. Independent and not catastrophic—not subject to a loss that would simultaneously affect many other similar loss exposures; not catastrophic
6. Affordable—premiums are economically feasible

[DA02747]

Fortuitous Losses

The second characteristic of an ideally insurable loss exposure is that the loss associated with the loss exposure should be fortuitous (occurring by chance) from the insured's standpoint.

Some causes of loss may be fortuitous from one point of view only. For example, vandalism and theft are intentional (and therefore not fortuitous) acts from the perspective of the individual or organization committing the acts. However, vandalism and theft are fortuitous (and insurable) from the victim's standpoint because the victim did not intend or expect these acts to occur. Other causes of loss are fortuitous regardless of the perspective from which they are examined. For example, naturally occurring events such as windstorms, hail, or lightning are fortuitous events whether one is the insurer, the insured, or any third party associated with the loss exposure.

For a loss to be fortuitous, the insured cannot have control over whether or when a loss will occur. If the insured has control, the insured might have an incentive to cause a loss. This is known as a moral hazard. For example, arson committed by an insured is not a fortuitous act. Ideally, insurance is suitable for situations in which there is reasonable uncertainty about the probability or timing of a loss without the threat of a moral hazard. If insureds were compensated for losses they cause, they might be encouraged to generate losses for property they no longer wish to own. This practice could undermine the pricing structure for insurance and increase insurance premiums for all policyholders.

Definite and Measurable

The third characteristic of an ideally insurable loss exposure is that it is definite and measurable.

Three components are required for a loss exposure to be definite: time, cause, and location. The insurer must be able to determine the event (or series of events) that led to the loss, when the loss occurred, and where the loss occurred. For example, Cindy parks her car in a public parking lot and upon returning to her vehicle discovers that its driver's side door is badly damaged. She could state that this happened on a certain date and within a certain period of time. It was clear from the damage and transfer of paint chips that another vehicle had hit her car. Therefore, the cause of the damage is known. Because Cindy parked her car in the parking lot, the location was established.

All insurance policies have a policy period that specifies the precise dates and times of coverage. A typical property-casualty policy has a policy period ranging from six months to one year. After receiving notice of a claim, the insurer usually needs to determine that the event occurred during the policy period. For some events, this may be a difficult process; insurers are reluctant to insure such events.

For example, an insurer is considering insuring a gas station against environmental pollution. A definite environmental pollution loss would be a fire that ruptured an underground gas tank and caused gas to leak into the surrounding soil. However, had no fire occurred and had the tank been slowly leaking for an indeterminate number of years, it would be impossible to pinpoint the exact date or the cause of the pollution. Therefore, it may be impossible to determine whether the event occurred during the policy period. Because they are not definite, these types of loss exposures are not ideally insurable.

A loss exposure also needs to be measurable to be ideally insurable. Insurers cannot determine an appropriate premium if they cannot measure the frequency or severity of the potential losses. For example, a house fire is a measurable loss exposure. Underwriters can analyze data from past fire losses to single-dwelling, wood-frame homes within a set geographic area. From the analysis, frequency and severity patterns are used to determine potential fire losses and the premium needed. In addition, the cost to repair or replace a house damaged by fire can be objectively measured before a loss, and coverage can be priced accordingly.

Conversely, contagious diseases are an example of a potential loss exposure that is difficult to measure. Flu viruses mutate constantly. The strength of the virus, as well as the age group susceptible, may vary from one flu season to the next. Also, the geographic territory where the virus strikes can vary from year to year. All these factors make it difficult for an underwriter to measure future losses. Insurers are reluctant to insure losses that are highly uncertain without receiving substantial compensation (high premiums).

Large Number of Similar Exposure Units

The fourth characteristic of an ideally insurable loss exposure is that the loss exposure is one of a large number of similar exposure units. Some common loss exposures that satisfy this requirement include homes, offices, and automobiles. Each exposure unit has a value that can be at risk when exposed to loss.

For example, Steve purchases a single-family home for $300,000. He faces loss exposures of fire, theft, burglary, windstorm, hail, collapse, and so forth. His exposure is the value of his home. If the home were destroyed by fire, he could not afford to replace it. This risk is transferred with the purchase of a homeowners insurance policy. The insurer does not want to insure only Steve's home, but rather thousands of single-family homes that face similar exposures. Based on past losses, the insurer knows that although all homes have a fire exposure, only a small percentage will experience a fire loss. The insurer can therefore spread the risk of fire loss over its entire pool of insured homes and thereby maintain manageable premium levels.

Independent and Not Catastrophic

The fifth characteristic of an ideally insurable loss exposure is that it is independent and not catastrophic. Independent means that a loss suffered by one insured does not affect any other insured or group of insureds. For example, Steve's home is located in a large subdivision of 1,000 homes and is surrounded by a wooded area. Steve's insurer would not want to insure all the homes in the subdivision because the forest fire loss exposure would put all 1,000 homes at risk of fire. The risk would not be independent for each home.

A catastrophic loss is severe; it involves numerous exposure units suffering the same type of loss simultaneously, with significant financial consequences for the insurer. Insurance operates economically because many insureds pay premiums that are small relative to the cost of the potential losses they could each incur. The cost can stay relatively small because insurers project that they will incur far fewer losses than the loss exposures they have. However, if a large number of insureds who are covered for the same type of loss were to incur losses simultaneously, the insurance mechanism would not operate economically and losses to the insurer could be catastrophic.

For example, to avoid a catastrophic hurricane loss, an insurer will diversify the homes and businesses it insures and will not have a large concentration in any one geographic area. Single events or a series of events can also present catastrophic risk to an insurer. Similarly, a small insurer should not insure a multimillion-dollar property, such as an oil refinery. Although the loss exposure may be independent of the other properties the insurer has chosen to insure, a loss at such a single location may cause the insurer severe financial difficulty.

Affordable

The final characteristic of an ideally insurable loss exposure is that the insurer is able to charge an economically feasible premium—one that the insured can afford to pay. Insurers seek to cover only loss exposures that are economically feasible to insure. Because of this constraint, loss exposures involving only small losses, as well as those involving a high probability of loss, are generally considered uninsurable.

Writing insurance to cover small losses may not make sense when the expense of providing the insurance probably exceeds the amount of potential losses. Insurance covering the disappearance of office supplies, for example, could require the insurer to spend more to investigate and to issue claim checks than it would for the insured to simply absorb the cost of replacing the supplies.

It also may not make sense to write insurance to cover losses that are almost certain to occur. The premiums would probably be as high as or higher than the potential amount of the loss. For example, insurers generally do not cover damage because of wear and tear on an automobile because automobiles are certain to incur such damage over time.

Apply Your Knowledge

Jim's summer job is to work as an intern for an insurance agency. When preparing a listing of the agency's homeowners book of business, Jim notes that seventy-five clients' homes are located within one-half mile of the river in a designated flood plain. Jim is concerned because one of the agents told him that flood exposure is not covered under the homeowners policy. Jim proposes to his manager that the agency sell a flood coverage endorsement to each of the homeowners clients. Jim's manager reviews with Jim the six characteristics of an ideally insurable loss exposure. Jim determines that the exposure of flood possesses only three of the six characteristics: pure risk, fortuitous losses, and definite and measurable.

If you were in Jim's position, how would you arrive at this determination?

Feedback: The exposure is a pure loss because a loss that occurs as a result of a flood does not result in financial gain for the insured; thus, there is either a loss or no loss. It is fortuitous because the insured does not have control over whether and when a flood loss will occur. It is definite in time, cause, and location, and flood data are available that can be measured. Conversely, there is not a large number of similar exposure units. Additionally, the loss is not independent because all of the homes in the flood plain will be exposed. Finally, because only those who believe they are at risk for a flood loss would purchase the flood endorsement, the insurer will not be able to offer an economically feasible premium.

SUMMARY

Property loss exposures are analyzed in these terms:

- Assets exposed to property loss
- Causes of loss to property
- Financial consequences of property losses
- Parties affected by property losses

Legal liability can arise based on torts, contracts, and statutes. Types of torts include negligence, intentional torts, and strict liability. Examples of liability based on contracts include hold-harmless agreements and warranties in contracts for sale of goods. Examples of liability based on statutes involve no-fault auto laws and workers compensation laws.

These are the three elements of liability loss exposures:

- Assets exposed to a liability loss, which include a defendant's property and future income
- Causes of liability loss, which could arise from various activities
- Financial consequences of liability loss, which include damages, defense costs, and damage to reputation

These are the three elements of personnel loss exposures:

- Assets exposed to a personnel loss, which include individual employees; owners, officers, and managers; and groups of employees
- Causes of a personnel loss, which include death, disability, resignation, layoffs, firing, retirement, and kidnapping
- Financial consequences of a personnel loss, which include loss of the value of an employee's contribution, replacement costs, loss due to negative publicity, and reduced productivity and increased illness caused by low morale

Net income loss exposures are characterized by these three elements:

- Assets exposed to a net income loss exposure—The future stream of net income of the individual or organization.
- Causes of net income loss—Direct property, liability, and personnel losses or business risks.
- Financial consequences of net income loss—These include a reduction in revenues, an increase in expenses, or a combination of the two.

These are the six characteristics of an ideally insurable loss exposure:

- Pure risk—Involves pure risk, not speculative risk.
- Fortuitous losses—Subject to fortuitous loss from the insured's standpoint.
- Definite and measurable—Subject to losses that are definite in time, cause, and location and that are measurable.

- Large number of similar exposure units—One of a large number of similar exposure units.
- Independent and not catastrophic—Not subject to a loss that would simultaneously affect many other similar loss exposures; loss would not be catastrophic.
- Affordable—Premiums are economically feasible.

Insurance Policies

Educational Objectives

After learning the content of this assignment, you should be able to:

▶ Explain the four elements of any valid contract.

▶ Describe the distinguishing characteristics of insurance policies.

▶ Explain how insurance policies can be structured using each of these alternatives:

- Preprinted and manuscript forms

- Self-contained and modular policies

- Endorsements and other related documents

▶ Given a specific policy provision, classify it into one of the following categories:

- Declarations

- Definitions

- Insuring agreements

- Conditions

- Exclusions

- Miscellaneous provisions

▶ Explain how property policy provisions typically address each of the following:

- Covered property

- Covered locations

- Covered causes of loss

- Excluded causes of loss

- Covered financial consequences

- Covered parties

- Amounts of recovery

9

▷ Explain how liability policy provisions typically address each of the following:

- Covered activities

- Covered types of injury or damage

- Excluded loss exposures

- Covered costs

- Covered time period

- Covered parties

- Amounts of recovery

Insurance Policies

ELEMENTS OF A CONTRACT

An insurance contract, called a policy, is an agreement between the insurer and the insured. An insurance policy must meet the same requirements as any other valid contract, which is a legally enforceable agreement between two or more parties.

If a dispute arises between the parties to a contract, a court will enforce only **valid contracts**. The validity of a contract depends on four essential elements. See the exhibit "Four Essential Elements of a Contract."

Valid contract
A contract that meets all of the requirements to be enforceable.

Four Essential Elements of a Contract

- Agreement (offer and acceptance)
- Capacity to contract
- Consideration
- Legal purpose

[DA07631]

If a court cannot confirm the presence of all four elements, it will not enforce the contract.

Agreement (Offer and Acceptance)

One essential element of a contract is that the parties to the contract must be in agreement. One party must make a legitimate offer, and another party must accept the offer. In legal terms, there must be "mutual assent." In insurance, the process of achieving mutual assent generally begins when someone who wants to purchase insurance completes an insurance application—an offer to buy insurance. The details on the application describe the exposures to be insured and indicate the coverage the applicant requests.

In an uncomplicated case, an underwriter (or an agent, acting on behalf of an insurer) accepts the application and agrees to provide the coverage requested at a premium acceptable to both the insurer and the applicant. The premium is the payment by an insured to an insurer in exchange for insurance coverage.

At this point, agreement exists; the insurer has accepted the applicant's offer to buy insurance.

In a more complicated case, an underwriter may not be willing to meet all the requests of the applicant. One of the underwriter's options is to accept the application with modification. The underwriter may be willing to provide coverage, but only on somewhat different terms. For example, an underwriter may insist on a higher deductible than the applicant had requested. When an underwriter communicates the proposed modifications to the applicant, these modifications constitute a counteroffer.

Several offers and counteroffers may be made before both parties agree to an exact set of terms. If the other essential elements of a contract exist, the mutual assent of the insurer and the applicant forms a contract. To be enforceable, the agreement cannot be the result of duress, coercion, fraud, or a mistake. If either party to the contract can prove any of these circumstances, a court could declare the contract to be void.

Capacity to Contract

For a contract to be enforceable, all parties must have capacity to contract. In other words, each party must have the legal capacity to make the agreement binding. Individuals are generally considered to be competent and able to enter into legally enforceable contracts, unless one or more of these characteristics applies:

- Being insane or otherwise mentally incompetent
- Being under the influence of drugs or alcohol
- Being a minor (person not yet of legal age)

However, minors are sometimes considered competent to purchase auto insurance, especially when auto insurance qualifies as a necessity. State laws vary in regard to issues involving minors.

Another aspect of legal capacity is that, in most states, an insurer must be licensed to do business in that state. If an insurer mistakenly writes an insurance policy in a state where that insurer is not licensed, the insured might later argue that the contract is not valid and demand the return of the premium. This demand would be based on the fact that the insurer did not have the legal capacity to make the agreement.

Consideration

Consideration
Something of value or bargained for and exchanged by the parties to a contract.

Consideration is something of value given by each party to a contract. For example, when an auto is purchased, the buyer gives money (consideration) to the seller who, in turn, provides the car (which is also consideration). Some contracts do not involve the exchange of one tangible item for another, but instead involve performance. For example, an author may sign a contract agreeing to write a book in exchange for payment by the publisher.

Performance can also involve a promise to perform some act in the future that is dependent on a certain event occurring. In an insurance contract, the insurer's consideration is its promise to pay a claim in the future if a covered loss occurs. If no loss occurs, the insurer is still fulfilling its promise to provide financial protection even though it does not pay a claim. In insurance contracts, two types of consideration are involved:

- The insured's consideration is the payment of (or the promise to pay) the premium.
- The insurer's consideration is its promise to pay claims for covered losses.

Legal Purpose

An enforceable contract must also have a legal purpose. Courts may consider a contract to be illegal if its purpose is against the law or against public policy (as defined by the courts). For example, an agreement to pay a bribe to a government official in exchange for receiving a government job would not be enforced by the courts because such an activity is against public policy.

Although most insurance policies do not involve a question of legality, certain situations do exist that may invalidate an insurance policy. Courts will refuse to enforce any insurance policy that is illegal or that tends to injure the public welfare. Insurance contracts must involve a legal subject matter. Property insurance on illegally owned or possessed goods is invalid. For example, property insurance covering illegal drugs would be illegal and therefore unenforceable. If fireworks are illegal in a particular state, then an insurance policy covering fireworks would be unenforceable in that state.

In addition, no insurance contract will remain valid if the wrongful conduct of the insured causes the operation of the contract to violate public policy. Thus, arson by an insured would render a property insurance policy unenforceable and would preclude recovery by the insured under the policy for a building the insured intentionally burned.

Apply Your Knowledge

Sam is an insurance producer. He is having several drinks with his friend Harry at a bar. Harry decides to leave. He asks Sam whether he'll insure him for auto liability, as he thinks he might need it going home. Sam nods his head. Which of the four elements of a valid contract may be questionable at this point?

a. Agreement (offer and acceptance)

b. Capacity to contract

c. Consideration

d. Legal purpose

Feedback: a., b., and c. To be valid, agreement requires mutual assent with an offer and acceptance. The offer is vague. For example, is coverage supposed to be for a standard policy term or just until Harry reaches his house? What is the limit of liability? The acceptance of Sam nodding is also vague. Was it Sam's intent to agree to provide coverage? Capacity to contract is a concern as well. Both parties may have temporarily lost their legal capacity to contract while under the influence of alcohol. Finally, consideration is questionable. Assuming Sam did intend to provide coverage, Harry has not paid or promised to pay any premium in exchange for the promise of coverage from Sam's insurer.

DISTINGUISHING CHARACTERISTICS OF INSURANCE POLICIES

Understanding what the distinguishing characteristics of an insurance policy are and being able to recognize when they apply is essential for an insurance professional who is held responsible for enforcing the policy.

All insurance policies are contracts. However, not all contracts are insurance policies. This unique subset of contracts has the same four essential elements that all contracts have, but, because of the specialized function it serves of transferring risk from an insured to an insurer, it also has certain distinguishing characteristics. Each of these distinguishing characteristics allows the transfer of risk to occur more efficiently. See the exhibit "Distinguishing Characteristics of Insurance Policies."

Distinguishing Characteristics of Insurance Policies

- Contract of indemnity
- Contract of utmost good faith
- Contract involving fortuitous events and the exchange of unequal amounts
- Contract of adhesion
- Conditional contract
- Nontransferable contract

[DA07629]

Contract of Indemnity

The purpose of insurance is to indemnify an insured who suffers a loss. To indemnify is to restore a party who has had a loss to the same financial position that party held before the loss occurred. Most property and liability insurance policies are contracts of indemnity.

Property insurance generally pays the amount necessary to repair covered property that has been damaged or to replace it with similar property. The policy specifies the method for determining the amount of the loss. For example, most auto policies, both personal and commercial, specify that vehicles are to be valued at their actual cash value (ACV) at the time of a loss. If a covered accident occurs that causes a covered vehicle to be a total loss, the insurer will normally pay the ACV of the vehicle, less any applicable deductible.

Liability insurance generally pays to a third-party claimant, on behalf of the insured, any amounts (up to the policy limit) that the insured becomes legally obligated to pay as damages because of a covered liability claim, as well as the legal costs associated with that claim. For example, if an insured with a liability limit of $300,000 is ordered by a court to pay $100,000 for bodily injury incurred by the claimant in a covered accident, the insurer will pay $100,000 to the claimant and will also pay the cost to defend the insured in court.

A contract of indemnity does not necessarily pay the full amount necessary to restore an insured who has suffered a covered loss to the same financial position. However, the amount the insurer pays is directly related to the amount of the insured's loss. Most policies contain a policy limit that specifies the maximum amount the insurer will pay for a single claim. Many policies also contain limitations and other provisions that could reduce the amount of recovery. For example, a homeowners policy is not designed to cover large amounts of cash. Therefore, most homeowners policies contain a special limit, such as $200, for any covered loss to money owned by the insured. In that instance, if a covered fire destroys $1,000 in cash belonging to the insured, the homeowners insurer will pay only $200 for the money that was destroyed.

Insurance policies usually include certain provisions that reinforce the **principle of indemnity**. According to the principle of indemnity, the insured should not profit from a covered loss. Insurance policies contain various provisions to clarify that the insured cannot collect more than the amount of the loss. For example, policies generally contain an "other insurance" provision to prevent an insured from receiving full payment from two different insurance policies for the same claim.

Similarly, insurance contracts usually contain subrogation provisions, which allow the insurer, after paying a covered loss, to assume the insured's rights of recovery against other parties who are legally responsible for causing the loss. For example, following an auto accident in which the insurer compensates its insured when the other driver is at fault, the subrogation provision stipulates that the insured's right to recover damages from the responsible party is transferred (subrogated) to the insurer. The insured cannot collect from both the insurer and the responsible party. If the insured is not fully indemnified by the insurer's loss payment, for example, because of a deductible, the laws of many

Principle of indemnity
The principle that insurance policies should provide a benefit no greater than the loss suffered by an insured.

states require the insurer to pay, out of its subrogation recovery, the additional amount needed to indemnify the insured. The insurer is entitled to keep the rest of the subrogation recovery.

Another factor enforcing the principle of indemnity is that a person usually cannot buy insurance unless that person is in a position to suffer a financial loss. In other words, the insured must have an insurable interest in the subject of the insurance. For example, property insurance contracts cover losses only to the extent of the insured's insurable interest in the property. This restriction prevents an insured from collecting more from the insurance than the amount of the loss he or she suffered.

A person cannot buy life insurance on the life of a stranger, hoping to gain if the stranger dies. Insurers normally sell life insurance when there is a reasonable expectation of a financial loss from the death of the insured person, such as the loss of an insured's future income that the insured's dependents would face. Insurable interest is not an issue in liability insurance because a liability claim against an insured results in a financial loss if the insured is legally responsible. Even if the insured is not responsible, the insured could incur defense costs.

Valued policy

A policy in which the insurer pays a stated amount in the event of a specified loss (usually a total loss), regardless of the actual value of the loss.

Some insurance contracts are not contracts of indemnity but valued policies. When a specified loss occurs, a **valued policy** pays a stated amount, regardless of the actual value of the loss. For example, a fine arts policy may specify that it will pay $250,000 for loss of a particular painting or sculpture. The actual market value of the painting or sculpture may be much smaller or much greater than $250,000, but the policy will pay $250,000 in either case. In most valued policies, the insurer and the insured agree on a limit that approximates the current market value of the insured property.

Contract of Utmost Good Faith

Because insurance involves a promise, it requires complete honesty and disclosure of all relevant facts from both parties. For this reason, insurance contracts are considered contracts of utmost good faith. Both parties to an insurance contract—the insurer and the insured—are expected to be ethical in their dealings with each other.

Concealment

An intentional failure to disclose a material fact.

Misrepresentation

A false statement of a material fact on which a party relies.

Material fact

In insurance, a fact that would affect the insurer's decision to provide or maintain insurance or to settle a claim.

The insured has a right to rely on the insurer to fulfill its promises. Therefore, the insurer is expected to treat the insured with utmost good faith. An insurer that acts in bad faith, such as denying coverage for a claim that is clearly covered, could face serious penalties under the law.

The insurer also has a right to expect that the insured will act in good faith. An insurance buyer who intentionally conceals certain information or misrepresents certain facts does not act in good faith. Because an insurance contract requires utmost good faith from both parties, an insurer could be released from a contract because of **concealment** or **misrepresentation** by the insured regarding a **material fact**.

Contract Involving Fortuitous Events and the Exchange of Unequal Amounts

While noninsurance contracts involve an exchange of money for a certain event, such as the provision of goods or services, insurance contracts involve an exchange of money for protection upon the occurrence of uncertain, or fortuitous, events. Insurance contracts involve an exchange of unequal amounts. Often, there are few or no losses, and the premium paid by the insured for a particular policy is more than the amount paid by the insurer to, or on behalf of, the insured. If a large loss occurs, however, the insurer's claim payment might be much more than the premium paid by the insured. It is the possibility that the insurer's obligation might be much greater than the insured's that makes the insurance transaction a fair trade.

For example, assume an insurer charges a $1,000 annual premium to provide auto physical damage coverage on a car valued at $20,000. The following three situations may occur:

- If the car is not damaged while the policy is in force, the insurer pays nothing.
- If the car is partially damaged, the insurer pays the cost of repairs, after subtracting a deductible.
- If the car is a total loss, the insurer pays $20,000 (minus any deductible).

Unless, by chance, the insurer's obligations in a minor accident total exactly $1,000, unequal amounts are involved in all three of these cases. However, it does not follow that insureds who have no losses—or only very minor losses—do not get their money's worth or that insureds involved in major accidents profit from the insurance.

The premium for a particular policy should reflect the insured's share of estimated losses that the insurer must pay. Many insureds have no losses, but some have very large losses. The policy premium reflects the insured's proportionate share of the total amount the insurer expects to pay to honor its agreements with all insureds having similar policies.

Contract of Adhesion

The wording in insurance contracts is usually drafted by the insurer (or an insurance advisory organization), enabling the insurer to use preprinted forms for many different insureds. Because the insurer determines the exact wording of the policy, the insured has little choice but to "take it or leave it." That is, the insured must adhere to the contract drafted by the insurer. Therefore, insurance policies are considered to be contracts of adhesion, which means one party (the insured) must adhere to the agreement as written by the other party (the insurer). This characteristic significantly influences the enforcement of insurance policies.

If a dispute arises between the insurer and the insured about the meaning of certain words or phrases in the policy, the insured and the insurer are not on an equal basis. The insurer either drafted the policy or used standard forms of its own choice; in contrast, the insured did not have any say in the policy wording. For that reason, if the policy wording is ambiguous, a court will generally apply the interpretation that favors the insured.

Conditional Contract

Conditional contract
A contract that one or more parties must perform only under certain conditions.

An insurance policy is a **conditional contract** because the parties have to perform only under certain conditions. Whether the insurer pays a claim depends on whether a covered loss has occurred. In addition, the insured must fulfill certain duties before a claim is paid, such as giving prompt notice to the insurer after a loss has occurred.

A covered loss might not occur during a particular policy period, but that fact does not mean the insurance policy for that period has been worthless. In buying an insurance policy, the insured acquires a valuable promise—the promise of the insurer to make payments if a covered loss occurs. The promise exists, even if the insurer's performance is not required during the policy period.

Nontransferable Contract

The identities of the persons or organizations insured are important to the insurer, because it has the right to select those applicants with whom it is willing to enter into contractual agreements. After an insurance policy is in effect, an insured may not freely transfer the policy to some other party (a practice called "assignment"). If such a transfer were allowed to take place, the insurer would be legally bound to a contract with a party it may not wish to insure. Most insurance policies contain a provision that requires the insurer's written permission before an insured can transfer a policy to another party.

Apply Your Knowledge

Evelyn's health had worsened to the point she no longer felt capable of driving and decided to sell her car. John agreed to buy it from her as long as she would assign her auto policy to him, as his poor driving record prevented him from buying auto insurance for an amount he determined to be reasonable. Before purchasing Evelyn's car, John took it for a test drive and collided with a wall, totaling the vehicle. John demanded Evelyn's insurer pay him for the value of the car. Which two distinguishing characteristics of Evelyn's insurance policy did John's demand fail to consider?

a. Contract of indemnity

b. Contract of utmost good faith

c. Contract involving fortuitous events and the exchange of unequal amounts

d. Contract of adhesion

e. Conditional contract

f. Nontransferable contract

Feedback: a. and f. John's demand failed to consider that Evelyn's insurance policy has the distinguishing characteristics of being a contract of indemnity and a nontransferable contract. The contract of indemnity characteristic requires John to have an insurable interest in the vehicle. That is, he must have an interest in the car that is not unduly remote and that would cause John to suffer financial loss when the collision occurred. Because John had not yet purchased the vehicle, he could simply apply the funds he would have paid Evelyn to purchase a vehicle from someone else. The nontransferable contract characteristic prevents Evelyn from assigning or transferring her policy to John without her insurer's written consent.

INSURANCE POLICY STRUCTURE

An insurance policy is a carefully written contract that describes the agreement between the insured individual or organization and the insurer. Insurers use different types of policy structure to meet insureds' particular needs.

Insurance policy structure can vary, depending on customer coverage needs. Most policies are issued using **preprinted forms**, but **manuscript forms** may be used when an insured has coverage needs that preprinted forms do not adequately address. Moreover, all policies can be classified as being either **self-contained policies** or **modular policies**. Another important aspect of policy structure is the incorporation of endorsements or other documents into the policy.

Preprinted and Manuscript Forms

Depending on whether the insurer can use a form already created or must create a new form for a customer, the policy can be either a preprinted form or a manuscript form.

Most insurers use standard preprinted policy forms, because it is not necessary to negotiate new contractual terms for each policy purchased. Insurance advisory organizations, such as Insurance Services Office, Inc. (ISO) and the

Preprinted form

An insurance form that meets the needs of many policyholders and is therefore printed in bulk for future use.

Manuscript form

An insurance form that is drafted according to terms negotiated between a specific insured (or group of insureds) and an insurer.

Self-contained policy

A single document that contains all the agreements between the insured and the insurer and that forms a complete insurance policy.

Modular policy

An insurance policy that consists of several different documents, none of which by itself forms a complete policy.

American Association of Insurance Services (AAIS), develop industry-wide standardized forms for different types of property-casualty insurance, and many insurers use these standard forms. Alternatively, an insurer may develop its own nonstandard, preprinted forms. For example, a person buying auto insurance may find that three small insurers are using the same ISO standard policy form but that one large insurer is using its own nonstandard, preprinted policy form for auto coverage.

When an insurer's preprinted forms do not provide the terms of coverage needed by a particular insured or a small group of insureds, the insurer (or in some cases the insured's broker) may draft a manuscript form to meet the customers' needs. For example, an insurer might develop a manuscript form to cover the unique liability exposures of a highly specialized profession. Because of the limited number of professionals requiring this coverage, insurers typically would not have preprinted forms available for that class of insureds.

Self-Contained and Modular Policies

Depending on the type and variety of coverages a customer seeks, a policy can be a single document (self-contained), or it may require a combination of documents to include all the agreements between the insured and the insurer (modular).

If the customer seeks coverage that is common to a large number of insureds, the insurer may choose to offer a self-contained policy. A personal auto policy is an example of a self-contained policy. Because most drivers have very similar auto insurance needs, a self-contained personal auto policy serves the needs of most insureds.

Conversely, if the customer seeks a variety of coverages that may not be common to a large number of insureds, the insurer may choose to offer a modular policy to tailor a policy to an insured's specific needs.

The ISO commercial package policy (CPP) is an example of a modular policy because it combines different **coverage parts** to meet the insured's particular needs. Commercial insureds' needs can vary, depending on the type of business insured. For example, some businesses may need commercial auto coverage, and others may not. See the exhibit "Components of the Insurance Services Office, Inc., Commercial Package Policy."

Each ISO-type CPP begins with two component documents: a set of common policy conditions and common declarations. Adding the necessary forms to make up the coverage parts that meet the insured's needs completes the policy. In most cases, a separate **declarations page** is included for each coverage part contained in the CPP.

Coverage part

A component of a CPP or a monoline policy that contains the policy provisions relating to a particular line of business, such as commercial property or commercial general liability; consists of the coverage part's declarations page, one or more coverage forms, applicable endorsements, and in some cases a general provisions form.

Declarations page (declarations, or dec.)

An insurance policy information page or pages providing specific details about the insured and the subject of the insurance.

Components of the Insurance Services Office, Inc., Commercial Package Policy

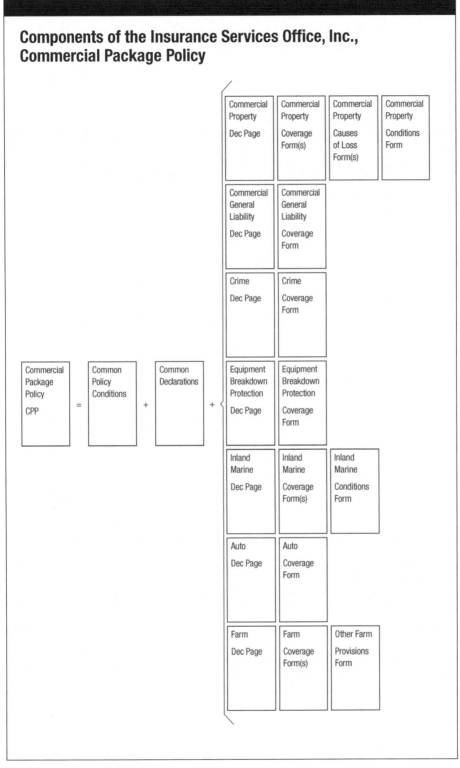

[DA00427]

Endorsements and Other Related Documents

Documents other than insurance forms can become part of a policy either by being physically attached to, or by being referenced within, the policy. Documents that can become part of a policy are the completed application, endorsements, the insurer's bylaws, and relevant statutory terms or provisions. See the exhibit "Related Insurance Policy Documents."

Related Insurance Policy Documents

Related document	Description	Example
Application	Documented request for coverage containing information about insured and loss exposures	Personal auto policy application containing relevant insured information pertinent to driving and vehicle(s)
Endorsements	Documents modifying basic policy form	Homeowners policy endorsement for home business coverage
Insurer's bylaws	Insurer's corporate bylaws	Attachment to policy issued by mutual insurer giving insureds corporate rights
Relevant statutory terms	Incorporation of statute by reference in policy	Workers compensation or no-fault auto insurance statutes

[DA00429]

An insurance application, the documented request for coverage, contains information about the insured and the loss exposures presented to the insurer. The insurer usually keeps the completed application in order to preserve the insured's representations. In some cases, misleading or false representations in an application can be grounds for denying a claim. Some state statutes require that any written application become part of the policy for some types of insurance.

Endorsement
A document that amends an insurance policy.

An **endorsement** adds to or modifies an insurance policy. An endorsement may be a few words handwritten into a policy, or it may be a separate document of one or more pages—preprinted, computer-printed, typewritten, or handwritten—that is attached to the policy.

An endorsement's provisions may conflict with the provisions of the policy to which the endorsement is attached. For example, a preprinted policy form may contain an exclusion, and an endorsement attached to the policy may delete the exclusion. If the policy and the endorsement contain conflicting terms, the endorsement takes precedence. Agreements between an insurer and insured, particularly handwritten alterations, tend to reflect true intent more accurately than do other, preprinted policy terms.

Some insurance contracts incorporate the insurer's bylaws or pertinent statutory provisions. For example, mutual and reciprocal insurance policyholders typically have rights and duties associated with managing the insurer's operations; the policy specifies these rights and duties by incorporating corporate documents.

Policies providing workers compensation insurance or auto no-fault insurance are among those that provide benefits required by state statutes. The insurance policy usually does not contain the relevant statutes but incorporates them by reference. For example, a standard workers compensation policy issued by the National Council on Compensation Insurance (NCCI) contains the following statement instead of detailing the types and amounts of benefits payable:

> We will pay promptly when due the benefits required of you by the workers compensation law.

Apply Your Knowledge

BNY Company has unique property and liability loss exposures that are not adequately insured under standard property-casualty insurance policies. What type of property-casualty policy would be the best solution for BNY?

a. Self-contained policy

b. Modular policy

c. Manuscript policy

d. Preprinted policy

Feedback: c. Because BNY Company has unique loss exposures, a manuscript policy would enable the insurer to draft a one-of-a-kind policy to address BNY's insurance needs.

POLICY PROVISIONS

Policy provisions are insurance policy statements communicating the terms of the insurer's and insured's coverage agreements. They describe and clarify the insurance policy's coverage, the types of losses the policy does not cover, and the parties' contractual responsibilities.

Each **policy provision** typically fits within one of six categories, depending on the provision's purpose. Some policy provisions appear in policy sections matching the provision's category, such as a definition located in the policy's definitions section. Other policy provisions may be interspersed throughout the policy.

Policy provision

Any phrase or clause in an insurance policy that describes the policy's coverages, exclusions, limits, conditions, or other features.

Common policy provisions fall within these six categories:

- Declarations
- Definitions
- Insuring agreements
- Conditions
- Exclusions
- Miscellaneous provisions

Declarations

An insurance policy first must identify the parties to the contract. Information specific to the policy, such as the insurer's and insured's names and locations and the subject of insurance, usually appear on the policy's first page, typically called the declarations page, or simply the declarations. See the exhibit "Categories of Property-Casualty Insurance Policy Provisions."

Categories of Property-Casualty Insurance Policy Provisions

Category	Description	Effect on Coverage
Declarations	Unique information on the insured; list of forms included in policy	Outline who or what is covered, and where and when coverage applies
Definitions	Words with special meanings in policy	May limit or expand coverage based on definitions of terms
Insuring Agreements	Statements containing insurer's promise to make payment	State circumstances under which the insurer agrees to pay
Conditions	Qualifications on promise to make payment	Outline steps insured needs to take to enforce policy
Exclusions	Provisions stating what the insurer will not cover	Eliminates coverage for excluded persons, places, things, or actions
Miscellaneous Provisions	Wide variety of provisions that may alter policy	Deal with the relationship between the insured and the insurer or establish procedures for implementing the policy

[DA00443]

The purpose of the declarations is to personalize a policy and tailor it to fit a particular policyholder's needs. The declarations contain (declare) information about the insured from the insurance application. They also summarize

the coverage provided under the policy, along with other information unique
to the policy. See the exhibit "Homeowners Policy Declarations."

Homeowners Policy Declarations

Homeowners Policy Declarations

POLICYHOLDER:	David M. and Joan G. Smith
(Named Insured)	216 Brookside Drive
	Anytown, USA 40000

POLICY NUMBER: 296 H 578661

POLICY PERIOD: **Inception:** March 30, 20XX
 Expiration: March 30, 20XX

**Policy period begins 12:01 A.M. standard time
at the residence premises.**

FIRST MORTGAGEE AND MAILING ADDRESS:

Federal National Mortgage Assn.
C/O Mortgagee, Inc.
P.O. Box 5000
Businesstown, USA 55000

**We will provide the insurance described in this policy in return for the premium and compliance with all applicable
policy provisions.**

SECTION I COVERAGES	LIMIT	
A—Dwelling	$ 120,000	**SECTION I DEDUCTIBLE:** $ 250
B—Other Structures	$ 12,000	**(In case of loss under Section I, we cover**
C—Personal Property	$ 60,000	**only that part of the loss over the**
D—Loss of Use	$ 36,000	**deductible amount shown above.)**

SECTION II COVERAGES	LIMIT	
E—Personal Liability	$ 300,000	**Each Occurrence**
F—Medical Payments to Others	$ 1,000	**Each Person**

CONSTRUCTION: Masonry Veneer	**NO. FAMILIES:** One	**TYPE ROOF:** Approved
YEAR BUILT: 1990	**PROTECTION CLASS:** 7	**FIRE DISTRICT:** Cook Township

NOT MORE THAN 1000 FEET FROM HYDRANT

NOT MORE THAN 5 MILES FROM FIRE DEPT.

FORMS AND ENDORSEMENTS IN POLICY: HO 00 03, HO 04 61

POLICY PREMIUM: $ 350.00   **COUNTERSIGNATURE DATE:**   **AGENT:** A.M. Abel

The declarations page typically contains these items:

- Policy number
- Policy inception and expiration dates
- Insurer's name
- Producer's name
- Named insured (policyholder's name)
- Named insured's mailing address
- Physical address and description of covered property or operations
- Numbers and edition dates of all attached forms and endorsements
- Dollar amounts of applicable policy limits
- Dollar amounts of applicable deductibles
- Names of persons or organizations whose additional interests the policy covers (such as mortgagees, loss payees, or additional insureds)
- Premium amount
- Any optional coverages the applicant has chosen

Scheduled coverage

Insurance for property specifically listed (scheduled) on a policy, with a limit of liability for each item.

Policy forms or endorsements also may contain information that qualifies as declarations, often in the form of **scheduled coverage**. For example, a home-owner might want increased limits of theft coverage for antique silverware stored in the home. A policy endorsement would list the details for such increased limits in a personal property schedule.

Definitions

Most insurance policies contain a definitions section defining policy terms to help clarify real or perceived ambiguity. This section is usually located near the beginning or the end of a policy.

A policy's definitions section defines words and expressions having specific meaning within the policy. In some policies, defined words may appear in boldface or within quotation marks every time the policy uses them with the specified meaning.

Insuring Agreements

Insuring agreement

A statement in an insurance policy that the insurer will, under described circumstances, make a loss payment or provide a service.

The purpose of an **insuring agreement**, which often follows the declarations and sometimes follows the definitions section, is to state in broad terms the insurer's promises to the insured. A policy providing more than one coverage can have more than one insuring agreement. For example, the Personal Auto Policy (PAP) contains provisions for liability, medical payments, uninsured motorists, and physical damage coverages, and each coverage has its own insuring agreement.

An insuring agreement usually introduces a coverage section, but it also can introduce other policy sections, such as coverage extensions, additional coverages, and supplementary payments.

An insuring agreement introducing a coverage section broadly states what the insurer agrees to do under the policy, subject to clarification in other parts of the policy, such as the policy definitions. Insuring agreements usually contain one or more defined terms crucial to understanding the coverage.

Conditions

A policy's **conditions** section clarifies the insurer's and insured's duties, rights, and options. Some policy conditions are included in a policy's conditions section; others may be found in the forms, endorsements, or other documents that together make up the entire insurance policy.

The insured must comply with conditions for a policy to cover a loss. The insurer is obligated to perform its promise only if the insured has fulfilled its contractual duties as specified in the policy conditions.

The insurer's obligations, as stated in the insuring agreement, may include these duties:

- To pay covered losses
- To defend the insured from lawsuits
- To provide other services to the insured

The insured's obligations, which stem from the policy conditions, include these:

- To pay premiums
- To report losses promptly
- To provide appropriate documentation for losses
- To cooperate with the insurer, as in legal proceedings, for example
- To refrain from jeopardizing an insurer's rights to recover from responsible third parties (subrogate)

If the insured fails to perform these duties, the insurer might be released from its policy obligations.

Exclusions

Exclusions are policy provisions that state what the insurer will not cover. The primary function of exclusions is not only to limit coverage but also to clarify the coverages granted by the insurer.

Condition
Any provision in an insurance policy that qualifies an otherwise enforceable promise of the insurer.

Exclusion
A policy provision that eliminates coverage for specified exposures.

An exclusion can serve one or more of these purposes:

- Eliminate coverage for uninsurable loss exposures—Some loss exposures are not generally insurable. Exclusions allow insurers to eliminate coverage for causes of loss that are difficult to insure, such as war, earthquake, or flood.

- Assist in managing moral hazards—Exaggerated or intentionally caused losses for the purpose of collecting insurance proceeds may be the result of **moral hazards** such as poor financial condition or a history of dishonesty. Exclusions help insurers minimize loss exposures that are affected by moral hazards.

- Assist in managing morale hazards—Losses often arise from carelessness or indifference because an individual is insured, reflecting **morale, or attitudinal, hazards**. Exclusions help insurers minimize loss exposures that are affected by morale hazards.

- Reduce the likelihood of coverage duplications—Sometimes two types of insurance policies may cover the same loss. Exclusions ensure that policies work together to provide complementary, but not duplicate, coverages.

- Eliminate coverages that the typical insured does not need—Exclusions can allow insurers to exclude coverage for loss exposures that typical insureds do not face. These exclusions eliminate the possibility that all insureds would have to share the costs of covering substantial loss exposures of relatively few insureds. For example, a policy might exclude coverage for destruction of a motorboat, because many insureds do not own motorboats. Watercraft policies or endorsements can provide coverage for this loss exposure.

- Eliminate coverages requiring special treatment—These coverages might require rating, underwriting, risk control, or other treatment that differs from that normally applied to the policy. An example is workers compensation coverage, which is normally provided in a self-contained policy.

- Assist in keeping premiums reasonable—Exclusions allow insurers to decline loss exposures that would increase overall insurance costs. By excluding such loss exposures, insurers can offer less costly premiums.

Exclusions typically appear in the exclusions section of the policy, but they may be contained in other policy sections, such as insuring agreements or definitions.

Miscellaneous Provisions

Insurance policies often contain miscellaneous provisions that do not qualify strictly as declarations, definitions, insuring agreements, conditions, or exclusions. Miscellaneous provisions may deal with the relationship between the insured and the insurer or may help establish procedures for implementing the policy. Miscellaneous provisions may affect coverage but do not have the force of conditions. Consequently, if the insured does not follow procedures

Moral hazard

A condition that increases the likelihood that a person will intentionally cause or exaggerate a loss.

Morale hazard (attitudinal hazard)

A condition of carelessness or indifference that increases the frequency or severity of loss.

specified in miscellaneous provisions, the insurer typically still must fulfill its contractual promises.

Apply Your Knowledge

Carol, an insurance agent, is analyzing an insurance policy that contains this provision:

> We cover (a) the dwelling on the "residence premises" shown in the declarations, including structures attached to the dwelling; and (b) materials and supplies located on or next to the "residence premises" used to construct, alter or repair the dwelling or other structures on the "residence premises".

This provision is best described as which of these?

a. Declarations
b. Insuring agreement
c. Condition
d. Miscellaneous provision

Feedback: b. The provision is an insuring agreement because it states that the insurer will cover the described types of property.

PROPERTY POLICY PROVISIONS

Insurance professionals must understand the provisions contained in property insurance policies because understanding these provisions is the foundation for developing essential policy-related skills, such as recommending appropriate property coverages and determining whether property policies cover particular claims.

A property insurance policy indemnifies an insured who suffers a financial loss because property has been lost, stolen, damaged, or destroyed. Generally, the policy must identify which property loss exposures are covered—that is, the types and locations of property, causes of loss, and financial consequences that are covered. Policies must also indicate which parties are covered and how much an insurer will pay in the event of a loss.

Covered Property

An insurance policy specifies what property is covered. Covered property is often described broadly and then refined through a series of limitations and exclusions. Exclusions and limitations are not the same thing; while exclusions eliminate all coverage for excluded property or causes of loss, limitations place a specific dollar limit on specific property that is covered.

In personal insurance, a residential structure is generally called a dwelling and is usually covered under a homeowners policy. A typical policy on a dwelling covers the residence premises. Usually, the policy definition of residence premises also includes other structures attached to the dwelling and materials located on or next to the dwelling used to construct, alter, or repair the residence premises. A freestanding, detached garage is not part of the dwelling. A separate insuring agreement for other structures covers such detached items. The coverage for the residence premises does not apply to land.

In commercial insurance, a permanent structure with walls and a roof is usually called a building. Other outdoor structures such as carports, antenna towers, and swimming pools are not considered buildings, but they can also be insured. A typical commercial property policy covers the building or structure described in the declarations. The policy definition of "building" may include additions that are either completed or under construction, as well as materials and supplies used for constructing the additions. Permanently installed fixtures, machinery, and equipment are also included as part of the building.

Personal property is another type of property covered by property insurance policies. Although buildings and personal property can be insured with the same policy, they are usually treated as separate coverage items.

Commercial property insurance policies usually refer to the contents of buildings as business personal property, which includes personal property of the insured located in or on the building described in the declarations, such as furniture, equipment, and stock.

Property insurance policies usually clarify what property is covered by listing property that is not covered. For example, policies that cover buildings and personal property typically show autos as property not covered because autos are more appropriately covered under auto insurance policies.

Property insurance policies often provide coverage for property that is owned by someone other than the insured. Homeowners policies provide coverage for the personal property of others, such as guests or employees, while the property is in the insured's home. Commercial property policies generally include limited coverage for the personal effects of officers, partners, and employees as well as for the personal property of others while it is in the care, custody, or control of the insured. The personal auto policy provides coverage for damage to a borrowed auto if the owner of the borrowed auto does not have physical damage coverage.

Covered Locations

Buildings are covered at the fixed location stated in the policy. However, in some instances, buildings do not necessarily remain at a fixed location. Portions of a building may be removed from the premises for repair or storage. For example, screens may be removed from the building's windows and placed in storage during the winter while storm windows are being used.

Some property insurance policies cover personal property that may not remain at a fixed location. For example, homeowners policies cover personal property of the insured while it is anywhere in the world. Auto insurance policies typically provide coverage while the insured's auto is in the United States, its territories and possessions, Puerto Rico, or Canada. Commercial property insurance policies are more restrictive; they typically provide coverage for the insured's business personal property while it is in the insured building or within 100 feet of the building. Commercial property policies often include a coverage extension that provides a certain limit, such as $10,000, of coverage for property off-premises; this extension, however, applies only to losses that occur in the specified policy territory, which is typically the U.S. and Canada.

A property insurance policy for covering personal property that moves from one place to another is often called a **floater** because it provides coverage that floats, or moves, with the property as it changes location. Policies covering movable property may have territorial limits such as the U.S. and Canada, or they may provide broader territorial limits such as "anywhere in the world." When insuring satellites or other property sent into outer space, a policy may cover property "anywhere."

Floater
A policy designed to cover property that floats, or moves, from location to location.

Covered Causes of Loss

Examples of covered causes of loss include fire, lightning, windstorm, hail, and theft. Many property insurance policies list their covered causes of loss. Such policies are commonly known as **named perils** policies because they name or list the covered perils. Usually, these policies also list the causes of loss that are excluded from coverage. Other policies cover all causes of loss except those that the policy specifically excludes. These policies are known by several different terms, including **special form or open perils policies**. The term "open perils" is used here.

Named peril
A specific cause of loss listed and described in an insurance policy. Also used to describe policies containing named perils.

Special form, or open perils policy
A policy that provides coverage for any direct loss to property unless the loss is caused by a peril specifically excluded.

An important difference between named perils and open perils coverage involves the burden of proof:

- With a named perils policy, for coverage to apply, the insured must prove that the loss was caused by a covered cause of loss.

- With an open perils policy, if a loss to covered property occurs, it is initially assumed that coverage applies. However, coverage may be denied if the insurer can prove that the loss was caused by an excluded cause of loss.

In the first case, the burden of proof is on the insured; in the second, it is on the insurer.

Personal and commercial property insurance policies on buildings and personal property are available with three different levels of coverage: basic form, broad form, and special form (open perils).

Reality Check

Effect of Burden of Proof When Determining Coverage

By shifting the burden of proof, an open perils policy can provide an important advantage to an insured who suffers a property loss by an unknown cause. For example, suppose that after a flood strikes a community, the insured's wrought-iron patio furniture is missing. Assume also that the patio furniture is clearly covered property. It is possible that the furniture was swept away in the flood, but it is also possible that the furniture was stolen following the flood. If a named perils policy covered theft but not flood, the insured would have to prove that the property had been stolen. Under an open perils policy, the insurer would have to pay the claim (even if the policy excluded flood losses) unless the insurer could prove that the property was swept away in the flood.

[DA07680]

Collision coverage

Coverage for direct and accidental loss or damage to a covered auto caused by collision with another object or by overturn.

Other than collision (OTC) coverage

Coverage for physical damage to a covered auto resulting from any cause of loss except collision or a cause of loss specifically excluded.

Specified causes of loss coverage

Coverage for direct and accidental loss caused by fire, lightning, explosion, theft, windstorm, hail, earthquake, flood, mischief, vandalism, or loss resulting from the sinking, burning, collision, or derailment of a conveyance transporting the covered auto.

Basic form covers approximately one dozen named perils, such as fire and lightning, windstorm, hail, aircraft, vehicle damage, riot and civil commotion, explosion, smoke, vandalism, sprinkler leakage, sinkhole collapse, and volcanic action.

Broad form adds several perils to those covered by basic form, such as falling objects; weight of snow, ice, or sleet; and sudden and accidental leakage of water from a plumbing system.

Special form covers all causes of loss that are not specifically excluded, thus providing broader coverage than even the broad form. For example, special form does not exclude theft by persons other than employees and therefore covers this cause of loss. Special form policies were once described as providing "all-risks" coverage, but this term is now less commonly used because it may be misinterpreted to mean that no causes of loss are excluded.

There are three types of auto physical damage coverage: **collision coverage**, **other than collision coverage** (or comprehensive coverage), and **specified causes of loss coverage**.

Excluded Causes of Loss

Property insurance policies typically exclude numerous causes of loss. Some perils that affect many people at the same time are generally considered to be uninsurable because the resulting losses would be so widespread that the funds of the entire insurance business might be inadequate to pay all of the claims. For this reason, almost all property insurance policies exclude coverage for losses from catastrophes such as war and nuclear hazard.

☑ Reality Check

Collision Coverage

Like other property, cars and trucks are subject to fire, theft, vandalism, and other perils. However, the most serious cause of loss to autos is collision. Insurance against collision costs considerably more than insurance against all other auto physical damage perils combined. Collision coverage is not included with other than collision coverage or specified causes of loss coverage and must be purchased as a separate coverage.

[DA07681]

Most policies providing coverage on buildings and personal property at fixed locations exclude coverage for earthquake and flood losses. An earthquake can be a catastrophe affecting many different properties in the same geographic area at the same time. Flood damage can also be catastrophic. However, floods can sometimes be predicted. For property in low-lying areas near rivers, creeks, or streams, the question is not whether floods will occur, but when. Insurers are generally unwilling to provide coverage for a loss that is certain to occur.

Property insurance policies also typically exclude loss from inherent vice and latent defect, as well as wear and tear and other maintenance perils. Such losses are generally uninsurable either because they are certain to occur over time or they are avoidable through regular maintenance and care.

Covered Financial Consequences

With regard to coverage for financial consequences, property losses can lead to a reduction in property value, lost income, and extra expenses. Property insurance policies must specify which financial consequences of a property loss are covered and which are not.

A reduction in the value of property is a **direct loss**. If the property is not restored, it is not worth as much after the loss as it was before. Homeowners policies and commercial property policies both provide coverage against direct physical loss to covered property by a covered cause of loss.

Another covered financial consequence is lost income, often referred to as **time element losses or indirect losses**. The longer a property is unusable, the greater the time element loss. Business income insurance protects a business from income lost because of a covered direct loss to its building or personal property. Coverage is provided for the reduction in the organization's **net income** that results from damage by a covered cause of loss to the property at the insured's location.

Direct loss

A reduction in the value of property that results directly and often immediately from damage to that property.

Time element loss (indirect loss)

A loss that arises as a result of damage to property, other than the direct loss to the property.

Net income

The difference between revenues (such as money received for goods or services) and expenses (such as money paid for merchandise, rent, and insurance).

Homeowners policies also provide coverage for lost income. When a covered cause of loss damages the part of a residence that an insured rents or holds for rental to others, "fair rental value" coverage in the homeowners policy indemnifies the insured for the loss of rental income until the rented portion of the residence is restored to livable condition.

Extra expenses

Expenses, in addition to ordinary expenses, that an organization incurs to mitigate the effects of a business interruption.

Additional living expense (ALE)

A coverage in homeowners policies that indemnifies the insured for the additional expenses that are incurred following a covered property loss so that the household can maintain its normal standard of living while the dwelling is being restored.

Named insured

A person, corporation, partnership, or other entity identified as an insured party in an insurance policy's declarations page.

Extra expenses are another covered financial consequence. The reason a business incurs extra expenses after experiencing a direct property loss is to continue its operations, which may also reduce the business income loss. **Additional living expense** coverage in homeowners and other policies covering dwellings is another example of extra expense coverage that applies if a direct loss to a dwelling makes it uninhabitable.

Covered Parties

Although a property insurance policy is a contract between the insurer and the **named insured**, the named insured is not always the only party that can recover in the event of an insured loss. Depending on the policy terms and conditions, property insurance can protect the insured and sometimes other parties that have an insurable interest in the property and that suffer a financial loss because covered property is lost, damaged, or destroyed.

Persons or organizations with an insurable interest in property can include property owners, secured lenders, users of property, and other holders of property. Insurance policies are written to cover these persons and organizations:

- The owner of a building is the named insured on a property insurance policy covering the building. Because the owner does not also occupy the building, typically there is no separate personal property of the owner's to insure at the building location.
- A party that owns and occupies a building is the named insured on a policy covering both building and personal property.
- A tenant occupies and uses rented space in a building and is therefore the named insured on a property insurance policy covering the tenant's personal property in that rented portion of the building.
- A secured lender, the party that provided funds to help finance purchase of an insured property, is usually not a named insured but is listed by name in the declarations (or in an endorsement) as a mortgagee or a **loss payee**.
- A bailee is the named insured on a bailee policy, which covers property of others that is in the bailee's custody.

Loss payee

A party entitled to share in whatever loss payment an insured receives.

Amounts of Recovery

When covered property is damaged by a covered cause of loss, how much will an insurer pay to an insured with an insurable interest? Any insurance policy providing property coverage must clearly address that question. The answer depends on policy provisions in these categories:

- Policy limits
- Valuation provisions
- Settlement options
- Deductibles
- Insurance-to-value provisions
- "Other insurance" provisions

When buying property insurance, the applicant usually requests a certain policy limit, which is the dollar amount of coverage. If the insurer agrees to provide that amount of coverage, the policy limit is established and the applicable policy limit is entered in the policy declarations.

A policy limit has several purposes. It tells the insured the maximum amount of money that can be recovered from the insurer after a loss. By comparing the policy limit to the value that may be lost, the insured can determine whether the amount of insurance is adequate. The policy limit is also important because it allows insurers to keep track of their overall obligations in any one geographic area and because the premium charged is directly related to the policy limit for most property insurance coverages.

Valuation provisions are used to set a value on covered property. The two most common valuation approaches in property insurance policies are replacement cost and actual cash value. A third approach, used for certain types of property, involves agreed value.

An insurer generally has these three settlement options when settling a loss:

- Paying the value (as determined by the valuation provision) of the lost or damaged property
- Paying the cost to repair or replace the property (if repair or replacement is possible)
- Repairing, rebuilding, or replacing the property with other property of like kind and quality instead of paying money

Property insurance policies usually contain a **deductible** provision, which serves several functions. Deductibles encourage the insured to try to prevent losses because the insured will bear a part of any loss. Shifting the cost of small claims to the insured also enables the insurer to reduce premiums. Handling claims for small amounts often costs more than the dollar amount of the claim. Thus, deductibles enable people to purchase coverage for serious losses at a reasonable price without unnecessarily involving the insurer in small losses.

Many property insurance policies include **insurance-to-value provisions**. Although total losses are much less frequent than partial losses, they do occur, and it is good risk management for property owners to insure their property

Deductible
A portion of a covered loss that is not paid by the insurer.

Insurance-to-value provision
A provision in property insurance policies that encourages insureds to purchase an amount of insurance that is equal to, or close to, the value of the covered property.

for its full value. Accordingly, insurers develop property insurance rates on the assumption that all policyholders will insure their property to at least 80 percent of its full value. If policyholders do not insure their property to that level, use of the insurer's property rates will result in premiums that are inadequate to cover all losses that the insurer must pay. Consequently, insurers encourage their insureds to buy insurance to value or to insure to a high percentage of the property's value. The traditional approach to encouraging insurance to value is to include a **coinsurance** provision in the policy.

In some cases, more than one insurance policy provides coverage for the same item of property, which can trigger "other insurance" provisions in either policy. If two or more insurers paid in full for the same loss, the insured could profit from the loss, violating the principle of indemnity. Most policies contain an "other insurance" provision to deal with this potential problem. When more than one policy covers a loss, the amount paid by each policy depends on the allocation procedure specified in the "other insurance" provisions of the policies.

Coinsurance

An insurance-to-value provision in many property insurance policies providing that if the property is underinsured, the amount that an insurer will pay for a covered loss is reduced.

LIABILITY POLICY PROVISIONS

Insurance professionals must understand the provisions contained in liability insurance policies because understanding these provisions is the foundation for developing essential policy-related skills such as recommending appropriate liability coverages and determining whether liability policies cover particular claims.

Liability insurance

Insurance that covers losses resulting from the insured's liability to others.

The insuring agreements of most policies that provide **liability insurance** make essentially the same promise: to pay damages (usually for bodily injury or property damage) for which an insured becomes legally liable and to which the coverage applies. The insurer also promises to pay related defense costs. To clarify the intent of the insuring agreement, which is usually a relatively brief statement, the provisions of a liability insurance policy must address the covered activities, covered types of injury and damage, excluded loss exposures, covered costs, covered time period, covered parties, and amounts of recovery.

Covered Activities

Property insurance claims usually involve only two parties: the insurer and the insured. Liability insurance claims involve three parties: the insurer, the insured, and a third party. The third party is the claimant making a claim against the insured for injury or damage allegedly caused by the insured. Although the claimant is not a party to the insurance contract, he or she is a party to the claim settlement. Under a liability policy, the insurer will pay damages only to those third parties who suffer injury or damage for which the insured is legally liable if the harm arose from a covered activity.

Liability insurance policies use two approaches to defining covered activities. Certain policies state the specific activity or source of liability covered, such as an auto insurance liability policy stating that it applies to claims that result from covered auto accidents. General liability insurance, in contrast, covers all activities or sources of liability that are not specifically excluded.

A commercial general liability (CGL) policy is an example of a policy that provides general liability insurance. The insurer agrees to pay damages "to which this insurance applies." However, the extent of coverage depends to a large degree on the exclusions. That is, general liability policies essentially cover those claims that are not excluded. General liability insurance policies specifically exclude coverage for claims that are better handled by other liability insurance policies, such as automobile liability, workers compensation, aircraft liability, watercraft liability, and professional liability. Exclusions dealing with difficult-to-insure exposures, losses expected or intended by the insured, and loss exposures that would be too costly to insure are also contained in general liability policies. For example, nearly all liability policies exclude coverage for losses that arise from war and nuclear hazard.

Covered Types of Injury or Damage

Liability policies typically cover claims for bodily injury and property damage for which the insured is legally liable. Other types of injury may also be covered; for example, the CGL policy also covers personal and advertising injury.

Bodily Injury

The standard CGL policy describes "**bodily injury**" as bodily injury, sickness, or disease sustained by a person, including death resulting from any of these at any time. This description indicates that, as used in the CGL policy, the term includes some things that may not be included in its everyday use. Sickness and disease are often considered forms of illness that do not involve injury. Death could be considered the severest form of injury, but unless it is specified in the policy, the applicability of bodily injury liability coverage may be questioned.

Bodily injury
Physical injury to a person, including sickness, disease, and death.

Property Damage

In typical CGL and homeowners policies, **property damage** includes physical injury to tangible property and loss of use of tangible property, whether or not it is physically injured. The definition of "property damage" in a typical CGL policy also specifies that data are not tangible property.

Property damage
Physical injury to, destruction of, or loss of use of tangible property.

Thus, according to both CGL and homeowners policies, property damage includes both direct losses and time element (or indirect) losses sustained by the claimant. For example, a fire at a store in a strip mall can cause indirect loss to the owners of surrounding businesses if they have to cease operations despite the fact that there might not be direct physical damage to their properties.

Personal and Advertising Injury

Personal injury

Injury, other than bodily injury, arising from intentional torts such as libel, slander, or invasion of privacy.

In addition to bodily injury, harm can be inflicted in ways such as damage to one's reputation. Although attorneys tend to use the term "personal injury" when referring to bodily injuries, in liability insurance policies, **personal injury** usually refers to a specific group of intentional torts. For insurance purposes, intentional torts are usually considered personal injury offenses and are either excluded from coverage or are covered separately.

Advertising injury, which is covered by most CGL policies, typically includes libel and slander; publication of material that constitutes an invasion of privacy; misappropriation of advertising ideas or business style; and infringement of copyright, trade dress, or slogan.

Because the definitions of personal injury offenses and advertising injury offenses overlap somewhat, current versions of the CGL policy include both personal and advertising injury in the same insuring agreement to avoid duplication of coverage. Coverage for personal injury liability (but not advertising injury) also can be added by endorsement to a homeowners policy.

Excluded Loss Exposures

No insurance policy can reasonably cover all loss exposures. The exclusions in liability insurance policies generally follow these broad guidelines:

- Avoid covering uninsurable losses. For example, war is a catastrophic event that is not economically feasible to insure.
- Avoid insuring losses that occur because of illegal activities, such as distribution of illegal drugs.
- Eliminate duplicate coverage provided by policies specifically designed to address particular exposures. For example, watercraft liability and aircraft liability are excluded under CGL policies and the liability section of homeowners policies.
- Eliminate coverage that most insureds do not need. For example, racing exclusions appear in personal and commercial automobile policies.
- Eliminate coverage for exposures that require specialized coverages and underwriting. The homeowners policy excludes coverage for professional services, such as those provided by physicians, architects, and lawyers.
- Keep premiums reasonable. For example, commercial liability policies generally exclude all but limited exposures from pollution. Businesses with more serious pollution liability exposures must purchase specialty policies to cover those exposures. If broad pollution coverage were provided under all liability policies, the coverage would not be affordable.

Covered Costs

Liability insurance policies typically cover these two types of costs:

*   The damages that the insured is legally liable to pay
*   The cost of defending the insured against the claim

In addition, liability policies commonly cover incidental expenses under the policy's supplementary payments provision and cover medical payments for injured persons, regardless of whether the insured is legally liable.

Damages

The CGL policy typically contains two insuring agreements that express the insurer's promise to pay damages on behalf of the insured:

> Coverage A: Bodily Injury and Property Damage Liability
>
> We agree to pay those sums that the insured becomes legally obligated to pay as damages because of "bodily injury" or "property damage" to which this insurance applies.
>
> Coverage B: Personal and Advertising Injury Liability
>
> We agree to pay those sums that the insured becomes legally obligated to pay as damages because of "personal and advertising injury" to which this insurance applies.[1]

A person who has suffered bodily injury, property damage, or personal and advertising injury for which the insured is allegedly responsible may make a claim for damages. The claim is most often settled out of court. Generally, out-of-court settlements, with the insurer paying the claimant on behalf of the insured, are attractive to both sides because they resolve cases quickly, spare the parties financial and emotional costs, and eliminate uncertainty about the outcome of a claim. In exchange for payment, the third party signs a **release**.

If a case goes to court, the claimant may be awarded two types of damages: compensatory damages and punitive damages (exemplary damages). Most liability insurance policies do not state whether punitive damages are covered. Some states do not permit insurers to pay punitive damages because the punishment is viewed as less effective if the responsible party does not personally pay the required damages. However, insurers will pay punitive damages if allowed by the state and not excluded by the policy.

Insurers, the court system, and society favor out-of-court settlements in general. Claim costs would soar if insurers had to resolve all liability claims through the courts, and the courts would be overwhelmed with cases and expenses. Society benefits when injured parties receive prompt compensation and when all parties put their legal disputes behind them.

Release
A legally binding contract between the parties to a dispute that embodies their agreement, obligates each to fulfill the agreement, and releases both parties from further obligation to one another that relates to the dispute.

Defense Costs

An insurer's duty to defend insureds against liability claims is often more important than its duty to pay damages. If the defense is successful, the court may award no damages or a smaller amount of damages. Most courts in the

United States interpret the insurer's duty to defend as requiring the insurer to pay the costs of defending an insured against any claim or lawsuit, even those without a legitimate basis, whenever a claimant's allegations (if proved) would be covered under the policy.

The insurer's duty to defend implies that the insurer will retain the attorneys and pay their fees and expenses. The insurer is also responsible for the costs of investigation, legal research, expert witness fees, and similar costs incurred in preparing and presenting the case.

Supplementary Payments

Supplementary payments

Various expenses the insurer agrees to pay under a liability insurance policy (in addition to the liability limits) for items such as premiums on bail bonds and appeal bonds, loss of the insured's earnings because of attendance at trials, and other reasonable expenses incurred by the insured at the insurer's request.

Liability insurance policies typically include a **supplementary payments** section describing various expenses that the insurer agrees to pay in addition to liability limits. Other costs that relate to the claim may also be included in the list of supplementary payments. Two examples are **prejudgment interest**, which may accrue between the time of the injury or damage and the time when a court awards a judgment to the claimant, and **postjudgment interest**, which accrues when an appeal to a higher court delays the payment of the judgment.

Prejudgment interest

Interest that may accrue on damages before a judgment has been rendered.

Postjudgment interest

Interest that may accrue on damages after a judgment has been entered in a court and before the money is paid.

Medical Payments

Liability policies may also provide **medical payments coverage**, which can help avoid larger liability claims. If a homeowners policy includes $1,000 of medical payments coverage, for example, a neighbor injured on the insured's property can receive emergency medical treatment up to that amount without having to sue the insured to recover the cost. In homeowners policies, this coverage is called "medical payments to others" and does not cover injuries to an insured or regular residents of his or her household. In personal auto policies, medical payments coverage does cover an insured's injuries, up to a specified limit.

Medical payments coverage

Coverage that pays necessary medical expenses incurred within a specified period by a claimant (and in certain policies, by an insured) for a covered injury, regardless of whether the insured was at fault.

Covered Time Period

Occurrence-based coverage

Coverage that is triggered by the actual happening of bodily injury or property damage during the policy period.

Personal auto insurance is often written for a six-month term, but other types of liability insurance are usually written for a one-year period. Depending on the type of liability insurance policy, coverage is usually "triggered" by either of these situations:

- Injury or damage that occurs during the policy period (in an occurrence basis policy)
- Claims made (submitted) during the policy period (in a claims-made policy)

From the insured's standpoint, **occurrence basis coverage** offers valuable protection for unknown and unforeseen claims. For example, if the claimant was injured in an automobile accident caused by the insured only a few hours before the policy period expired, the resulting claim would be covered, even if the claim is not submitted until after the policy expired. For the insurer, however, occurrence basis coverage means that liability claims may surface long after a policy has expired. This particular problem contributed to the development of claims-made coverage.

Although personal liability insurance policies and most commercial general liability insurance policies are written on an occurrence basis, **claims-made coverage** is sometimes used to insure businesses that face certain types of liability loss exposures, such as medical malpractice, professional liability, or liability for especially hazardous products. Under such a liability policy, the covered event must occur on or after a specified date (called a **retroactive date**) and before the end of the policy period.

Covered Parties

Liability insurance policies provide coverage for the named insured and others. A liability policy generally gives the broadest protection to the named insured. Coverage for others is generally based on their family or business relationship with the named insured. Therefore, liability insurance policy provisions must define the relationships that determine coverage. For example, the liability coverage of a typical homeowners policy applies to the named insured and these persons:

- The named insured's spouse, if the spouse is a resident in the household
- Relatives of the named insured or spouse, if the relatives reside in the household
- Full-time students who were residents before moving out to attend school, if under twenty-four and a relative or under twenty-one and in the care of an insured

Commercial liability policies also cover the named insured and certain others, depending on their relationship to the named insured. For example, one provision usually contained in a CGL policy defines others who may be covered because of their business relationship to the named insured and the circumstances under which they are covered. The parties who are insureds under this provision include these:

- The named insured's employees and volunteer workers
- Real estate managers for the named insured
- Any organization that is newly acquired or formed by the named insured for up to a certain number of days after it is acquired or formed

If several named insureds are listed in the declarations of a commercial liability policy, a policy provision usually stipulates that the first named insured is the insured with whom the insurer has contact for payment of premiums, claim reporting and claim payment, notices of cancellation or nonrenewal, or interim policy changes.

Claims-made coverage form

A coverage form that provides coverage for bodily injury or property damage that is claimed during the policy period.

Retroactive date

The date on or after which bodily injury or property damage must occur (or a personal and advertising injury offense must be committed) in order to be covered.

Amounts of Recovery

When a liability claim is covered, an insurer does not necessarily pay the full amount of the judgment awarded. The extent of the insurer's payment depends on these policy provisions:

- Policy limits
- Defense cost provisions
- "Other insurance" provisions

Policy Limits

Predicting the dollar amount of liability insurance needed to cover an insured's future claims can be difficult. Legal obligations depend on uncertain future events in a changing legal environment. Still, it is necessary for the insured and the insurer to agree on some dollar amount of coverage. As with property insurance, policy limits help an insurer measure the extent of its obligation. Limits also provide options to the insured, who must decide not only how much coverage is desirable but also how much is affordable. Liability insurance limits are generally round numbers such as $100,000, $500,000, or $1 million and can be expressed in different ways, such as an **each person limit**, **each occurrence limit**, or **aggregate limit**.

Separate limits for bodily injury and property damage liability coverage are known as **split limits**. For example, a personal auto policy may provide bodily injury liability coverage with a $100,000 limit for each person and a $300,000 limit for each occurrence, and with a separate limit of $50,000 for each occurrence for property damage liability coverage. A **single limit** applies to any combination of bodily injury and property damage liability claims arising from the same occurrence. For example, a $300,000 single limit covers a bodily injury loss up to $300,000, a property damage liability loss up to $300,000, or any combination of bodily injury and property damage arising from a single occurrence up to $300,000. See the exhibit "Examples of Split Limits and Single Limit."

Defense Cost Provisions

Most liability policies place no dollar limit on the defense costs payable by the insurer. The only limitation is that the insurer is not obligated to provide further defense once the entire policy limit has been paid in settlement or judgment for damages. Stated differently, defense costs are usually payable in addition to the policy limits, and policy limits include only payment for damages. Some liability policies place defense costs within the overall policy limit. In such policies, for example, if the policy limit is $100,000 and the insured has a covered claim involving damages of $90,000 and defense costs of $30,000, the insurer would pay a total of $100,000 for both the damages and the defense. The insured would be responsible for the additional $20,000.

Each person limit

The maximum amount an insurer will pay for injury to any one person for a covered loss.

Each occurrence limit

The maximum amount an insurer will pay for all covered losses from a single occurrence, regardless of the number of persons injured or the number of parties claiming property damage.

Aggregate limit

The maximum amount an insurer will pay for all covered losses during the covered policy period.

Split limits

Separate limits for bodily injury and property damage liability coverage.

Single limit

A single limit of liability for the combined total of bodily injury and property damage from any one accident or occurrence.

Examples of Split Limits and Single Limit

Split Limits

Jessica has a personal auto policy with the following split limits:

Bodily Injury:

- $100,000 each person
- $300,000 each occurrence

Property Damage:

- $50,000 each occurrence

Jessica is liable for a covered auto accident resulting in injuries to Richard, the driver of the other car, and Marcy, his passenger. When the case went to trial, the court awarded $200,000 in bodily injury damages to Richard and $150,000 to Marcy. In addition, the damage to Richard's car amounted to $10,000, which Jessica was also ordered to pay. Jessica's insurer would pay $110,000 to Richard ($100,000 each person limit for bodily injury plus $10,000 for property damage) and $100,000 to Marcy (the each person limit). Thus, the insurer would pay a total of $210,000 for this accident (plus Jessica's defense costs, which are paid in addition to the policy limits in a personal auto policy). Jessica would have to pay the remaining bodily injury damages of $150,000.

Single Limit

If Jessica's personal auto policy instead had a single limit of $300,000 in lieu of the split limits, her insurer would pay a total of $300,000 to Richard and Marcy for both bodily injury and property damage (plus defense costs) in the accident. (A determination of exactly how much each party receives would depend on the circumstances of this particular claim.)

In this situation, Jessica's insurer would pay more under the single limit policy than the split limits policy, but such is not always the case. For example, if three people had had bodily injury of $150,000 each plus the $10,000 property damage, the insurer would have paid a total of $310,000 under the split limits policy ($100,000 bodily injury for each person plus $10,000 property damage); under the single limit policy, the insurer would pay only $300,000, the maximum payable for any one occurrence.

[DA02540]

"Other Insurance" Provisions

In some cases, two or more policies may cover the same claim. Liability insurance policies contain "other insurance" provisions to resolve this problem and preserve the principle of indemnity. Several approaches can be used, and the applicable approach depends on the wording of the policies, which, depending in the facts of the situation, usually provides a formula for sharing the cost of damages.

SUMMARY

A valid insurance contract has four essential elements:

- Agreement (offer and acceptance)
- Capacity to contract
- Consideration
- Legal purpose

If any of these elements is not satisfied, the contract is not enforceable.

Although all of the rules of contract law apply to insurance policies, certain special characteristics distinguish insurance policies from other contracts. An insurance policy is all of these:

- A contract of indemnity
- A contract of utmost good faith
- A contract involving fortuitous events and the exchange of unequal amounts
- A contract of adhesion
- A conditional contract
- A nontransferable contract

Depending on customers' coverage needs, insurers may use either preprinted or manuscript forms to assemble insurance policies, and policies may be either self-contained or modular. Various documents may either be attached to the policy (such as an endorsement) or be incorporated by reference (such as statutory provisions).

Policy provisions communicate the terms of an insurer's and an insured's agreements as to coverage. They fall within six categories: declarations, definitions, insuring agreements, conditions, exclusions, and miscellaneous provisions.

Common characteristics of property insurance policies include: covered property, covered locations, covered causes of loss, excluded causes of loss, covered financial consequences, covered parties, and amounts of recovery.

To clarify the intent of a liability insurance policy's insuring agreement, the policy provisions typically address covered activities; covered types of injury or damage, including bodily injury, property damage, and personal and advertising injury; excluded loss exposures; covered costs, including damages, defense costs, supplementary payments, and medical payments; covered time period; covered parties; and amounts of recovery, including policy limits, defense cost provisions, and "other insurance" provisions.

ASSIGNMENT NOTE

1. Commercial General Liability Coverage Form (CG 00 01 12 07), copyright, ISO Properties, Inc., 2011.

Index

Page numbers in boldface refer to pages where the word or phrase is defined.